savory sweets

savory
sweets

From Ingredients to Plated Desserts

Amy Felder, CEPC

John Wiley & Sons, Inc.

Published by John Wiley & Sons, Inc., Hoboken, New Jersey
Published simultaneously in Canada

For general information on our other products and services or for technical support, please contact our Customer Care Department within the United States at (800) 762-2974, outside the United States at (317) 572-3993 or fax (317) 572-4002.

Wiley also publishes its books in a variety of electronic formats. Some content that appears in print may not be available in electronic books. For more information about Wiley products, visit our web site at www.wiley.com.

Library of Congress Cataloging-in-Publication Data:

Felder, Amy, 1961–
        Savory sweets : from ingredients to plated desserts / Amy Felder.
            p. cm.
        Includes bibliographical references and index.
        ISBN-13: 978-0-471-74058-2
        ISBN-10: 0-471-74058-6
    1. Desserts.   I. Title.
    TX773.F38 2007
    641.8'6—dc22

                                                                2006038983

Printed in the United States of America

10 9 8 7 6 5 4 3 2 1

For my mother,
my first (and best) baking teacher

table of contents

table of contents

introduction

Traditionally the culinary (or savory) world and pastry world have been viewed as two separate entities. The culinary world with its pungent herbs and spices, proteins, and vegetables utilizes a wide range of cooking techniques. The pastry world utilizes a rather more limited list of ingredients and uses baking as its primary cooking technique. There is a new world of flavor possibilities for the pastry chef who begins to fuse savory ingredients and cooking techniques into his or her pastries. This merging of the savory and the pastry worlds is a type of fusion cuisine.

Fusion cuisine itself is nothing new. For years chefs have been borrowing from one type of cuisine, in terms of either ingredients or cooking styles, and developing variations of familiar dishes. Picture a spring roll made with Asian cooking styles and spices but with a filling of typically Western ingredients. This is one type of fusion cuisine. In this instance the chef is no longer confined to one type of ingredient; suddenly his/her pantry becomes much larger. The great thing about fusion cuisine is that it allows the chef to expand his or her flavor repertoire; old techniques and products are reinvented and new depths of flavor are discovered.

Savory Sweets rests on the concept that the savory world offers pastry chefs a new approach to flavor; specifically to the development of flavor in plated desserts. However, for pastry chefs to reap the flavor rewards offered by the culinary side of the kitchen, they must first have an understanding of the many facets of the culinary world. Fusion cuisine is effective only when the chef understands the nature of each of the worlds that he or she is fusing together. Fusion cuisine should never consist of raiding the spice cabinet and adding ingredients together without first understanding the nature of each of those ingredients. The goal of this book is to establish a firm understanding of the culinary world, its ingredients, and its cooking styles. Once that knowledge is in place, a true fusion of the two worlds can begin.

This book is divided into four parts. The parts are designed to lead the reader through the process of analyzing flavor, manipulating flavor through cooking techniques, understanding culinary ingredients, and, finally, constructing specific plated desserts. Part 1 establishes a vocabulary and offers graphic blueprints for analyzing flavor. Before flavor can be manipulated, its nature must be understood. This section will start the reader on the road to increased palate acuity. The tools offered in this section are applicable to any dish or ingredient used in either the savory or the pastry kitchen.

The second part discusses various culinary cooking techniques. Each technique is analyzed in terms of the flavor it can contribute to a final dish. The third part is to be used as an ingredient resource. It examines herbs, spices, vegetables, dairy, and dry pantry ingredients that are most often associated with the culinary world. The flavors and origins of each ingredient are explored and a list of complementary ingredients is included. The goal of *Savory Sweets* is to fully understand the culinary world's many flavor resources. Thus, the ingredients in Part 3 are those primarily associated with the culinary world. The typical battery of pastry and/or dessert ingredients is not included here. These ingredients can, however, be found in all of the individual "partner with" lists.

Part 4 is the culmination of the information presented in the previous three sections. It traces the development of eight plated desserts. The vocabulary, cooking techniques, and ingredients discussed in the previous three sections are all applied to these specific plates. The thought process behind the design of the plates is explored and all of their recipes and methods of preparation are included.

Although the parts of the book were designed to be used sequentially, they can be used out of context just as effectively. The discussions of flavor and flavor development in Parts 1 and 2 can be especially useful in a culinary, as well as in a pastry class. Although the book's focus is on plated desserts, culinary chefs will benefit equally from the discussions of flavor analysis, flavor development, and individual ingredients. Just as pastry chefs are enjoying the flavor rewards of raiding the culinary side of the kitchen, so too will culinary chefs benefit from looking at familiar ingredients with new eyes (and a new palate).

For instructors of this material there is an *Instructor's Manual* (0-470-04514-0). It contains chapter learning objectives, detailed chapter outlines, classroom demonstrations and exercises, and a bank of test questions. Please contact your Wiley representative or visit www.wiley.com/college to request a copy.

Acknowledgments

Thanks to all of the bachelor degree students in my plated dessert classes over the years. Their ability to look outside of the pastry box and borrow liberally from the culinary world when designing desserts was the impetus for this project. Most notable among those students is Reginald Abalos who took pen in hand and breathed life into my plated dessert descriptions. He is an artist with both a paintbrush and a chef's knife.

Heartfelt thanks to the culinary faculty and administration at Johnson & Wales Charlotte campus. They welcomed me warmly into my new North Carolina home and supported me in a hundred different ways throughout this endeavor. I am especially grateful to Catherine Rabb who looked at and critiqued early drafts and kept pushing me along with her enthusiasm, and Jerry Lanuzza who made my desserts look great.

Gwendolyn Valcourt tested the recipes, although any final mistakes are mine alone. She went above and beyond and did so with a smile on her face.

Thanks also to those reviewers who reviewed the book proposal and manuscript and offered many helpful and encouraging insights. They are Martha Crawford, Johnson & Wales University; Vincent Donatelli, Asheville-Buncombe Technical Community College; Catherine Hallman, Walters State Community College; Paul Krebs, Schenectady County Community College; and Virginia Olson, Anne Arundel Community College. And to my family and friends who understood my lack of social graces while I was writing, thank you.

savory sweets

vocabulary of flavor

the nature of taste

Taste is both a physical and a mental process. It is also a process that differs from person to person. Because of its subjective nature tasting is often a confusing subject to clearly comprehend. This chapter discusses the physical process of tasting as well as its emotional and personal attributes. An understanding of the nature of taste is the first step in becoming an analytical taster. The next step, an analysis of the vocabulary of taste, is presented in Chapters 2 and 3.

taste: a physical process

Taste is a physical process. We place food in our mouths, chew, and miraculously we "taste" the food. Something happens in our mouth that allows us to experience the flavor of the food we are eating. Although similar in texture, an apple does not taste the same as a pear.

On the most basic level taste begins with our taste buds. Look into a mirror and stick out your tongue. Contrary to what you may believe, the bumps or small dots you see are not your taste buds. They are papillae. A single papillae can hold a cluster of anywhere from 2 to 250 taste buds. Although most taste buds are centered on the tongue, they are also found throughout the mouth.

Each taste bud has a pore in its center. Saliva is vital to the tasting process as it is responsible for carrying taste molecules into the crevices of the papillae and into the central opening of the taste bud. A single taste bud is composed of up to one hundred taste cells. The number of taste cells that people have will affect the manner in which they taste.

Tasters are divided into three groups. These divisions depend on the number of papillae and, consequently, the number of taste cells an individual possesses. The groups are labeled as tasters, nontasters, and supertasters. To analyze the number of taste cells a person has, researchers swab a small section of the tongue with a blue dye and count the number of papillae that stand out.

Those individuals with a high percentage of papillae are referred to as supertasters. About 25% of the population falls into this category. Supertasters have an approximate density of 165 taste papillae per square centimeter. Children are, for the most part, supertasters. Not only do they have a great density of taste buds, but their taste buds also cover a larger area than those of an adult. A child's taste buds are found not only on the tongue but also on the insides of the cheek and on the soft palate located on the roof of the mouth. This may well explain children's preference for bland foods. When a child says that they do not like a particular item it is often because they taste the flavor much more intensely than adults. Children are also genetically predisposed to like sweet tastes. This is certainly connected to the sweetness of breast milk. This preference for sweet typically decreases as the child reaches adolescence. The term "supertaster" can be misleading. It does not mean that supertasters have an advantage in being able to analyze flavors. Contrarily, supertasters have a great sensitivity to bitter and, to a lesser degree, sour. Thus, most supertasters tend to be extremely picky eaters, enjoying primarily bland foods. Interestingly, more women than men are supertasters.

Compared to supertasters with 165 papillae per square centimeter, normal tasters have approximately 127 papillae per square centimeter. Approximately half of the population is found within this category. Nontasters have about 117 papillae per square centimeter and, like super tasters, about one-quarter of the population falls within this category. Nontasters certainly do experience taste but not to the degree of tasters and supertasters. They tend to enjoy strongly bitter or sour food, as those tastes do not affect them, as they would supertasters. No matter to which category an individual belongs, analytical tasting is an acquired skill, and like any other skill utilized in the kitchen, practice will bring greater proficiency.

the sense of smell

The physical process of tasting is not only dependent on taste buds, but is also connected to the sense of smell. A large percentage of what we label as taste is actually aroma. Humans are only aware of five tastes: sweet, sour, salt, bitter, and umami (see Chapter 2 for more information on the five tastes) but we are able to detect thousands of aromas. One-day-old infants have been observed to express their unhappiness when offered rotten eggs to smell. Nursing infants are able to pick out their mother by scent alone. The sense of smell is so important to the tasting process that when we have a cold and our nose is stuffed up we declare, "I cannot taste a thing." It is the decrease in sensitivity to aroma that causes the elderly to feel that they are losing their sense of taste. It is estimated that approximately 80% of those eighty years of age or older have some major loss of smell sensitivity. It is this loss that causes our taste acuity to weaken as we age.

So how does the relationship between aroma and taste actually work? Our olfactory or smell receptors are found in the olfactory membrane located at the top of the nasal cavity. There are almost 100 million of the receptors located at this site. That sounds like a lot until you realize that a dog has over one billion smell receptors. The receptor cells are connected by neurons to the brain. Some are connected to the hypothalamus, which controls appetite and emotions, while others follow pathways to the hippocampus, which is connected to memories.

There are two ways in which an individual can experience aroma, either ortho or retro nasally. An ortho nasal perception of aroma comes from an outside aroma—for example, the wafting aroma that hits your nose when you are presented with a bowl of hot lobster bisque. In this case the aroma is released directly from the food and enters the nasal cavity through the nose.

Alternatively, the aroma from the food can be released as the food is chewed and warmed in the mouth. This is a retro nasal perception of food. The vapors of the warmed food move up the pharynx to the nasal cavities via a retro nasal path. Not all food items will affect the taster's ortho nasal perception, but all food, as it warms in the mouth, will affect the taster's retro nasal perception.

Distinguishing Between Ortho and Retro Nasal Perceptions of Flavor

Prepare a batch of simple syrup. Use 3 parts water to 1 part granulated sugar by volume (1 cup of water to $\frac{1}{3}$ cup of sugar). Add fresh lemon juice and a bit of zest until the water is lightly flavored. Do not make lemonade! The water should have a noticeable but gentle lemon flavor. Bring the mixture up to a boil and then let cool.

Divide the liquid into two cups. Plug your nose with one hand and sip from cup #1. Pay close attention to the flavor, or lack thereof. Release your nose and notice that you are suddenly encompassed with the flavor of lemon. This is an example of a retro nasal perception of flavor. The vapors produced as the liquid warms in your mouth are pushed up to the nasal cavities through a retro nasal path.

Spray a floral perfume or an air freshener in the air. Make sure that the spray is not lemon scented. I have a lime spray that I use for this experiment. Lean in and sniff the aroma as you sip from cup #2. Notice that your perception of the liquid's flavor has changed. The clear lemon flavor is lost amid the aromatic perfume. Your perception of the liquid's flavor moves from lemon to lime. This is an example of an ortho nasal perception of flavor. An outside aroma has altered your perception of flavor.

Alternatives to Making a Simple Syrup

Another way to experience a retro nasal perception of flavor is to taste a scoop of sorbet or ice cream. Notice that the sorbet itself does not have an appreciable aroma. As the sorbet or ice cream warms in your mouth, you perceive the aroma retro nasally and thus, experience its flavor.

Another way to experience an ortho nasal perception of flavor is to sip a cup of beef consommé while leaning over a pot of chicken stock or visa versa. Your perception of the consommé's flavor will undoubtedly change as the beef flavor gives way to chicken.

Taste buds and aroma form the basis for our physical understanding of taste and flavor. Successfully and analytically tasting in the kitchen requires constant awareness of the interrelationship between aroma and taste. It is much like any other skill acquired in the kitchen: it requires practice and concentration. The first step is to come to the tasting with a clean mouth. Drinking coffee, smoking cigarettes, chewing gum or breath mints will all interfere with the way in which you will perceive taste. Although you may no longer be able to taste the coffee, cigarette, gum, or breath mint it is, nonetheless, influencing the way in which you taste. Traces of a breath mint or of a cigarette will remain on your taste buds and affect everything else you taste retro nasally. Therefore, it is important to drink a lot of water and rinse your mouth out often with water or to take a bite of a plain cracker to cleanse your palate between tastes.

Avoid wearing perfume or aftershave, as both will affect your ortho nasal perception of flavor. Avoid tasting a product directly over a hot steaming pot. The aromas released in the steam will affect the flavors you perceive. When tasting a soup, for example, step away from the stove. Also be wary of an ortho nasal perception of flavor when you taste something warm or hot that is going to be served cold. This is especially important when tasting a sorbet or ice cream base, for example.

Be careful of the "painted room syndrome." Think about entering a freshly painted room. At first, the smell is overpowering. After a few minutes, however, the smell seems to dissipate. Someone then enters the room and asks how you can stand the stench. You realize that you are no longer aware of the smell. This same phenomenon occurs when tasting. Consider making a base for fresh ginger ice cream. You have already tasted the anglaise a few times and have added some additional fresh ginger. You are still unsure, however, if the taste of the ginger is strong enough. A colleague tastes the base and remarks that the ginger flavor is almost overwhelming. You have, in essence, blown out your palate. Just like the freshly painted room, you are no longer aware of the tastes around you. Thus cleansing your palate with water is vital. It is also important to take breaks and to sniff fresh air between tastings (some suggest sniffing coffee beans as a way of neutralizing or cleansing your olfactory nerves). It is also helpful to take several small sniffs of the product being tasted rather than large deep breaths.

the effect of fat on flavor

Fat plays an important role in one's ability to taste. Fat coats taste buds. That creamy, silky mouth feel that comes from eating something with fat in it is, in reality, clogging up your papillae (along with your arteries). As the papillae become coated with fat, it becomes increasingly hard for the palate to be able to detect flavors. When tasting more than one product, start with the item containing the least amount of fat. If you taste something fatty and then switch to a less fatty item, the fat from the first item will block your taste perception of the second item being tasted.

Experiencing the Effect of Fat on Flavor Perception

Make a batch of chocolate sorbet and chocolate ice cream (see Appendix for recipe). Scoop out a small portion each of the sorbet and ice cream. Allow both portions to sit out at room temperature for a few minutes so that their flavors can be more readily perceived. Start with the chocolate sorbet. Notice the clear intensity of the chocolate flavor. It starts out sweet and then immediately moves to the bitter astringency associated with cocoa powder. The chocolate flavor, or chocolate essence, is not subtle. It is strong and forthright. Once you swallow, a humming of bitterness remains in your mouth.

Now taste the chocolate ice cream. It too begins with a sweet note. It quickly moves to a silkiness, which is a result of the heavy cream and egg yolks used in the anglaise. Some heavy creams contain as much as 40% butterfat and an egg yolk is composed of approximately 80% fat. While there is a perception of chocolate, it is more subtle than that found in the sorbet. In the case of the ice cream the fat in the recipe smooths out that bitterness. While the ice cream has a chocolate flavor it lacks the intensity of the chocolate sorbet—the fat dulls the bitter astringency.

Think, for a moment, of the flavors as shapes or colors. The chocolate flavor of the sorbet is sharp and jagged while the fat of the ice cream has rounded out those jagged edges. One is not necessarily better than the other; they are simply different. Do not place a value judgment on either product; simply note the role of fat (or lack thereof) in each.

This point can be further illustrated through clear caramel and classic caramel sauces. (See the Appendix for recipes.) Start the tasting with the clear caramel sauce. The sauce begins with a sweet note, which quickly moves to a slightly bitter caramel taste. Now try the classic caramel sauce. While it too begins with sweetness, it moves quickly into a buttery richness lacking in the clear caramel sauce. The bitterness at the end is barely noticeable in the classic caramel sauce as the fat begins to coat the tongue and its papillae.

tasting: a mental process

The physical nature of taste is only one side of the coin. Tasting is also a mental or emotional process. Because individuals are distinct and unique, this aspect of taste can easily become confusing. To fully understand and analyze taste, you must become aware of its emotional nature.

Tasting can be an incredibly personal experience. The taste of a particular product often serves as a conduit for an individual's emotions and memories. Taste is often related to the memories of both the physical and emotional environment in which the product was first sampled. For example, when I bite into the first crisp fall apple I am flooded with childhood memories. I remember the excitement of the first day of school; the joy of jumping in a pile of freshly raked leaves, and the feel of approaching winter in the air. The memories come to mind completely unbidden; the taste of an apple is enough to call them to mind.

Because memories differ from person to person, each individual will perceive the flavor of a particular product in a slightly different fashion. Both positive and negative experiences influence the way in which a product's flavor is perceived. These experiences become part of the lenses through which each individual will forever view the world of flavor. Remembering the overcooked liver of one's childhood can, for example, prevent the adult taster from fully enjoying liver's flavor.

The professional chef must be constantly aware of the personal aspect of tasting. It is important to remember that despite the memories that one may associate with certain flavors, there are no inherently good or bad tastes. (This refers to foodstuffs that are nonpoisonous. Many poisonous plants possess an extremely bitter or "bad" taste as a warning system to potential diners.) A chef must be able to separate the qualities of a particular dish from their personal perception of the dish's flavor. "It tastes good" or "It tastes bad" are not remarks that reflect a true analysis of a dish's flavors. As a professional chef, it is important to make the distinction between what is an inferior or improperly made product and a product that we simply, on a personal or emotional level, do not like.

Professional chefs do not have the luxury of making only products they personally like or enjoy. We must focus on whether the flavors work together and whether they make sense. I have created desserts that are very popular with customers although I personally do not care for their flavors. For instance, I hate white chocolate. As a pastry chef I have tasted dozens of white chocolates and while I can appreciate their qualities, strengths, and weaknesses, I personally do not enjoy them. As a professional chef I cannot allow my personal prejudices to lose potential customers. It is, therefore, vital that chefs be aware of the mental component of tasting.

your individual flavor box

Your flavor box, or flavor personality, consists of your life experiences and their effect upon the emotional aspect of your tasting process. Your flavor box derives from your present environment as well as all of the previous environments in which you have lived. The way in which you taste is an outgrowth or product of these environments. It is part of your flavor personality.

Family often has the biggest impact on an individual's flavor personality. Your family, your town, the surrounding community and region, and the way in which you were raised all join together to form your flavor box. I grew up in the Midwest, surrounded by a family with deep Croatian roots. At home we ate a large variety of Croatian dishes. Throughout my childhood, this style of food was simply part of our family life and I grew up assuming that other families were eating similar foods. I was in middle school before I realized that my schoolmates had never heard of, let alone tasted, dishes like paletchinka (a type of thin pancake filled with cheese and jam), sarma (sour cabbage stuffed with ground pork and veal), or paprikash (a stew rich with paprika, vegetables, and chicken). These dishes were normal dinner fare in our household. Their flavors were subconsciously defining my taste personality, my flavor box.

Your flavor box is not a stagnant entity. Think of it as a box with slightly fluid and constantly moving walls. With each new taste

Consider that a mother's breast milk carries with it the flavors of the foods she eats. Thus, the connection between a child's predispositions to the flavors of his/her childhood begins almost from birth. Some theories also propose that because the flavor of a mother's breast milk will change from day to day, due to variances in her diet, a breastfed child is exposed to a greater variety of flavors than a child who is not breastfed. Some believe that lack of such exposure leads to children who grow up to be picky eaters. To date, no conclusive studies have been done on the long-term effect of a varied diet in a child as he or she matures.

experience the walls of the box are inexorably altered. As an adult my flavor box has expanded beyond my Croatian heritage. I have lived in many different regions of the United States as well as in Europe. These experiences have influenced my flavor box. Each physical change of locale has brought me into contact with new ingredients, new cooking methods, and new ways of tasting foods. All of these factors serve as the foundation for new food memories.

Consider how tomatoes can be made into a sauce in Italy . . . in Mexico . . . in California? Each exposure to new cultures or new ingredients adds depth and breadth to your flavor box. For instance, the Japanese have dozens of words to define the textures of tofu. For most Americans, this is somewhat hard to comprehend; yet such descriptors are inherent to the Japanese flavor box. Tofu, and all its varieties, is intrinsic to the Japanese culture. It is important to be aware of the limits your culture places on your flavor box. Strive to keep your mind and palate open to new taste possibilities, to new ways of expanding your flavor repertoire.

As a chef it is vital to be aware of and able to define all of the components of your flavor box. It is essential to be cognizant of your prejudices, likes, and dislikes, as well as their sources. This knowledge will help to make you a better taster. Perhaps the flavors you have always labeled "good" are, in reality, triggers for positive food memories while the flavors themselves are flat and underdeveloped. You may love the supermarket birthday cakes of your childhood. Each bite brings with it wonderful memories of birthday parties and a table full of presents. In reality, the cakes are usually overly sweet with a waxy, vegetable shortening-laden frosting. The flavor is too sweet and ultimately flat and undesirable; the vegetable shortening coats your tongue and the roof of your mouth. However, since your perception of the flavor is good because of the happy memories it recalls, this sweet flavor is then labeled good in your flavor box. It is therefore imperative that chefs are aware not only of the contents of their flavor box, but also of the emotional and personal context of those flavors.

Defining Your Individual Flavor Box

An understanding of your personal flavor box is a vital step in becoming an analytical taster. Start by simply defining and describing your flavor box's contents. In two columns list the products you like and those you dislike. It is perhaps easiest to start with the extremes. What foods do you absolutely love? Which foods do you hate? Try to establish the reasons behind your preferences and your prejudices. For instance, if you dislike a product is it because of its texture, its flavor, or its association to negative memories? Try to be as specific as possible. Do you like hot, spicy food because it is the food of your childhood? The more detailed and more specific you can make these lists, the more they will aid in your palate development. I keep my lists and refer to them every six months or so. It helps me to remain aware of my palate development. An awareness of the contents of your flavor box as well as the emotions and memories associated with those contents will help you to differentiate between the actual flavors of a product versus your personal prejudices for or against a particular product. This awareness is vital for all professional chefs.

As you begin to define your flavor personality, your individual flavor box, you may find that there is a difference between the way in which you taste on a personal level and the way in which you taste as a professional or when you are cooking for others. My career as a professional chef has dramatically altered the way in which I taste food. My professional flavor box is much more diverse than my personal flavor box. This may be true for you as well.

Your flavor box is not stagnant; think of its walls as fluid and constantly moving. This is because your emotional and mental environment is constantly changing and evolving. Therefore, each time you taste, that flavor is being placed into a slightly new and altered flavor box. Even if it is a familiar product, there is a new part of the flavor box into which that flavor must be deposited. Thus repetition becomes a vital component of the tasting process and to the development of your flavor palate. Repetition should be applied in the course of one tasting as well as in the overall number of tastings. You can never say, "I know how that tasted, I don't need to taste it again." Repetition and concentration are the most important steps to increasing one's flavor repertoire. Stay alert to nuances and differences between each sampling of a flavor. I can taste the same product a hundred different times, and each time I notice something new, something different. Like any skill in the kitchen, tasting requires constant practice. With practice, the otherwise confusing nature of taste becomes easy to understand. Once you understand the nature and contents of your individual flavor box, you are well on the way to becoming an analytical taster.

flavor profile

Language defines the way in which we view the world. It also influences the world of taste and flavor. To better be able to analyze flavor, you must possess and be comfortable with the correct vocabulary. I once took an eight-week wine and spirits course. Much of that time was spent in frustration. I sat in the back of the room enjoying the wines but unable to clearly define each particular taste and nuance. The growth of my palate was contingent upon the growth of my vocabulary. Through a series of guided tastings I was finally able to associate the sensations on my tongue and palate with actual words. I had been "tasting" all along but needed someone to help me name the physical sensations my palate was experiencing. Becoming an analytical taster is dependent on connecting a vocabulary of flavor with experiences on your palate.

Gaining an understanding of the language of flavor is vital to be able to analyze and manipulate it in the kitchen. Once you are comfortable with the vocabulary, the analysis of what you taste becomes easier to understand and improve. With practice the relationship between the vocabulary of flavor and the sensations in your mouth will become second nature.

The concept of flavor profile is the first step in establishing a language of flavor. A flavor profile consists of three components: taste, aroma, and trigeminal response. This chapter defines each of these elements and shows how to apply those terms when analyzing specific plated desserts.

taste

The first element of flavor profile is taste. Taste is the physical response we experience in our mouth as we eat. Recall the discussion in Chapter 1 as to the physical nature of taste. There are five tastes: sweet, sour, salt, bitter, and umami. For many years it was believed that taste buds were neatly organized on the tongue. Sweet taste buds were found on the extreme tip of the tongue, followed closely by salt. Sour taste buds were found along the edges with bitter buds located at the back of the tongue. Today we know that all taste buds are capable of responding to stimuli from all of the tastes. Some buds, however, are more receptive to specific tastes than to others.

Sweet

We tend to perceive sweet at the tip of our tongue or at the front of our palate. There are two ways in which a food product becomes sweet. The product itself can be inherently sweet, as in the case of sugar, molasses, or honey. Alternatively, the product can undergo a cooking process that increases its sweet qualities. The difference between a raw carrot and one that has been slowly roasted to release and caramelize its natural sugars is an example of this type of sweetness. Refer to Chapter 4 for more information on various cooking methods and their relationship to flavor.

The pastry world often looks for sweetness in the most obvious places. Is something not sweet enough? Then simply add more sugar. It is important to remember, however, that each sweetener has its own unique flavor as well.

Take, for example, a fruit coulis. After cooking the fruit you find that it is not very flavorful. You, therefore, add more sugar or simple syrup to the purée. The fruit flavor still seems weak. You add more sugar. Eventually the flavor of the sugar or simple syrup will take over the natural flavors of the fruit. In this case, more is not always better.

Sour

We tend to perceive sour at the sides of our tongue and mouth. Many children love sour because of the all-encompassing physical response it solicits. Biting into a sour candy causes our mouth to salivate and the sides of our jaws to tingle and often results in comical facial expressions.

Not all sour comes in the extreme form of sour candies found at the grocery store. In the right proportion sour can be a wonderful addition or counterpoint to the sweetness of most desserts. Some common sources for sour are certainly citrus fruits, but it can also be found in some wine and wine reductions, vinegars, fruit juice reductions, and tamarind. See Chapters 7–11 for more examples of sour ingredients.

The addition of a sour or acidic element can often boost a product's original flavor. This is especially true when working with fresh fruit. Remember that fruit is an agricultural product and as such its flavor will change according to the season and region in which it is grown. Fruit at its peak of ripeness has an intrinsic sweet and sour balance. Therefore, adding some sour notes as well as sweeteners will replace the fruit's natural flavor balance. Rather than using a recipe or formula for a coulis, instead let your palate be your guide. Taste the puréed fruit and if it needs a sweetening boost, then add some sweetener. When you feel that the resulting flavor is about 75% of the way there, it needs just a bit more sweetener, then stop. Instead of adding more sugar, simple syrup, or honey, add an acid—a sour note. Citrus fruits are a great source of such flavor. A few drops of lemon, lime, orange, or grapefruit juice, a bit of finely grated citrus zest and the resulting bloom in the flavor of the coulis will astound you.

Salt

Salt, like sweet, is perceived in the front of the mouth. It can add a wonderful boost to the flavor of a dish. Salt's primary source is, well, salt. There are many types of salts on the market today. Each has its own personality and nuances. Try to sample and use as many as possible.

There are also ingredients with a high salt content that can be used in a dish in much the same way as salt. Bacon and cured meats, soy sauces, and some cheeses can all be used as salty additions. Keep in mind that, just like sugar, too much salt will overpower a product's intrinsic flavor.

Bitter

We often associate bitter as an undesirable taste; it catches us at the top of the throat and at the back of the roof of our mouth. Have you ever bitten into a piece of unsweetened chocolate? That lingering flavor that hits you at the top of your mouth is bitter, from the cocoa powder. Other sources of bitter are the white pith of an orange or the overwhelming astringency of a burnt caramel. Bitter is perhaps an unexpected addition to pastry work but, as we'll see later, it can be a wonderful counterpart to a sweet dish.

Umami

Umami is considered by many to be the fifth taste. While relatively new to the American culinary world, it has been part of the Asian culinary world for thousands of years. Asians have used umami to describe flavors that are savory or almost meaty. The essence of tenderloin aged perfectly and cooked to perfection, the sensation of eating a plum tomato straight off of the vine at the height of tomato season, the pungency of a wonderfully aged blue cheese, and MSG are all examples of umami. Umami is an expression of savoriness. It describes a product's depth of flavor. Umami translates as "delicious" and although Western scientists are still trying to understand exactly how it affects our taste receptors it is believed to be linked to the presence of sulfur-containing amino acids. These amino acids are found in many salt-cured and fermented products.

experience sour versus bitter

Slice a ripe orange into quarters. First eat the meat or flesh of the orange. It is slightly sweet with a wonderfully full orange flavor, or orange essence, and a pleasing bit of sourness. Not the Mr. Lemonhead shake your head and lift up your shoulders kind of sourness; instead, it is simply a light tingle at the sides of your tongue and at your jaw bone followed by a rush of saliva into your mouth. Now bite into the white pith of the orange. It is not at all sweet and there is no orange flavor. Instead, what you experience is a physical sensation in your mouth. A dryness or kind of astringency hits you at the back of your mouth, the roof of your mouth, or the top of your throat. This is bitter. Realize that while this is an example of bitter in a negative sense, there are some instances of bitter being a positive presence in a plated dessert. More information on the important role of bitter in desserts can be found in Chapter 3.

experience sweet and sour in fresh fruit

Experiment with the sweet–sour balance in a fruit coulis. You can use ready-made purées or purée fresh fruit yourself. Taste the purée. Add simple syrup or granulated sugar until you feel that the fruit flavor has grown somewhat but is still a bit weak. Then add a few drops of fresh lemon juice and taste. Continue to add lemon juice, or any other citrus juice, depending on the flavor of the purée, until the original fruit flavor has reached its peak. Make sure to taste the fruit purée after each addition of the lemon juice. In this way you will experience how the fruit flavor blooms with the addition of an acidic ingredient.

experience sweet and bitter

Tasting a variety of chocolates is a wonderful way to experience the roles of sweet and bitter. Start with a variety of chopped chocolates. This variety should include only couverture chocolates, chocolates with at least 33% cocoa butter. At the bare minimum include white, milk, dark, and unsweetened chocolate, or cocoa liquor. If possible get a range of dark chocolates with various percentages of cocoa liquor, i.e., dark chocolates ranging from 33 to 100%.

Taste each type of chocolate in the following manner. Place the chocolate in your mouth and chew vigorously three to four times. Once the chocolate begins to melt, push it to the top of your mouth with the flat of your tongue. Continue to push the chocolate to the roof of your mouth paying attention to the many nuances of flavor that will result.

A brief note about chocolate and chocolate percentages: Couverture chocolates are those with a large percentage of cocoa butter and little or no other fats. These chocolates are used in candy making, for garnishes, and as ingredients. Their high cocoa butter content gives them a shine and snap not seen in lower-quality chocolates. Couvertures must contain at least 33% cocoa butter, as opposed to coating chocolates in which the more expensive cocoa butter is replaced with vegetable shortening. The percentage on a package of chocolate refers to the percentage of cocoa liquor, the amount of cocoa butter, and cocoa powder in the total mass of the chocolate. Thus, white chocolates are not given a percentage since they possess no cocoa powder. A chocolate labeled 52% has more cocoa liquor and is, therefore, more bitter than a chocolate labeled 33%. For more information concerning the exact breakdown of cocoa powder and cocoa butter within a specific percentage for a specific chocolate, contact the individual chocolate manufacturer.

Start with the white chocolate. You will immediately get a sensation of sweet, followed closely by the flavor of dried milk solids. The chocolate is a couverture and so it will melt quickly and evenly in your mouth, with no greasy or waxy residue. Pay attention to the way in which the flavor moves through your mouth, starting with a strong sweetness, then moving to a milky creaminess, and then simply stopping.

Next try the milk chocolate: it also starts with a strong sweetness. Although it has some milkiness, there is not as strong a presence as that found in the white chocolate. Following the milky creaminess, the milk chocolate introduces a chocolate essence. This essence is the flavor that is identifiably chocolate. That chocolate essence comes from cocoa powder. Unlike the white chocolate, there is a slight lingering of chocolate flavor in one's mouth after the chocolate is swallowed. There is also the small beginning of something bitter. Physically your mouth feels clean but the bitter taste will linger or continue to hum. That humming is caused by the cocoa powder's bitterness.

Move to the dark chocolates. Taste these chocolates moving from the lesser to greater percentages of cocoa liquor. As you taste the dark chocolates you will find that the taste takes longer to bloom in your mouth. Unlike the white or milk chocolate, you will have to chew the chocolate longer before any kind of taste is released. This is because dark chocolates have less sugar than milk or white chocolates. The less sugar there is in a product, the longer it takes for the taste to be perceived. Sugar gives the taster immediate impact, introducing the essence of the product's flavor in a loud and clear voice. Thus, a bite into a white chocolate, with its high sugar content, results in an immediate perception of flavor. With dark chocolates, especially those with a high percentage of cocoa powder (which means, consequently, that the chocolate has less sugar), you will have to chew the chocolate longer before its true flavor is released. A chocolate of 50 or 73% takes longer to introduce itself to your palate than one with 42%.

This theory is borne out even more clearly with the 100% chocolate or cocoa liquor. This is chocolate in its purest form, consisting of only cocoa powder and cocoa butter. Once you start chewing the chocolate you will find that it takes quite a while before any flavor is released into your mouth. The complete absence of sugar prevents the flavor from being noticed. Once the chocolate is almost completely chewed, ready to be swallowed, only then does the true flavor of the chocolate come out. There is an overwhelming sense of bitterness. The rather enjoyable light humming experienced after swallowing the earlier dark chocolates has now become a large, uncomfortable banging of drums. The bitter flavor stays in the mouth long after the chocolate is swallowed. The bitterness of the cocoa liquor leaves a drying sensation at the roof of your mouth and/or at the top of your throat.

Be careful to not make any value judgments as to which chocolate is good and which is bad. Instead, concentrate on the movement of sweet to bitter in your mouth as each chocolate is tasted. Often the chocolate one enjoys in a chocolate tasting is not the one that works best as an ingredient in the kitchen. I once had the chance to taste some single-origin chocolates from many different countries around the world. I fell in love with a particular chocolate made by a small plantation in South America. The chocolate had some wonderful smoky tobacco notes, which I found intriguing. Excitedly I rushed back to the kitchen to start using this chocolate in products. Much to my dismay the same smoky notes that had so attracted me in the tasting were completely obliterated when the chocolate was mixed with other ingredients. So be careful. A chocolate tasting is a wonderful way to familiarize yourself with the role of sweet and bitter, but it is not always the best way in which to pick a chocolate for use in your kitchen. Try the chocolates, and then make mousse or ganache with them before committing yourself to a purchase from your purveyor. There is no good and bad here, they are what they are. See the following chapter on Plate Profile for a deeper discussion of the movement of flavor from sweet and salt to sour and bitter.

Like wine, cocoa beans reflect the nature of the country in which they are grown: the soil, surrounding plant life, weather, etc. Single-origin chocolates are chocolates that are manufactured with just one bean; there is no blending. For this reason single-origin chocolates often have wonderful nuances of flavor that are undetectable when the same beans are blended with others. These chocolates are more expensive than blended chocolates but often worth the additional expense. Some chocolate companies designate their single-origin chocolates with a Grand Cru label.

aroma

The second aspect of a flavor profile is aroma. As previously discussed in Chapter 1, flavor is perceived both ortho and retro nasally. The importance of aroma to the perception of flavor cannot be overstated. To experience retro nasal perception of flavor, separately grate some raw onion and some raw apple. Have someone blindfold you and as you plug your nose have him or her hand you first a small spoonful of one product and then a small spoonful of the other. (This can also be tried with an apple and parsnip, carrot and apple, or lemon and orange. Products that are similar in texture will work best.) You will find that with your nose plugged you will be unable to clearly separate one taste from the other. You have blocked the retro nasal passage. Once you unplug your nose, however, such distinctions become easy to make. We taste all foods retro nasally as they warm up in our mouth. In the context of flavor profile, aroma refers only to the ortho nasal perception of flavor. Recall that an ortho nasal perception of flavor is triggered by an aroma outside of the mouth. The wafting of steam from a bowl of clam chowder, for example, will affect the taster ortho nasally.

trigeminal response

The last component of a flavor profile is trigeminal response. Trigeminal response is sometimes referred to as feeling factors or chemical feeling factors. It is the response in your mouth to a particular chemical in the item you taste. The following scenario is a good example of eating a food that causes a trigeminal response. You are at a Mexican restaurant and as you wait for your food, the waiter brings over some chips and salsa. The salsa is at room temperature. You are hungry and begin to eat. After a few chips you find that the inside of your mouth is burning. Has the salsa changed temperature? Has it miraculously heated itself up? The answer, of course, is no. Instead the capsicum in the jalapeno peppers in the salsa have triggered a chemical response in your taste buds and you now feel as if your mouth is burning. Cinnamon, fresh ginger, and wasabi are other examples of foods that will cause a warming sensation when eaten.

A trigeminal response does not always involve heat. Sometimes the chemical response in your mouth is exactly the opposite. Chew some mint gum, especially one of the super ice brands. As you chew, your mouth feels as if it is freezing, yet if you were to take the temperature of your mouth and of the gum you would find that they are both at regular body temperature. Again, a chemical in the gum, in this case menthol, is reacting to the nerve endings in your mouth and you perceive your mouth to be freezing cold. Anise and fennel are other examples of foods that will cause a cooling sensation in your mouth.

Not all products will produce a trigeminal response. And not all trigeminal responses are hot or cold. The burn from alcohol and the tannin from red wine or from an under-ripe green banana are additional examples of this chemical response. The role of trigeminal response is discussed further in Chapter 3, Plate Profile.

A flavor profile consists of taste, aroma, and trigeminal response. A plate possessing most of these components is said to have a full flavor profile. In the following exercise you will taste each component of a flavor profile, ending with a product that has a full flavor profile.

This tasting works best with whole blanched almonds. They have a softer, more neutral flavor than other nuts and thus the other ingredients in the tasting are allowed to be the primary focus. You will need six almonds per person. One of the six almonds should remain raw while the rest should be roasted.

Once the almonds are roasted set aside one per person. Place a teaspoon or so of pasteurized egg whites in a bowl and lightly whisk. Pasteurized egg whites are used here for convenience's sake. The nuts are going to be roasted again so fresh egg whites would also be fine in this circumstance. Add the almonds to the whites and mix to coat. The almonds should be just lightly moist to the touch. Remove the almonds from the bowl one at a time. Dredge the first almond in coarse or rock sugar, the second in sea salt, the third with ancho chilli powder, and the last almond with a combination of all three. Place the nuts on a sheet pan and return to the oven. Roast until they are a rich caramel color. Once the nuts have cooled, you are ready to taste.

Start with the raw almond. As you chew the almond, notice that it does not have a lot of crunch and texture to it. If you were blindfolded, it would be difficult to recognize the nut as an almond. There is not a lot of almond flavor there.

Taste the plain roasted almond. It crunches as you take your first bite and you are immediately hit with the buttery flavor and texture associated with almonds. The almond flavor is the nut's essence. This essence is the nut's distinguishing characteristic. It is what differentiates the almond from other nuts. See Chapter 4 for more information on the power of roasting and its effect on flavors.

Try the nut that has been dredged in sea salt. You will get an immediate salty impression. The

The nuts should be roasted in a 350°F (180°C) oven on a sheet pan. There is no need to spray the pan or line it with parchment paper. The almonds will begin to turn a light golden color and start to look oily. As the nuts become increasingly fragrant, shake the pan every few minutes and continue to roast until the nuts are all the color of a light golden honey. Remove from oven.

salt is the first flavor that you perceive, followed by the buttery roasted almond. The fourth nut, the sweet one, will give you much the same impression. That is, you perceive the sweetness before you perceive the almond flavor. This progression of flavor will change with the fifth nut, the one dipped in chilli powder. You will first experience the almond essence and then the smokiness of the chilli and, finally, the trigeminal response. It is possible that you may not perceive any trigeminal response until after you have swallowed. You should experience some heat in the back of your throat from the chilli pepper.

The last nut is a combination of all of the above sensations. You will get sweet and salt first, then the almond, along with a bit of smoky flavor from the ancho, and then the trigeminal response from the pepper.

This exercise provides you with a familiarity of the concept of flavor profile, as well as an understanding of the four tastes and how they are perceived on your palate. As the tastes move throughout your palate they also move from simple to complex. The last almond has many components to it. The salt and sweet enhance the nut's essence while the chilli powder complements the almond flavor. An item with a full flavor profile has a depth, complexity, and richness of flavor not experienced in the nuts with fewer tastes and little or no aroma and trigeminal response.

After participating in the orange, chocolate, and almond tastings, you have experienced the movement of flavor in your mouth and the role of sweet, salt, bitter, sour, and trigeminal response.

Now that the various elements of a flavor profile have been defined and experienced, the concept can be put to use in analyzing specific plates. The following chart offers a visual representation of a flavor profile. Each individual component of a plated dessert is placed into the chart and analyzed in terms of its taste, aroma (remember that only an ortho nasal perception of aroma is considered here), and trigeminal response. As you look at the chart you will realize that not every component fills in every section of the chart. Every individual component will not have all the aspects of a full flavor profile. Do not try to force your components to fill in all of the sections of the chart. Simply put N/A (not applicable) for those sections that do not relate to your individual components.

For example, the last nut in the almond tasting would fill out the flavor profile chart in the following manner.

	SWEET/SOUR/ BITTER/SALT	AROMA	TRIGEMINAL RESPONSE
Roasted almond with sugar, salt, and ancho chilli powder	Sweet: sugar Salt: sea salt Bitter: a touch from the roasting process	N/A	Ancho chilli powder

When designing a plate the overall goal is to experience a full flavor profile when all of the components of the dessert are tasted. A full flavor profile is one in which the four tastes, the aroma, and any trigeminal response are all balanced, with no one element overpowering the rest. Be careful: it is easy to have desserts that are top-heavy on the sweet side with no contrasting tastes. Utilizing the following chart when composing plates can be extremely helpful. The chart makes it clear if you have too many items that are sweet, sour, or with too much trigeminal response, competing aromas, etc.

The first dessert to be analyzed is a classic American favorite, apple pie. In this case the pie is served warm with a scoop of vanilla ice cream. Here is its flavor profile chart:

	SWEET/SOUR/ BITTER/SALT	AROMA	TRIGEMINAL RESPONSE
Warm apple pie	Sweet: sugar in the filling Sour: from the granny smith apples	Warm apple and spice aroma	N/A
French vanilla ice cream	Sweet: sugar	N/A	N/A

The chart reveals that many pieces of a full flavor profile are missing. The result is a pie with a lot of sweet elements but not much else. In this case a full flavor profile could be creating by adding a sour element, perhaps some cranberries or tart dried cherries to the pie, in addition to the apples, or bitter, in the form of a dark caramel sauce, or even a trigeminal response, some fresh ginger in the ice cream. Any of these additions will give the plate greater depth, which will enhance the pie's natural flavors.

The next dessert to be analyzed is a bit more complex. An analysis of this dessert clearly shows the depth of flavor that can be derived when a full flavor profile is used. The dessert consists of a warm gingerbread cake served with pears, which have been sautéed with fresh ginger. The cake is served with a red wine and pear reduction and a salty caramel and curry sauce. A pear sorbet, a dried pear chip, and a salted caramel corkscrew are the dish's accompaniments and garnishes.

To analyze the plate's flavor profile, each element is broken down and placed in the following chart. Charting out the flavor profiles of each component of a dessert, or culinary dish, makes it clear if the tastes are balanced.

	SWEET/SOUR/ BITTER/SALT	AROMA	TRIGEMINAL RESPONSE
Entrée: Warm gingerbread cake with sautéed pears with fresh ginger	Sweet: molasses, sugar, honey, and natural sugars in the pears	From warm gingerbread cake as well as from the pears	From the heat of the fresh ginger
Sauce #1: Red wine and pear reduction	Sweet: from pears, wine, and honey Sour: from pears and wine Salt: N/A Bitter: N/A	N/A served at room temperature	A bit of tannin from the red wine
Sauce #2: Salted caramel sauce with a touch of curry and fresh ginger	Sweet: caramel Sour: N/A Salt: sea salt Bitter: caramel	N/A served at room temperature	A bit from the heat of the fresh ginger and the curry powder
Frozen component: pear sorbet with pear William	Sweet: honey and pear purée Sour: pear and a touch of orange Salt; N/A Bitter: N/A	N/A served frozen	Slight burn from the alcohol in the pear Williams
Crunch: dried pear chip	Sweet: pear and simple syrup Sour: small note in the pear Salt: N/A Bitter: N/A	N/A as it is served at room temperature	N/A
Garnish. salted caramel corkscrew	Sweet: caramel Salt: sea salt Bitter; caramel Sour: N/A	N/A as it is served at room temperature	N/A

The above plate was designed to illustrate a full flavor profile. When designing plated desserts it is important to have components that contrast against the sweet elements. In this plate the sour found in the pears, red wine, and orange as well as the salt and bitter found in the caramel all work to offset what would otherwise be an overwhelmingly sweet plate. Trigeminal response is found in the heat from the fresh ginger and curry powder and the tannin from the red wine. This offers yet another type of contrast to the rest of the tastes on the plate. Note that some components affect the consumer through an ortho nasal perception of flavor (the heat of the warm gingerbread and pears).

A full flavor profile offers a depth of taste. The overall flavor of the sweet molasses laden gingerbread cake is greatly enhanced with the addition of the spicy and slightly sour fresh pears. The sour and trigeminal response offers a wonderful backdrop for the cake. Their nonsweet qualities heighten the taste of the cake itself. Think back to the chocolate tasting. Recall the movement of flavor that occurred when tasting the dark chocolates. A plate with a full flavor profile will provide the consumer with a similar sort of movement.

The ability to isolate and define the elements of a flavor profile is a critical first step in building a vocabulary of flavor. You must be comfortable with this step before proceeding to the next chapter. Practice analyzing plates you have made in class or tried in a restaurant. Isolate each component and fill in the following chart. Continue this exercise with as many plates as possible. Practice will make this type of analysis easier. The next chapter uses the concept of flavor profile and applies it in a new context.

	SWEET/SOUR/ BITTER/SALT	AROMA	TRIGEMINAL RESPONSE
Entrée:			
Sauce:			
Sauce:			
Frozen component:			
Garnish:			
Crunch factor:			

chapter 2   flavor profile

plate profile

 The concept of plate profile is the final step in establishing a vocabulary for analyzing flavor. In Chapter 2 the idea of flavor profile was presented. Analyzing a dessert's flavor profile helps chefs to isolate and clearly define the strengths and weaknesses of their creations. This concept is taken a step further in this chapter's discussion of plate profile.

Once a chef understands the concept of plate profile, he/she can then separate the individual components of a particular dish to answer the questions, What is missing? and What does this plate need? The analysis required to develop a plate profile is not unique to the pastry world and should be used by all chefs when they taste and evaluate their dishes.

A plate profile consists of a description of a product's flavor from when it is first smelled until after it is swallowed. The movement of flavor in the mouth is referred to as the top, middle, and base notes. A plate is said to have a full plate profile when it possesses all three of these notes.

top notes

The top note of a dish is the initial impression it gives the consumer. The top note can appear in three different forms: through an ortho nasal aroma, or via sweet or salty elements of the dish. Let's begin with the ortho nasal aroma. Recall that retro nasal perception of flavor is always present as a by-product of the tasting process. Thus, only an ortho nasal aroma is considered to be a top note. We smell the waft of apples from the slice of warm apple pie and get an immediate initial impression of the pie's flavor, even before our fork touches the plate. This aroma is a top note.

Other sources of top notes are found in sweet and salty elements. Think back to the almond tasting in Chapter 2 and the almonds coated with sugar and/or salt. The sweet and salt was perceived before the actual flavors of the almond. These are top notes.

Top notes provide instant impact. Ortho nasal aroma reaches us before we even eat the pie. Likewise, sugar and salt hit the front of the palate before we get a true impression of the product's true essence or flavor. The majority of top notes are volatile flavors; they evaporate quickly and have little or no staying power. While their impact is almost instantaneous, it dissipates quickly.

middle notes

Middle notes provide the actual staying power of any particular flavor. These notes are the essences of the flavor. The middle note *is* the product's flavor. In the nut tasting, the middle note was the almond essence or almond flavor of each nut. Recall the orange tasting in Chapter 2. In that case, the middle note was the orange flavor or essence.

In many instances fat will help to hold and carry a middle note. The following exercise helps to illustrate this point.

Middle Notes and Caramel

Caramelized sugar is one of the few products whose flavor can be anticipated by its color. The longer the caramel is cooked, the bitterer it becomes. For the most part, Americans are used to a rather anemic caramel, sugar cooked until it is a light honey color. This is caramel that is simply sweet (it is, after all, sugar) but with little other flavor. If, however, the caramel is cooked until it becomes quite a bit darker (the color of dark ground cinnamon) a wonderful bitterness begins to emerge.

Prepare both the clear and classic caramel sauces using the recipes in the Appendix. Begin by tasting the clear caramel sauce. Because there is no fat in this sauce, you will fully experience the bitter sweetness of the caramel. The top note of sweetness hits your palate first. The middle note consisting of the actual flavor of caramel, or caramel essence, follows. The caramel will have a nutty richness to it. The bitterness of a dark caramel is the base note. In this context bitterness is not a negative; it gives the caramel a full nutty flavor. Take another taste and concentrate on the movement of the flavor through your mouth: sweet—caramel nuttiness—bitter.

Now try the classic caramel sauce. Again, you are initially hit with the sweetness, followed by the flavor of the caramel. In this instance, however, that flavor is dimmed or blurred by the fat that is also in the sauce. The caramel has a rich, buttery flavor with less nuttiness. A fatty richness accompanies the caramel flavor. The bitter end of the sauce, unlike the clear caramel sauce, is much shorter and not nearly as strongly recognizable. This is a good example of the role of fat. Again, this is neither good nor bad, it simply is what it is. Follow the movement of flavor in your mouth: sweet—buttery richness—caramel nuttiness—faint hint of bitter.

Let's take this tasting a step further. Divide both the clear caramel and the classic caramel into three batches. For each (clear and classic) keep one batch as is, to the second batch add a bit of sea salt, and to the last portion add a bit of ancho chilli powder. Taste the three clear caramel sauces first and then the classic caramel sauces. Taste the sauces in the following progression: plain (no additions), salt, and then chilli. As you taste, concentrate on the way in which the flavors move through your mouth. For both the clear and classic caramels, you will find the salt hits your palate first followed closely by the sweetness of the caramel and then the bitter last note. The caramels with chilli are especially interesting, as they leave not only a back note of bitter from the caramel but also a wonderful trigeminal response from the ancho chilli powder. Pay close attention to the movement of flavor through your mouth as you taste each sauce.

For each sauce the movement in your mouth should feel something like this:

Clear caramel sauce: sweet—caramel nuttiness—bitter

Clear caramel sauce with salt: salt—sweet—caramel nuttiness—bitter

Clear caramel sauce with ancho powder: sweet—caramel nuttiness—earthiness from the ancho chilli powder—bitter—heat from the chilli powder

Classic caramel sauce: sweet—buttery richness—caramel nuttiness—hint of bitter

Classic caramel sauce with salt: salt—sweet—buttery richness—caramel nuttiness—hint of bitter

Classic caramel sauce with ancho powder: sweet—buttery richness—caramel nuttiness—hint of bitter—hint of heat

Notice that the flavor and heat of the ancho chilli powder is really smoothed out and somewhat dulled in the classic caramel sauce. The chilli's earthy qualities are not nearly as recognizable as they are in the clear caramel sauce counterpart.

$\circlearrowleft$ base notes

Base notes are the last impression a flavor leaves in your mouth. Base notes are found in products with a sour or bitter taste or in those with a trigeminal response. Often base notes leave a humming of flavor in the mouth. Recall the dark chocolates with their strong bitter finish. As the chocolates became increasingly bitter, their finish, or base note, became steadily stronger. Consider the almond coated with ancho chilli powder that too had a strong base note.

The following balloon diagrams are very helpful in the analysis of plate profiles. The ability to analyze a dish's plate profile is vital to an understanding of taste and flavor. All chefs, not only pastry chefs, use this skill. The plate profile diagram is based on the image of a water balloon.

Consider a water balloon. Although it is pliable and flexible, it can contain only a limited amount of liquid. If you were to pull on one end of the balloon its oval shape would be shifted. Instead of the majority of water creating a bulge in the middle of the balloon, that bulge would move to one or the other of the balloon's sides. In this way, moving one portion of the balloon affects the entire balloon.

A plate profile operates in a similar fashion. A full plate profile is one in which the top note introduces the larger middle note, which is followed by a softer base note. Adjusting any one of these notes will affect all of the notes in the plate profile. The following plate profiles are diagrams for items you tasted in Chapter 2.

Top Note: Roasted Sugared Almond

Note that the large top note supplied by the sugar coating on the almond leaves little room for a base note. After the almond flavor is gone the palate is clear. In this case there is no humming or resonance of flavor.

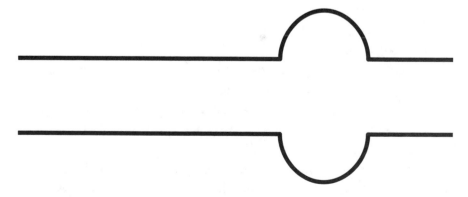

FIGURE 3.1

The top note of a roasted sugar almond.

chapter 3   plate profile

Middle Note: Plain Roasted Almond

In this case the plate profile consists solely of a strong middle note. The buttery rich flavor of the almond fills the entire plate profile. There is little top or base note here, just the flavor of the roasted almond.

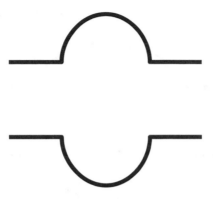

FIGURE 3.2

The middle note of a plain roasted almond.

Base Note: Unsweetened Chocolate or Cocoa Liquor

In Chapter 2 you experienced the overwhelmingly strong base note of unsweetened chocolate or cocoa liquor. There is no sugar in this chocolate and, thus, no top note. Additionally there is not much of a middle note because it takes so long to develop any flavor. Throughout the tasting of this chocolate one is left with a strong base note of bitterness.

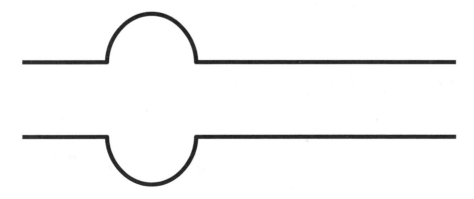

FIGURE 3.3

The base note of unsweetened chocolate or cocoa liquor.

Full Plate Profile: Roasted Almond with Sugar, Salt, and Ancho Chilli Powder

In this instance, it is clear that the nut has a full plate profile. The sweet and salt supply a top note, the almond flavor is the middle note, and the trigeminal response caused by the ancho chilli powder is the base note. Note that a full plate profile has a gentle introduction and conclusion to the strength of the flavor, which makes up the middle note.

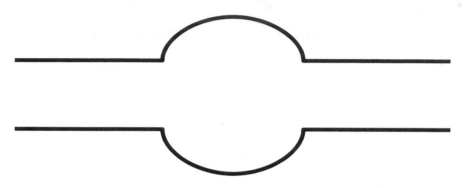

FIGURE 3.4

The full plate profile of roasted almonds with sugar, salt, and ancho chilli powder.

Remember that a water balloon can hold only a finite amount of liquid. Thus, one must be careful that the three parts of the balloon are aligned. If there is too much of a top note, there will be less room for a middle and base note. Likewise, if the base note is too large, the top and middle note will be pushed to the side. The goal is to have the top note lead into the main singer, the middle note, and then exit with a humming of the base note. There cannot be three (or more!) lead singers; there can be only one, the middle note.

These balloon diagrams can be used for analyzing full plated desserts. You can either graph out each component of the dish or the dish as a whole. The following diagram is for the apple pie previously discussed on page 22.

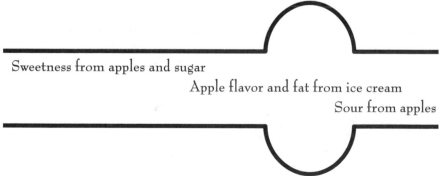

Sweetness from apples and sugar

Apple flavor and fat from ice cream

Sour from apples

FIGURE 3.5

The full plate profile of apple pie.

TOP NOTES:

Sugar from the pie filling
Natural sweetness from the apples
Sugar in the ice cream

MIDDLE NOTES:

Apple flavor
Fat in ice cream

BASE NOTES:

Slight sour note from the apples

Like the flavor profile chart, the plate profile balloon diagrams show the faults of this dessert. It is clear that its top note is too heavy. The dessert is too sweet.

The ideal plate profile has an introductory top note, a larger middle note, and a base note with the same relative strength as the top note. This is often hard to accomplish. The goal is best met through all of the components on a particular dish rather than through each individual component. In some restaurants chefs are directing their customers as to how to eat a particular dish. They are, in essence, directing the customer to the "perfect bite," or a full plate profile.

When diagramming a more complex dish, it is probably best to establish a plate profile for each individual component. The following balloon diagrams illustrate the plate profile for the gingerbread cake discussed in Chapter 2. The entrée is a warm gingerbread cake served with freshly sautéed pears. The cake is accompanied by a pear chip, pear Williams sorbet, a salty caramel corkscrew, red wine and pear reduction sauce, and a salty caramel sauce with curry powder and fresh ginger.

FROM THE CHEF'S MIND TO THE CUSTOMER'S PALATE

The mechanics in the kitchen are meaningless if an explanation of the plate and the chef's goals are not articulated to the consumer. Developing any type of dish takes a great deal of time. As the plate evolves, the chef has a clear concept of the order in which each of the elements should be eaten. This information must be conveyed to the customers before they begin to eat their dessert.

The customer can be guided in a number of ways. The simplest method is to physically construct the plate so that the customer has no recourse but to eat the components in the desired order. Stacking the various components one upon the other is one way in which this can be accomplished. For instance, if I know that I want the customer to experience the ancho chili ice cream in the same bite as the Mexican chocolate ganache, then I need to build those components one on top of another. Perhaps I could make them both into small bricks resembling a Mayan pyramid. The pyramid fulfills two functions. It forces the customer to eat both the ice cream and the ganache with each bite, and the visual image reinforces the Mayan flavor theme of the dessert.

Alternatively, the consumers can be guided in their flavor journey by the wait staff. The wait staff is, in turn, guided by the chef. In this scenario the wait staff relays to the customer the chef's suggestion for the best way to eat a particular dish. For instance, if the corn tortilla broth "shooter" was meant to be the first step in the dessert course, this should be explained to the customer. If there is a clear progression from one element of the plate to the next, the customer should be informed of that as well.

Communication between the chef and the wait staff is vital. It is important that the wait staff knows not only the order of the components of the dish, but, more importantly, why the components should be eaten in that order. It is up to the chef to educate the front of the house staff. They must be included in all of the tastings, and the whys and wherefores for each component must be clearly articulated. The wait staff will then continue this educational process as they speak with the customers, insuring that each consumer experiences the perfect bite, the perfect plate profile.

Aroma from the cake and pears
Sweet from the cake and pears
Gingerbread cake and pear essence
Sour from the pears
Heat from the fresh ginger

FIGURE 3.6

The plate profile of gingerbread cake with freshly sautéed pears.

The entrée item has a fairly complete plate profile. This will not always be the case.

Sweet from simple syrup and pear's sugars

Pear flavor

Slight sour, depending on type of pear used

FIGURE 3.7

The plate profile for a pear chip.

Note the change in the structure of the balloon. The strong top note means that there will be a resulting decrease in the middle and/or base note. In the case of the pear chips, the base note is diminished. The sweetness of the chips detracts from the natural sourness of the pear.

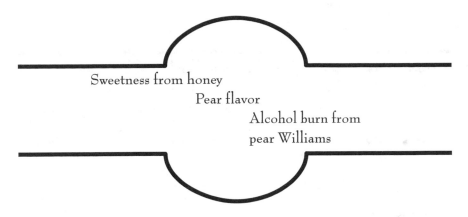

Sweetness from honey
Pear flavor
Alcohol burn from
pear Williams

FIGURE 3.8

The plate profile for pear Williams sorbet.

There is a strong pear presence in the sorbet. The middle note is, therefore, quite large. Consequently, the plate profile balloon must adapt with smaller top and base notes.

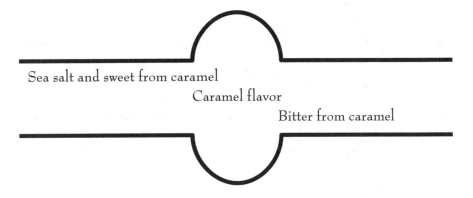

Sea salt and sweet from caramel
Caramel flavor
Bitter from caramel

FIGURE 3.9

The plate profile for a salty caramel wave.

The salt and sweetness from the caramel make for an intense top note. The strength of the top note is offset, to an extent, by the bitterness in the caramel itself. The breadth of the top and base notes means that there is little room for a commanding middle note. This is borne out when eating the salty caramel. The taste moves from salty—sweet—a bit of caramel flavor, and is immediately followed by the bitterness of the caramel itself.

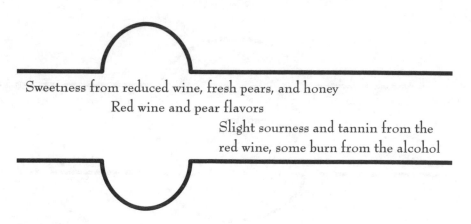

Sweetness from reduced wine, fresh pears, and honey
Red wine and pear flavors
Slight sourness and tannin from the
red wine, some burn from the alcohol

FIGURE 3.10

The plate profile for a red wine and pear reduction.

The deep base note in the reduction sauces means that there will be a resulting shorter top note. As a result the sauces are more sour or tart than they are sweet.

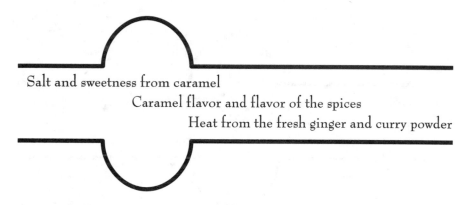

Salt and sweetness from caramel
Caramel flavor and flavor of the spices
Heat from the fresh ginger and curry powder

FIGURE 3.11

The plate profile for salty caramel sauce with curry and fresh ginger.

The plate profile of the salty and spicy caramel sauce is similar to that of the salty caramel garnish. The base note for the sauce has increased depth with the addition of the heat supplied by the fresh ginger and the curry powder.

The gingerbread plate is a good example of a well-balanced plate profile. There is a strong middle note in the gingerbread cake. The sauces and the garnishes all work to accentuate and draw attention to the lead singer, the gingerbread cake. There is a nice distribution of top and base notes as well, with no one note overpowering the others. When designing dishes, this should always be your goal. If you don't have the time to diagram each separate component, the entire plate can be charted onto a single balloon.

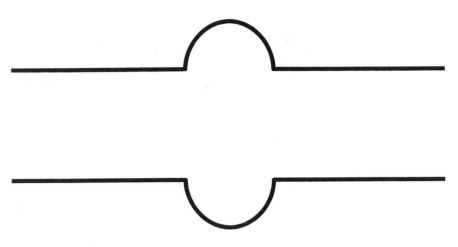

FIGURE 3.12

Plate profile practice diagram.

Whether you chart the entire plate or each individual component, the result will be the same. You will immediately know if the plate profile is balanced or not. Use the following blank diagram as a guide for analyzing the plate profiles of the plates you have made or enjoyed in a restaurant.

mechanics of flavor

chapter 4

cooking methods and culinary techniques

Cooking revolves around the ability to control heat. The discovery of fire led to the realization that applying heat to mastodon meat transformed its flavor. Suddenly, the raw meat became more palatable. Although cooking methods have become a tad more sophisticated, they still transform the flavor of the product being heated. Traditionally, the baking and pastry world used baking as their primary cooking method. For the pastry world, baking changes a raw product into something edible. However, an interpretation of culinary cooking methods with an eye toward flavor will reveal that cooking methods outside of baking have much to offer the flavors of plated desserts.

A QUICK REVIEW OF THE STEPS IN THE BAKING PROCESS:

1. *Gas formation and expansion:* Carbon dioxide, steam, and air are the gases that provide leavening to raw doughs and batters. Some gases will be produced at room temperature. Once the product's internal temperature reaches 170°F (75°C), however, the rise produced by these gases is halted.

2. *Coagulation of proteins:* The final structure of the baked good becomes set as the proteins begin to coagulate. This occurs at 140–160°F (60–70°C). The proteins are formed by either egg proteins or gluten.

3. *Gelatinization of starches:* Starches begin to gel and strengthen, becoming firm. This occurs once the internal temperature of the baked good reaches 140°F (60°C) and will continue until the temperature reaches 200°F (95°C).

4. *Evaporation of water and gases:* This occurs as the internal temperature of the dough reaches 212°F (100°C).

5. *Crust formation and caramelization:* Once water evaporates, the surface of the crust becomes dry. The sugar and starch on the surface will begin to caramelize at about 266°F (130°C).

It is important to note that the items being cooked for plated desserts are not meat–protein based. We have forgone the mastodon filet and, instead, are primarily cooking fruits, vegetables, nuts, starches, dairy, and egg proteins. In the case of fruits and vegetables, the products are cooked solely for flavor development as they can be eaten in their raw state with no ill effects, unlike a raw cake batter or bread dough.

Culinary cooking categories are divided into three categories: (1) dry heat, (2) moist heat, and (3) a combination of dry and moist. Dry heat transfers heat to the food product without the addition of any liquid. The heat is transferred through a hot pan, hot oil or fat, or hot air or radiation. Moist heat transfers heat to the food through some kind of liquid. In most cases this liquid is flavored and those flavors are transferred to the food during the cooking process. Combination cooking usually begins with dry heat and uses moist heat to complete the cooking process.

caramelization and maillard browning

The role of temperature in various cooking processes will prove to be extremely important to the development of flavor. Caramelization refers to a specific stage in the sugar cooking process. When sugar reaches 325–330°F (163–166°C), it begins to caramelize. Simply meant, the sugar turns brown. The longer it is allowed to cook, the darker the sugar will become. As it darkens, the sugar develops its characteristic caramel flavor. Caramelization gives a plate strong top and base notes: sweet and bitter.

Maillard browning refers to the browning that many products undergo as they are cooked. This concept of browning was discovered and defined by Louis Camille Maillard in 1910. He found that interactions between carbohydrates and amino acids, when in the presence of proteins, lead to full, deep flavors and brown color. In short, Maillard browning takes place in foods that are not primarily sugar based. The flavors of products that have undergone Maillard browning are full bodied and rich. They far transcend the simpler caramel sugar flavor associated with caramelization. Maillard browning helps a plate to develop strong, resonant middle notes.

Temperature plays an important role in both caramelization and Maillard browning. High temperatures (Maillard browning for some foods begins at 220°F (104°C)) are needed for either of these processes to occur. Water boils at 212°F (100°C). Unless a pressure cooker is being used, the temperature of any moist cooking method will not rise above water's boiling temperature. Cooking techniques can, therefore, be divided into those that will trigger Maillard browning and caramelization and those that will not. Cooking techniques using temperatures much lower than 220°F (104°C) will not impart Maillard browning. Thus, none of the moist heat techniques will develop the flavor found in either caramelization or Maillard browning.

When considering a specific plated dessert it is necessary to consider whether the richness and strong middle notes contributed by Maillard browning are desirable. The context of the specific component within the plated dessert will define the manner in which heat should be applied to the product.

dry heat sautéing

Sautéing uses high heat and a small amount of fat. The fat is used to prevent the food from sticking to the pan and does not, necessarily, impart flavor to the product. This is a fast cooking method and is consequently not used for products that, due to their size and/or toughness, need to be cooked for a long period of time. The quick application of heat means that most of the food's natural flavor is captured. Juices that are extracted in the cooking process are caught in the sauté pan and will often form the base for a pan sauce (see Chapter 5). Fruits or vegetables that are being sautéed will result, for the most part, in an al dente or fork-tender product. Their internal temperature will, in most cases, not reach 212°F (100°C), which means that their cell walls have not yet completely broken down.

In plated desserts sautéing works well when the fruit or vegetable is fairly ripe. A hard, relatively tasteless, not quite yet ripe pear will not suddenly become flavorful through the sautéing process. Use this cooking method with ripe fruit for the best results. This method can also be used for soft fruits, such as strawberries and raspberries, when prolonged cook-

COOKING FRUITS AND VEGETABLES

Cooking fruits and vegetables breaks down their cell walls. Fruits and vegetables contain a great deal of water. As the fruit/vegetable cooks, the water pressure inside the cells increases and the cell walls break down. The internal water pressure will burst the cell walls at 140°F (60°C). When the cell walls burst, the water inside of them is released. At this stage the fruit or vegetable is tender to the bite, yet still al dente. As the fruit/vegetable reaches the boiling point (212°F or 100°C), the cell structure breaks down even more and the resulting texture is fairly soft. Further boiling will reduce the fruit/vegetable to a purée.

Bear in mind that fruits and vegetables contain sugars. As the product's cell walls break down, these sugars are more evenly dispersed and thus more readily perceived by the consumer. Depending on the cooking method, some of those sugars may become caramelized and/or undergo Maillard browning.

Cooking fruits and vegetables gives them a deep full flavor, unlike the clear crispness they possess when they are raw. On the whole, cooked fruit or vegetables are both more tender and sweeter than their raw counterparts. In the development of plated desserts there are times when both attributes (sweet and tender versus crisp and less sweet) are needed. Whether a fruit or vegetable should be cooked or kept raw depends upon the plate profile of the specific plated dessert in which it is being used.

ing will break the fruit down, causing it to lose its integral shape. A quick sauté, finished with a sprinkle of granulated sugar will result in fruit with a clear, shiny, and sweet "glaze." (See Corny Ice Cream Sandwich for a plated dessert that uses this cooking method.)

Sautéing relies on a hot pan. It is vital that the pan is hot before adding a small amount of fat and that the fat is hot before adding the item to be sautéed. Using a cold pan or cold fat will result in the sautéed item absorbing too much fat, altering its end taste and texture.

grilling

Grilling is done on an open type of grid with heat radiating from below. The heat source can be either gas or wood. Cooking with wood obviously imparts a smokiness to the product. Occasionally herbs are burnt along with the wood to infuse the item being grilled with more flavor. In this cooking method the juices extracted from the product are reduced directly on its outer surface. The result is a charred exterior composed of a flavorful, caramelized crust. (See page 126 for an example of a plated dessert using this cooking method.) Grilling a thick slice of fresh pineapple, for instance, will result in a crusty sugar crust surrounding the soft fruit, encasing its flavorful juices. Consider marinating the fruit or vegetable before grilling or brushing the fruit or vegetable with a juice or liquor marinade while it is grilling. Either technique will result in a product with an even greater depth of flavor. Grill marks can add some visual excitement to the plate as well, as in the case of grilled polenta cakes branded with a perfect cross-hatch grill pattern. Grilling will not work well with smaller soft fruits. Their size makes them easy to lose them between grid openings and their soft texture means they will break down too much over the high heat of an open flame.

pan-frying/deep-frying

In both pan-frying and deep-frying, the heat of the oil or fat cooks the food rather than direct contact with a dry heat source (such as a pan). Deep-frying is traditionally used for larger items, whereas pan-frying works best for smaller items. If a large item is pan-fried make sure that at least half of the product is covered in oil. This way, when it is flipped over the middle of the item is fried twice insuring that it is completely cooked.

Products are often dredged in a breading and/or a flour and egg mixture, or sometimes dipped into a batter prior to frying. This coating locks in the food's natural juices. Sauces for deep- or pan-fried items are, therefore, made separately. Take the example of assorted tempura fruits. For this plate, fruits such as strawberries and slices of peaches, pineapple, or even pears and apples are covered with a light batter and fried. The contrast of the crispy coating and the softer, juicy fruit works well. The batter seals in the fruits' juices, requiring that any accompanying sauce be made separately. (See page 160 for a plated dessert that utilizes this technique.)

Starchy vegetables can be fried without any type of protective barrier. The natural starches of potatoes or squash, for instance, allow these vegetables to be deep fried without first being covered with a batter. Consider a plated dessert of a soft applesauce spice cake and brown sugar ice cream with an accompaniment of deep-fried sweet potato matchsticks dredged in cinnamon sugar. This is a modern pastry twist on the classic American French fry.

roasting and baking

Although classically most roasting was done on a spit, modern roasting more closely resembles baking. Both cooking techniques take place in a closed environment. Roasting is usually done for longer periods of time than baking. The product being roasted is often placed on a rack to ensure that it will be entirely encompassed by the circulation of hot air. Items being baked are not placed on a rack but, rather, contained within a dry heat environment. As a product roasts, its natural juices rise to the surface and turn to steam. That steam, in turn, penetrates the food as it cooks. The product's natural sugars begin to caramelize on its surface and the result is a product with deep, intense flavor. The sweet richness of a roasted vegetable or fruit is incomparable. In the pastry world, roasting is primarily done with fruits, vegetables, and nuts. Recall the depth of flavor achieved when almonds were roasted.

Roasting a fruit or vegetable can also form the base of a sauce. The pan drippings, or fond, can be deglazed (with liquor or juice) and further reduced. The result is a sauce full of intense, caramelized flavor. (See page 128 for a plated dessert using this cooking technique.)

smoking

Smoking is a culinary cooking technique not often used in the pastry world. There are many reasons for this. A smoked flavor and aroma can easily overpower a plate, especially a dessert plate. Additionally, the smoked flavor is hard to control. In contrast to meat products, fruits and vegetables readily and quickly absorb smoked flavor.

To have more control over the strength of the smoked flavor, it is sometimes best to smoke the sweetener rather than the fruit or vegetable. This technique works well for sugars and honey. Pour the honey or sugar into a pie tin or hotel pan and place in the smoker. Taste at frequent intervals. The resulting smoky sweetener can be stored in a covered container at room temperature. Having the smoke in the sweetener makes it easy to control the level of smoky flavor in the end product. When used with a gentle hand-smoked sugar or honey can add a wonderfully full back note to a plated dessert as well as a hint of aroma for a top note. If a free-standing smoker is not available, smoking can be done on the stovetop or in the oven. Use a tightly closed hotel or roasting pan for this. Experiment with different types of wood chips. These will offer your plate additional woody notes.

The earthiness of a smoky note works well when combined with a fruit or vegetable that has been roasted. The strength and depth of the roasted flavor allows the smoky sweetener to harmonize with the plate rather than overwhelming it.

moist heat

Moist heat uses some type of liquid to transfer heat to the product being cooked. Recall that water boils at 212°F (100°C). Moist cooking methods do not rise above the boiling temperature of water. Therefore, caramelization and Maillard browning, which both occur at temperature higher than 212°F (100°C), are not present in these moist cooking methods.

Poaching

A poached product is one cooked in a flavored liquid. In this cooking process the flavors of the liquid are infused in the product as it cooks. Traditionally, poaching is used for delicately flavored food items as these will more easily absorb the flavor(s) of the poaching liquid. Enough liquid should be used so that the item being poached is completely submerged. Poaching generally takes place between 160 and 185°F (71–85°C). This relatively low temperature means that fragile items can be poached without disintegrating.

Certainly the most familiar dessert using poaching is that of poached fruit. In this instance, the fruit is gently cooked while being infused with flavors from the poaching liquid. Consider the many alternative uses for poaching liquid. It can be used as a sorbet base, the beginning of a reduction sauce, or a consommé or made into a gelée. Alternatively, it can simply be refrigerated and used in the future to poach more fruit. (See page 132 for an example of a plated dessert using this cooking method.)

Simmering

Simmering occurs between 185 and 200°F (85–93°C). The increased heat means that denser and less fragile items can be used than those used in poaching. Technically, therefore, many poached fruit desserts are in reality simmered fruit. This is especially true of poached apples or pears. The strong structure of these fruits allows them to be cooked at high temperatures. There is a greater amount of flavor transfer from liquid to product in simmering than in poaching. Just as with poaching, the liquid can be utilized for other products such as sauces, sorbet bases, and gelées.

Boiling

Boiling takes place at 212°F (100°C). This cooking method is used often for grains and pastas. Items such as polenta, grits, risotto, and farina all employ boiling as part of their preparation. Most boiling is accomplished with plain water. In this method the liquid is not usually flavored as is the case in poaching or simmering. And unlike poaching or simmering, the liquid used in boiling will often be completely absorbed by the item being cooked. For some pastry work a dairy product such as milk or heavy cream may replace a portion of the water. Polenta, for instance, may be cooked with lightly sweetened water, and heavy cream may be added toward the end of the cooking process. The result is a rich, luxurious polenta that can be used in a multitude of forms on a plated dessert (see page 130 for an example). A risotto made in much the same way can form the base of a flavorful dessert risotto or the base of a rice pudding.

combination methods

Combination cooking utilizes both dry and moist cooking processes. The method begins with a dry cooking method and ends with the addition of some kind of liquid that transfers heat to finish the cooking. Beginning with dry cooking means that the combination method adds some caramelization and/or Maillard browning to the products being cooked.

Braising

Traditionally, the items to be braised are first seared. Searing is the dry portion of the cooking method. When working with fruits and vegetables, searing the food product allows for the formation of a caramelized crust. This crust will add to the depth of flavor in the end product (see page 176). After the product has been seared it is placed in a pan with some liquid. This is the moist heat cooking method. Not a lot of liquid is added, just enough to cover about one-third of the product. The mixture is then covered and placed in an oven with low heat until it is completely cooked. The liquid is used as the base of the sauce. Items such as beets, fennel, carrots, pears, apples, and pineapple all acquire deep, luxurious flavors when braised with a bit of liquid. Some examples of flavor pairings include beets and carrots with fresh orange juice, fennel with a dry white wine, pears with bourbon and a touch of maple syrup, apples with fresh apple cider, or pineapple with Malibu rum. The flavor combinations in all of these dishes are deep and full bodied. The resulting liquid, along with the pan fond, or drippings can be made into an accompanying sauce.

Stewing

Stewing differs from braising in a number of ways. First, the products being stewed are cut into small pieces. Next, they are completely covered with a liquid, unlike the smaller quantity of liquid used in the braising method. The mixture then remains on the stovetop and continues to cook uncovered. In the case of stewing, the liquid becomes part of the dish. No additional sauce is required. Both braising and stewing are used with tougher items that both require and can withstand a long cooking time.

In some respects, a compote is a type of stew. The fruit is in small pieces and a liquid is added as the fruit is cooked. In this case the fruit's natural pectin will thicken the "stew," which is most often used as a sauce for plated desserts. Fresh raspberries cooked with red wine and a bit of orange juice and honey served over a lemon buttermilk ice cream is an example of a combination cooking method being incorporated into a plated dessert.

experience the effect of cooking methods on a product's flavor

Try the following experiment to more fully understand the way in which cooking methods affect the flavors of any one particular product. Clean and peel some carrots. Cut the carrots into strips of approximately ½ inch by 3 inches. Set aside a few strips. These will be tasted raw. Divide up the remaining strips into nine piles. Each pile will be cooked separately. One pile will be poached, one simmered, and one boiled. As each batch is finished, set it aside to cool. Sauté one pile with a touch of butter, grill one pile, fry a pile with a light tempura batter, stew another pile, roast another, and braise the final pile with fresh orange juice. Make sure to clearly label each pile as they are being cooked.

You are now ready to taste. Begin with the raw carrot. Notice not only its crunchy texture but also its lightly sweet and crispy clean flavor. Now taste the poached, simmered, and boiled carrots, respectively. While the poached carrot still has some of the clean flavor of its raw counterpart, those notes are lost the longer that it has been cooked. The heavy overly cooked flavor of the boiled carrot bears little resemblance to its raw cousin in both texture and taste.

The sautéed carrot, although cooked, has a bit more sweetness than the first batches, which were prepared with wet cooking methods. The same is true for the grilled carrot. Its slightly caramelized crust serves to intensify its sweet carrot flavor. The flavor of the fried carrot most closely resembles that of the sautéed carrot. It is slightly al dente with a light, crispy coating. The natural carrot flavor is fairly subtle. The roasted carrot is the sweetest thus far. This is a prime example of Maillard browning. The carrot has a deep, rich flavor. Raw carrot flavor times ten! Its strong inherent sweetness does not need any help from outside sources such as sugar or honey. Slow braising or stewing also contributes markedly intense carrot flavor to the end product. The addition of a liquid, in this case some orange juice, serves to somewhat dilute that intensity but it does bring out the carrot's inherent citrus notes.

Consider cooking techniques as not only a way of transforming a raw product into something more palatable but, more importantly, as a way of developing and expanding the elements of flavor in any one particular dish. Using the proper cooking technique can help to develop a full plate profile. One method of cooking is not necessarily better than another. When deciding which method to employ, the plate profile of the entire dessert must be taken into account.

The following chapters take these cooking techniques one step further. They are used to develop even more varied nuances of flavors in the development of assorted plated desserts.

sauce work

Sauce work is integral to the overall composition of plated desserts. Sauce is an important part of a dish's appeal, both visually and in terms of flavor. Visually, a sauce's presence on a plate can contribute an aesthetic excitement that would otherwise be absent. More importantly, sauces are one of the easiest methods of completing a full plate profile. They can be used to add yet one more harmonizing flavor to a particular dish.

When developing sauces for a specific plated dessert, the role of fat must be taken into account. Examine the plate profile of your dessert. Is the entrée's middle note full of fat? If so, then choose a sauce whose middle note is carried by its clean flavors, not its fat-laden ingredients. Consider the classic dessert sauce, sauce anglaise. Sauce anglaise is a sweet, dairy-based sauce that is thickened by egg yolks. Its middle note is carried by the fat of the heavy cream and egg yolks. Consequently, anglaise is a sauce that should not be used when the dish's entrée item also contains a large amount of fat. Think about a traditional Bavarian cream, or a rich chocolate mousse accompanied by sauce anglaise. The dessert's plate profile has a huge middle note that does not allow room for a top or base note. On the other hand, if the entrée item of your plated dessert does not have much fat, then a creamy sauce will help to round out the dessert's middle note.

This chapter offers some modern alternatives to classic dessert sauces. The focus of all of these sauces is flavor. You will notice that they all contain little or no fat. The absence of fatty middle notes allows the strong, true flavors of each sauce to be fully appreciated. Most of the sauces have loud top and/or base notes. These sauces offer an easy way of completing a dessert's full plate profile.

reworking classic sauces

Sauce anglaise is not the only classic dessert sauce with a fat-laden middle note. A classic chocolate sauce is made with ganache, a combination of heavy cream and chocolate (sometimes with the addition of butter). Recall the classic caramel sauce tasted in Chapter 1 with its full middle note of butter and heavy cream. Sabayon, egg yolks and sugar, is yet another example of these traditional rich, fatty dessert sauces. Consider using infusion as a way of developing a bit more depth into the middle notes of these sauces. The result will be a rich sauce with some harmonizing background notes of flavor.

infusion

Infusion can be defined as extracting flavor from a fresh or dried herb or spice. Infusing flavor is similar to making a cup of tea. Tea leaves impart more flavor to a warm liquid than to a cold liquid. The flavor of tea becomes stronger the longer the tea leaves remain in contact with the liquid, the longer it steeps.

Similarly, there are two steps to infusion in the culinary and pastry world: heating and steeping. To extract the optimal amount of flavor, the herb or spice must be placed in a warm liquid rather than a cold liquid. The longer the herb or spice remains in the liquid—the longer it steeps—the stronger the resulting flavor. This process requires constant tasting and cannot be done by simply following a recipe or formula. The time required to extract flavor from any one particular product is dependent, for the most part, upon its freshness. Freshly zested orange rind will, for instance, infuse into a dairy base quicker than a dried cinnamon stick. Remember the importance of repetition and taste the infusion throughout the production process.

When flavoring through infusion, always consider how the resulting flavored liquid is going to be used in the final product. For instance, if the finished product contains a large amount of fat (an anglaise ice cream base, or a Bavarian cream, for example) make sure that the initial infusion is strong. (Keep in mind the classic caramel and clear caramel sauce tasting on pages 26–27.) If the initial infusion has a wonderful gentle hint of lemon, realize that it will completely disappear as the other fattier elements of the recipe are added, such as egg yolks or heavy cream.

Infusions Versus Extracts

Using infusions brings a greater depth of flavor to the end product than using an extract or flavoring compound. Although there are some good extracts available, there is no comparison between a manufactured, distilled flavor and the real thing.

The advantage of extracts is their convenience. They can be easily measured and weighed and will offer consistent results with little effort on the part of the chef. Flavoring with extracts also means that the end result can be quickly adjusted. If a taste of the anglaise reveals that the almond flavor is too weak, for example, more extract can be easily added. Once an anglaise is made with an infusion, however, it is not possible to resteep the cream to increase its flavor as doing so will most likely break the sauce. Infusion requires more finesse from the chef, constant vigilance, and tasting throughout the process. Despite all of these factors, the flavor rewards of using an infusion are great.

modern dessert sauces

The following sauces borrow techniques from the culinary/savory world. In most cases the sauces have little or no fat, which makes them the perfect accompaniment to an entrée item made with lots of heavy cream, eggs, or butter. Additionally, their lack of fat results in strong top or base notes. These sauces are a wonderful way in which to complete a dessert's full plate profile.

Reduction Sauces

Reduction sauces are as simple as reducing down a liquid. The liquid can be a juice, liquor, or poaching liquid. A reduction sauce is thickened through evaporation. Some, or all, of the water in a juice, liquor, etc., is evaporated, which, in turn, transforms the remaining liquid into a syrup-like consistency. Slow simmering will allow the sauce to thicken on its own. As the water evaporates the flavors of the sauce intensify. Do not use a slurry to thicken reduction sauces, as it is the process of evaporation that intensifies the flavors of the sauce while it thickens the sauce. The concentration of flavors is what makes a reduction sauce so special.

Pan Sauces

Pan sauces are the result of other either dry or combination cooking methods, such as sautéing, roasting, or braising. After the products are cooked, remove them from the pan. Deglaze the pan with the desired liquid, scraping up the fond. Reduce the mixture to desired consistency. Strain (if desired) and serve. Sometimes cold butter is added to the sauce, which adds a sheen and buttery mouth feel to the end product. Be wary of this step if the dish's entrée item already contains a large amount of fat.

Clear Sauces

Clear sauces are those made without any fat. The "clear" refers to the crisp, clean, clear flavors that result when fat is left out of a recipe. You have already tasted a clear sauce in Chapter 1, the clear caramel sauce. In this case, water was added to the caramelized sugar instead of the more traditional heavy cream and butter. You experienced the depth of flavor, the full deep plate profile that was the result. Consider infusing the liquid for a clear sauce with an herb or spice to make this sauce even more flavorful. Liquids such as fruit juices, liquors or purées can be substituted for the water.

Herb Clear Sauces

The idea of clear sauces is continued with these herb clear sauces. There are two types of herb clear sauces and in both cases they consist of only an herb and a sweetener. The sauces' composition allows the true nature and flavors of the herb to shine through. Both methods of preparation offer strong herb flavors; in the first sauce the herbs are cooked and the second sauce they are left in a raw state.

Infused Herb Clear Sauces

Infusing fresh herbs into a simple syrup is one way of producing an herb clear sauce. Rinse the herbs and pat them dry. Add the herbs to a simmering simple syrup. Continue to simmer the sauce until the desired flavor is reached. Strain the syrup and store the sauce in the refrigerator until needed for service.

There are both advantages and disadvantages to making an herb clear sauce in this manner. The heating/steeping process brings a depth of flavor to the sauce as well as some great back notes. This is certainly an advantage. The disadvantage is that the heating process also gives the herbs a distinctly cooked flavor. They lose their fresh grassy notes. Once the herbs have been strained from the simple syrup, the resulting sauce is relatively colorless and fairly thin. Because simple syrup forms the base of this sauce, further reduction can sometimes cause the sugar to crystallize. A grainy or crystallized sugar syrup is certainly not desired in sauce work.

The sauce's colorless and thin nature makes this a good sauce to use in tandem with another sauce. It works especially well together with a thicker or denser sauce. A few drops of the clear sauce can be placed on top of another thicker sauce in a tie-dye or oil spill type of pattern. This technique works best when two sauces of different densities are used. The thick sauce is placed on the plate first, followed by the thinner sauce. In this way the thinner sauce is held in place. You can then use a toothpick or the point of a paring knife to create a pattern between the two sauces. Alternatively, the sauces can be left alone to form a type of tie-dye pattern on the plate. Remember that the flavor of the sauce being used is of primary importance. If the sauce tastes great but is too thin, do not despair. There are many beautiful ways of incorporating that sauce into your final plate design.

Uncooked Herb Clear Sauces

An alternative to an infused herb clear sauce is an uncooked herb clear sauce made with a light corn syrup base. Blanch the fresh herbs quickly. Place the herbs in a chinoise before blanching. This makes it much easier to move them in and out of the boiling water and the ice bath. Pat the herbs dry with paper towels immediately upon removing them from the ice water. Place herbs and light corn syrup in a robot coupe or food processor and blend until a vibrant green syrup is formed.

Like the infused herb sauces, there are both advantages and disadvantages to this type of sauce. The advantage is that this sauce maintains the integrity of the fresh herbs' flavor. This sauce is saturated with the herbs' crisp, fresh, grassy flavors. It has a thick viscosity and a deep, dark green color. While the infused sauce may be a bit subtler, flavorwise, the fresh sauce is a loud burst of fresh herb flavor. The disadvantage of using raw herbs is that the sauce lacks the greater depth of flavor that is achieved when the herbs are infused.

Think about the flavors of the entire plated dessert when making the decision as to which herb clear sauce to use. Either used alone or in tandem with a more traditional dessert sauce, a full plate profile will be achieved when these sauces are employed.

 foams

Traditionally foams have always formed a part of the pastry chef's repertoire. Whipped cream and meringues are just two examples. Air is whipped into a liquid, either heavy cream or egg whites, and the result is a frothy set of stabilized bubbles. They hold up fairly well at room temperature and both are strong enough to be piped through a pastry bag. But what about foams with no fat—with strong clear flavors?

Foams as a Sauce Alternative

Foams can take many forms, but in all cases they are a liquid composed of a multitude of bubbles. The stability of these bubbles is what will dictate the ultimate form and look of the foam. The simplest form of a foam is made by incorporating air into ice-cold whole milk. The result is a foam with large light bubbles. The bubbles resemble soap bubbles. They are clearly delineated from each other.

Heat milk to infuse desired flavors. Allow to steep if needed. Chill milk until icy cold and then vehemently whisk when needed for service. The resulting bubbly foam can be spooned off the top of the milk and placed on the plate as a sauce. These bubbles have a short life span and will dissipate quickly. The large, clear bubbles resulting from aerated foam offer a beautiful visual contrast both on the plate itself and on the palate. They give texture to sauce work and are light and airy on the tongue. Such foams will work as top notes.

A light foam is not always desired. Sometimes the chef wants a foam with smaller bubbles, a foam that will not dissipate so quickly on the plate or on the customer's tongue.

Foam ISI Canister

Since foams are simply aerated liquids, the smaller and tighter the bubbles, the heavier and more stable the foam will become. An ISI canister pumps gas into a liquid base and is one way of creating small bubbles out of a liquid. The resulting foam is much more tightly packed than a simpler hand aerated foam. An ISI foam can be piped and will still hold its shape. Although the ISI canister has traditionally been used to make whipped cream, fat-free intensely flavored waters, juices, and liquors can also be used with great results.

Stabilized Foams

Foams stabilized with gelatin are quite strong. They will hold their shape for a long time, which allows them to be made before service. Additionally, such foams can be scooped and frozen. The following method of preparation is based on the fact that as bloomed and dissolved gelatin cools, it begins to thicken. (For exact measurements see the Appendix.)

Prepare the liquid. Some options include infusing water or dairy and lightly sweetening. Take approximately two-thirds of the liquid and place in a freezer. The liquid must be icy cold to achieve the best results. Storing the liquid in a metal container will facilitate the cooling process. Rehydrate or bloom the gelatin sheets by covering them with cold water. Wring out the excess water. Heat the remaining one-third of the liquid; add the rehydrated gelatin. Stir to dissolve gelatin. Place the gelatin mixture in a 5-quart KitchenAid mixer with the whip attachment. Start the mixer on speed 3 and slowly drizzle in the remaining two-thirds of icy cold liquid.

The theory behind this foam is simple. The addition of the icy liquid to the warm gelatin mixture means that the gelatin will start to solidify or to set up. By whipping the mixture on speed 3, the gelatin is being broken up into tiny pieces as it chills. The result is a foam with relatively small, yet clearly visible individual bubbles. It is extremely stable and will remain stable for quite a while. The mixture will continue to gel and solidify as it sits out at room temperature. For a clean look on the plate, simply scoop or quenelle the foam onto a parchment lined sheet pan and hold for service.

designing plates with modern dessert sauces

Using these new sauces will increase the flavor and plate profiles of your plated desserts. The sauces' lack of fat means that they possess strong top and/or base notes. Visually, however, the sauces can be challenging to work with. We know a sauce anglaise is cooked when it reaches the nape stage. The sauce gently coats the back of a spoon. The resulting sauce is easy to use in a squirt bottle. It will hold its line and allows the chef to design intricate sauce patterns without worrying that the sauce will not hold its edge.

Modern dessert sauces are not always cooked. And when the sauces are cooked, their flavor tells the chef when they are done, not their consistency.

Often these sauces are not at a nape stage when they are used for plating. The sauces may not flow easily from a squeeze bottle, being either too thick or too thin. The chef must, therefore, be prepared to attack the plates from a new visual angle. Consider using more than one sauce on a dish as alternative densities may often hold the thinner sauce in place. Do not force these sauces to hold the same tight lines that classic sauces would hold. It is better to develop new plate designs, new sauce patterns to accommodate these new flavorful sauces. You want your plates to look like you had intended the spatter of sauces as part of your design, rather than to have the design look simply messy and incomplete. Look at the photos in the glossy insert as well as the drawings in Chapters 8–11 for ideas as to how to use these modern dessert sauces to their best advantage.

texture and flavor

Thus far in our discussions of plate profiles, we have discovered that dishes with full plate profiles are by far the most satisfying for consumers. Desserts with full plate profiles offer a great depth and richness of flavor. Up to this point we have discussed only the flavors of specific ingredients in terms of their relationship to a plate profile. This chapter takes the concept of plate profile one step further. Here we explore the idea of altering a product's placement in the plate profile by manipulating its texture.

Consider the following two products: a piece of roasted peanut brittle and a scoop of peanut ice cream. Imagine biting into the peanut brittle. You are hit immediately with sweetness—roasted peanut flavor—and then a light humming of bitterness from the caramel. The physical nature of the brittle forces all of those flavors to linger on your palate. Even after the actual piece of brittle is swallowed, some of the sweet caramel peanut flavor remains.

Now imagine tasting a spoonful of roasted peanut ice cream. It too begins with sweet moving to roasted peanut flavor. Compared to the brittle, however, the ice cream begins to melt the moment it enters your mouth. In this case, once you swallow, the flavors of the ice cream dissipate, unlike the heavier brittle, and there is no lingering flavor on your palate. The very nature, the physical composition of these two products affects their overall placement in a plate profile. The following plate profile diagrams make this clear.

The concept of altering the position of a product in a plate profile solely by manipulating its texture opens up a whole new world of flavor possibilities. Through manipulation of texture it is possible that an item

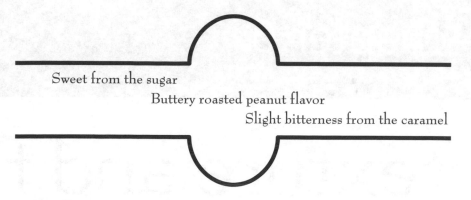

Sweet from the sugar

Buttery roasted peanut flavor

Slight bitterness from the caramel

FIGURE 6.1

The plate profile for roasted peanut brittle.

with a strong top note can be pushed to the base of a plate profile. And, conversely, if an extremely bitter or sour item is easily diffused on the palate, its normal base note qualities can become perceived by the consumer as top notes. Manipulating textures within a dish requires planning and forethought. It is vital that the plate profiles of all the components are plotted out and graphed before any alteration of their textures takes place.

The chef's goal is to have a fully developed plate profile. Manipulating the texture of some, or all, of the dish's components can often fill gaps in the plate profile chart. Sometimes the question of what is missing can be answered by simply adjusting the texture of some of the plate's components. The following techniques are especially helpful in this regard. Their utilization can help the chef to insure a full plate profile, not by changing the product's flavors but by altering its texture.

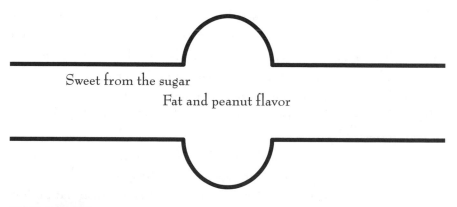

Sweet from the sugar

Fat and peanut flavor

FIGURE 6.2

The plate profile for roasted peanut ice cream.

 top notes

Powders

Powders are both a flavorful and a colorful addition to any plated dessert. They can consist of a ground vegetable, fruit, or brittle. The physical attributes of a powder means that it dissolves almost instantly on the tongue. Using a powder is, therefore, one way of insuring that the plate has a strong top note.

There are a number of ways to make a fruit or vegetable powder. The quickest method is to dry strips, slices, and/or peels of fruits or vegetables under a heat lamp or in a dehydrator. The fruit can also be dried in a low oven or in the microwave. Alternatively already made fruit or vegetable chips can be ground into a powder.

The following method of preparation works well for drying fruits or vegetables in a microwave. Slice the fruit/vegetable thinly and lay the slices in a single layer on a piece of paper towel. Place in the microwave for quick 10- to 15-second bursts (this will, of course, depend on the strength/power of your specific microwave). Flip the chips and allow to cool completely. Once the chips are cooled, return to the microwave and cook again for 10–15 seconds. Continue until the chips are crisp with no color. They will continue to crisp as they cool. Once they are crisp, grind the chips in a spice grinder and then push through a fine sieve. The resulting powder can be used to dust a plate, sprinkle on a tuile cookie before it is baked, or sprinkle on top of a mousse, Bavarian cream, or a scoop of ice cream. Store the powder in a tightly covered container at room temperature. (See the photo of Beef Meets Chocolate for an example of a beet powder.)

To make a powder from a nut brittle, grind the brittle in a spice grinder. Be careful not to grind for too long, or the ensuing heat will cause the sugar to start to melt. The result will be a sticky mass rather than a delicate powder. This works best if the original brittle is thin rather than thick. Thinner brittle will grind up quickly, thus reducing the chance of producing a gummy mess. Once you have a fine, sweet powder, use as you would a fruit or vegetable powder. Make sure to store powders in air-tight containers at room temperature.

"Chef-Made" Aromas

Because most plated desserts are not served piping hot, it is often hard to incorporate aroma as a top note. The chef must, therefore, manufacture an aroma that will push the desired top notes to the front of the consumer's experience. This can be accomplished in a number of ways, but most methods entail manufacturing an aroma outside of the individual components of the plate. For instance, serving a small cup of flavorful hot tea for the customer to smell and enjoy before taking the first bite of dessert. Alternatively, place the dessert plate on top of a larger underliner plate holding an assortment of dried ingredients. Their aromas are released with the addition of hot water added tableside by the wait staff.

Imagine a dessert composed of sweet corn cake, strawberry and cilantro salsa, lime-tequila clear caramel sauce and Mexican chocolate sorbet. In this instance all of the plate's components are either room temperature or frozen. A large pasta-type bowl is used as an underliner for the dessert plate. The bowl is filled with some cilantro leaves, lime zest, fresh cornhusks, vanilla beans and Mexican cinnamon. The plate with the dessert is placed on top of this underliner. Once the plate is presented to the customer the waiter fills the underliner pasta bowl with hot water. The customer is encouraged to lean over and deeply inhale the aroma before the first bite of the dessert is taken. Voila! The chef has manufactured aroma, a strong top note in the plate's overall plate profile. Although the smells harmonize with the flavors of the dish, they have been manufactured outside of the dish's individual components.

There are countless options for manufacturing aroma as a top note. Instead of hot water, a tea can be added to the bowl. Alternatively, present a small teacup on the side of the plate filled with a warm liquid to be sipped and enjoyed before eating the dessert. Think about aromatics. Burn a sprig of a dried flower or herb so that the smell wafts to the customer with every bite. Use your imagination—the variations are countless. Manufacturing an aroma does require a certain amount of logistical maneuvering but the resulting full top notes are worth the effort.

Flavored Water "Shooters"

The use and manipulation of flavored waters is another way in which a top note can be introduced to a plated dessert. It also offers a way for the chef to introduce the main theme of the plate. This is especially helpful when the flavors of the plate may be something with which the customer is not overly familiar. The easiest way to serve the water is in a shot glass. Remember that this is just an introduction to the plate, only a sip or two of the liquid is needed. The quantity should be small enough that, like a shooter, the customer can drink the water in one gulp. The result is a wash of flavor over the palate. Water shooters are also a good way of announcing the transition from the main course to the dessert.

These shooters are simply infusions. They can be lightly sweetened. For example, imagine a sweet corn-based dessert. It consists of grilled polenta cake with fresh mangoes, corn cream ice cream, and an ancho chilli caramel sauce. The water in this case is made by simply infusing the corn-cobs in water with just the smallest hint of honey. The result is a water-color of flavor, a refreshing and slightly sweet corn flavor. The water cleanses the palate while simultaneously preparing it for the next course. Flavored waters should be served at room temperature for maximum flavor. (See the Tomato Trio for an example of a plated dessert using this technique.)

 foams

Consider foams as a way of altering the texture of a sauce. Suddenly a sauce can be placed firmly as a top, middle, or base note, depending on the consistency of the foam in which it is made.

Foams as a Top Note

Foam can be placed as a top note when its bubbles are large and easily dissipated. This type of foam is most often made by simply incorporating air into ice-cold, flavored milk. No special equipment is needed, only a hand whisk and a bit of elbow grease. Spoon the bubbles off the top of the milk and place as desired on the plate. Make this foam as needed for service and use quickly. Its loose structure means that the large bubbles have a short life span. The bubbles dissipate quickly. The large bubbles of this type of foam resemble soap bubbles and visually they look lovely on a plate. Texturally they melt quickly on the tongue. Such foams work well as top notes.

Foams as Middle Notes

A light foam is not always desired. Sometimes the flavors of a foam are those that the chef wants to place as a middle note. Changing the foam's consistency can allow its flavors to linger longer on the palate.

Foam ISI Canister

This is perhaps the foam with which we are most familiar. The consistency of this foam is such that it can be piped out into rosettes. Although most commonly used for chantilly cream, the ISI canister will stabilize water-based liquids as well. Compared to the hand-whisked foam, the ISI canister produces tiny air bubbles. The ensuing foam is fairly firm. The desired mixture can be placed in the canister at the beginning of service and will last throughout the evening. The physical strength of this foam means that it takes a while to dissolve on the tongue. Thus, the flavors used in such a foam, even those without any fat, will become part of the plate's middle note.

Foams Stabilized with Gelatin

Foams stabilized with gelatin are quite strong; they will hold their shape for a long time. They can be made before service and will hold up well throughout the evening. These foams are so stable that they can be scooped or shaped into quenelles. The method of preparation for such foams is straightforward and is outlined in the Appendix.

This foam will continue to set after it is made. Once the gelatin reaches the desired consistency, it can be scooped onto a parchment-lined sheet pan and placed in the refrigerator until required for service. Alternatively, the mixture can remain in a bowl and be lightly whisked just before being scooped out onto the plate. This will loosen the foam if it has become too dense.

The scoops of foam can also be frozen. The result is lighter than a sorbet because of the large incorporation of air. This is a versatile product, and its density places it as a firm middle note.

water-based middle notes: gelées

Remember the Jell-O jigglers of your childhood? Gelée is simply a fancy form of Jell-O. Their firm texture places them at one extreme of the gelée spectrum. Experiment with the recipes in the Appendix (see pages 238–239). The various ratios of liquid to gelatin allow the chef to control the length of time that any one particular flavor will stay on the customer's palate. Also experiment with the size of each individual gelée. These can range anywhere from the familiar Jell-O jiggler cubes to a small brunoise diced "jewel." Gelling a coulis, a consommé, or a flavored water are all possibilities for allowing nonfat flavors to linger on as a middle note. The more dense the gel, the stronger presence it will have in the plate profile. (See page 75 for an example of a dessert that uses a gelée.)

base notes

A full plate profile should have a strong, but not overwhelming, base note. A number of techniques can be used to insure that the flavors used in a plated dessert will resonate on the consumer's palate.

Water-Based Frozen Lozenges

A flavorful ice cube is perhaps the clearest description of a frozen lozenge. The liquid for the lozenge is similar to the liquid used in a flavorful water shooter. Alternatively, water can be used to encase a fresh herb or dried spice. Unlike an ice cube, the lozenge should be small. The entire thing should be easily consumed in one bite. As the customers suck on the lozenge, the flavors of the dessert wash over their palate. Unlike the flavored water shooter, the frozen lozenge requires more effort and time for its flavors to be released. The flavors involved, therefore, will remain on the consumer's palate for a longer period of time.

The lozenge can be offered at any time in the course of the dessert. It is, however, most effective when offered at the end of the dessert course. In this way the lozenge can mirror the wash of flavors introduced at the onset of the dessert course by the flavored water shot or shooter. Alcohol can be added to the lozenge if a somewhat softer texture is required. Make these lozenges in small molds. Remember, a delicate wash of flavor is desired—this is not a Popsicle.

Sugar as a Base Note

Imagine biting into a piece of peanut brittle or English toffee. There is a lot of chewing involved. The flavors incorporated into this type of hard sugar remain on your palate for a relatively long time. In this way, sugar can move from its original spot as a top note, to a position as a base note on a plated dessert.

Infuse the caramel with flavors from the dessert. Be cautious, however, about adding items with a high water content. Remember that sugar is hygroscopic. It has the ability to absorb moisture from its environment. Adding an item with too much water will soon result in a sticky unappetizing caramel mass. The water content of fruits and vegetables will eventually dissolve the caramel.

The following method of preparation is a great way to make a flavorful sugar addition for your dish. Make a caramel using either the wet or dry method of cooking sugar. Spices, salts, ground nuts, fruit and vegetable powders can all be added to the caramel to reinforce the driving flavors of the dish. Pour the flavored caramel onto a Silpat. Cool at room temperature. Best results are achieved with a thin caramel. Pouring the caramel onto a hot Silpat will make it easier to get a thin sheet. Once the sheet of caramel is cool, break it into pieces. Using a food processor, grind the shards to a powder. Sprinkle the powder on a Silpat and place in a 350°F oven. The caramel dust will melt in the oven after a few minutes. Once it is completely melted remove from the oven. Cool caramel for just a minute and then pull it into beautiful, free form, abstract shapes. (See

Chocolate in India on page 186 for a plated dessert that uses this technique.) Alternatively, a stencil can be placed on the Silpat and filled with the caramel dust. Remove the stencil, place the Silpat in the oven, and the result is beautiful, sharp-edged caramel garnishes. Even though a paper-thin layer of caramel is used, the result will be flavors that resonate on the palate as base notes.

Flavor is always the driving force of any plated dessert. It is the flavors of the dish that form the plate's overall plate profile. When designing your next plated dessert consider some of the techniques discussed in this section. Utilizing these techniques means that suddenly the inherent tastes of a product serve as only a starting point. It is ultimately the texture of a product that will dictate its placement in the dessert's plate profile.

In the following chapters, the skills and techniques discussed thus far are applied to specific ingredients as well as to specific plated desserts. You will see how cooking techniques can be employed to manipulate the flavor and texture of individual ingredients. The flavor partners of a multitude of ingredients are explained. Dozens of examples of specific plated desserts are also given. Use these examples as the starting point for your own creations.

constituents
of flavor

Traditionally the repertoire of ingredients used in the pastry world is fairly small. It is often the methods of preparation a pastry chef uses, rather than the ingredients themselves, that separate one product from another. The goal of the next four chapters is to increase the ingredient list used in the construction of plated desserts. These chapters look at some familiar, and some new, ingredients with one goal in mind. What does that particular ingredient bring to a dish in terms of flavor? The ingredients discussed include an assortment of vegetables, herbs, spices, dairy products, and dry pantry products. The flavor of each ingredient is examined, and a list of other flavors that partner well with the ingredient is included. Additionally, a plated dessert has been designed that showcases each ingredient. Use the following chapters as a resource in your flavor journey.

chapter 7

vegetables

Vegetables may initially seem like an odd choice of ingredient to use in a plated dessert. The wide variety of flavors they offer, however, make them an important flavor choice. The vegetables chosen for this chapter all offer the pastry chef new flavor possibilities. Some of the vegetables gain flavor through cooking processes; others are best used raw. Whether roasted or raw, there is no doubt that an examination of the farmer's market will bring a greater depth of flavor to your dishes.

beets

While their bright magenta color certainly makes them unique, it is the flavor of beets that makes them truly memorable. Beets combine a relatively high sugar content with a deep, musky earthiness. Their robustness makes them a wonderful addition to other fatty components. The classic example of this combination is borscht, a combination of intense beet flavor paired with sour cream.

Roasting intensifies both the sweetness and the flavor of beets. To roast a beet, cut off its leaves and rub the beet with a bit of vegetable or olive oil. Wait to peel the beet until after it has been roasted. This will increase its flavor and also facilitate the peeling process. Wrap the beet loosely in aluminum foil and place in a 350°F (175°C) oven for about 45 minutes or until fork tender. Remove the beet from the foil, peel, and slice or dice. Proceed according to the recipe. Beets also make great dried chips and a superb powder.

Partner with

· ·

Fruits: lemons, oranges

Vegetables: carrots, daikon, fennel, garlic, horseradish, onions

Dairy: buttermilk, cream cheese, crème fraîche, mascarpone cheese, ricotta cheese, sour cream

Sweeteners: brown sugar, caramel, honey

Nuts: hazelnuts, pecans, walnuts

Dried fruits: apricots, raisins

Liquors: beer

Beverages: black tea, coffee

Chocolate: milk, white

Baking spices: allspice, anise seed, caraway, cloves, ginger (dried), nutmeg

Culinary spices: Chinese five spice, dill, fennel seed, garlic, mustard (dried), peppercorns, star anise

Pantry ingredients: balsamic vinegar, olive oil

FIGURE 7.1

Beet sampler plate: pickled beet foam with pickled beet slaw, flourless chocolate timbale, borscht "shooter," and orange cheesecake (from left to right).
Illustration by Reginald S. Abalos.

The beet on this plate is used as an accompaniment to dessert items with which the guest is more familiar. Beet is first introduced to the guest in the form of a borscht "shooter." This is a thin beet purée with a dab of sour cream on top. The portion is tiny: the guest should be able to comfortably drink the shot in one swallow. The earthy beet flavor is evident but not overpowering. The bit of sour cream helps to round it out as does the slightest hint of orange. The plate's remaining components are a flourless chocolate timbale and an orange cheesecake. The beets are used in a pickled beet foam and pickled beet slaw. The idea is to have the guest eat a bit of foam or slaw with each bite of chocolate or orange cake. The foam and slaw are both pickled, which prevents the beet flavor from getting overwhelmed by the fat of the cakes. The pickled beet foam dissipates quickly in the mouth while the slaw's crisp texture means that it will linger longer on the palate.

Pickling beets: Roast the beets, peel, and slice into thin matchsticks. Place the beet sticks in a jar and cover with a warm mixture of vinegar, sugar, water, and traditional pickling spices. Cover the jar and let stand until the beets have been completely infused with the pickled flavor. The slaw consists merely of the pickled beet matchsticks. The foam is made by straining the spices out of the liquid and proceeding as for a gelatin cloud foam. The liquid will have picked up some color from the beets and the result is a glorious magenta-colored foam.

carrots

The idea of using carrots in the pastry world is not new; consider their traditional use in a cake or quick bread. The natural sweetness of carrots makes them a logical choice for use in desserts. Raw, sautéed, steamed, roasted, or fried—carrots in almost any form lend a flavorful component to any plated dessert.

The flavor identity of a carrot changes vastly according to the manner in which it is cooked. Using carrots in their raw state preserves their crisp, clean notes. The natural sweetness of the carrot is evident but is not overwhelming. When using raw carrot, think of other clear, crisp flavors that will accompany rather than overpower its grassy notes. Cucumbers, dill, and chilli and bell peppers are just a few suggestions.

Roasting the carrot brings all of its natural sugars to the surface and when roasted long enough, these sugars will caramelize. Magically, the crisp clarity of the raw carrot is transformed into something with much more body. Think of the raw carrot as a watercolor and the roasted carrot as an oil paint. Not only does the roasted carrot taste sweeter, it also has a greater depth of "carrotness" to it, and some earthy notes begin to be evident. With a strong carrot middle note, a roasted carrot will hold up to the addition of fat, some heat, and some of the earthy, dusty spices such as coriander and cumin.

Partner with

Fruits: apples, apricots, grapefruit, kiwi, kumquats, lemons, limes, oranges, passion fruit, peaches, pears, pineapple

Vegetables: beets, bell peppers, cucumbers, garlic, onions, pumpkin, squash (acorn and butternut)

Dairy: Asiago cheese, cheddar cheese, cream cheese, crème fraîche, goat cheese, mascarpone cheese, Parmesan cheese, sour cream, yogurt

Sweeteners: brown sugar, caramel, honey, maple syrup

Nuts: almonds, coconut, hazelnuts, pecans, walnuts

Dried fruits: apricots, figs, raisins

Liquors: bourbon, white wine

Beverages: green tea

Baking spices: cinnamon, cloves, dried ginger, mace, nutmeg

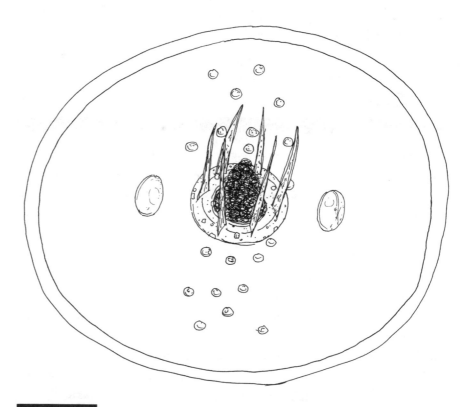

FIGURE 7.2

Orange Bavarian cream with an inlay of coriander roasted carrots accompanied by a fresh carrot foam, carrot chip, caramelized, spicy carrot "jewels," and a carrot–dill sorbet. Illustration by Reginald S. Abalos.

Culinary spices: basil, cilantro, chilli peppers (fresh and dried), Chinese five spice, coriander, cumin, dill, ginger (fresh), marjoram, mint, oregano, peppercorns, rosemary, sage, tarragon, thyme

Pantry ingredients: balsamic vinegar, sweet soy sauce

This plate presents carrot in many textures, utilizing varying cooking methods. The plate includes the heavy sweet notes of roasted carrots as well as the fresh, clean flavor of raw carrots.

The carrots in the center of the Bavarian cream have been roasted. Their earthy sweetness is accentuated by the addition of coriander. The tart orange zing of the Bavarian cream contrasts nicely with the deep roasted carrot–coriander flavor. The foam and sorbet are both made from fresh carrot juice and display the crisp, clean, grassy nature of raw carrots. The grassy, clean notes are further accentuated in the sorbet with the addition of fresh dill.

The carrot "jewels" are steamed carrots cut into a small dice. These cubes are then sautéed quickly with a bit of granulated sugar. The result is a beautiful shiny, glazed orange jewel full of sweet carrot flavor. These are sprinkled with a pinch of salt and pepper, which help to offset the sweetness of the carrots and emphasize their flavor.

 corn

Some of my best childhood memories are of eating sweet corn straight off of the grill. With its inherent sweetness, it is no wonder that corn is the preferred vegetable of many children. That natural sweetness makes it a welcome addition to the pastry world. There are a myriad of ways in which corn can be utilized, either in a fresh or in a ground state.

Fresh roasted corn kernels can be folded into a mousse or cake. They add a burst of grassy sweetness with each bite. If a grill is not readily available, the corn can be roasted over a gas burner. Shuck the corn and use tongs to hold it over the flame. Rotate the cob as the kernels become black. The kernels can then be cut off the cob and added to the recipe.

Don't throw away the cob. It can add corn flavor to an infusion. Place the cob into a saucepan of heavy cream. Reduce over low heat until the desired thickness and flavor is reached. This cream can be used as is for a sauce, it can be aerated to make a frothy foam, or it can be used in place of heavy cream in a recipe (ice cream, for instance). It is a great example of the amazing sweetness of fresh corn. Let the cream cool overnight in the refrigerator. The next day it will be thick enough to be scooped and/or quenelled. It is an extremely rich, yet flavorful addition to a dessert plate.

The kernels can be made into true "candied corn." Steam the kernels until they are completely cooked. Then simmer in simple syrup until the kernels are saturated with the sugar mixture. You will know they are done by tasting a kernel or two. They should have strong sweet top note with a middle note of corn. Strain the kernels out of the simple syrup and place on a Silpat-lined sheet pan. (Don't throw away the simple syrup. It can be used as a sorbet base.) Arrange the corn in a single layer, not one large clump. Place the sheet pan in a low oven (300°F/150°C or lower). Continue to cook, shaking the pan every 6 minutes or so, until the kernels are crispy. The candied corn kernels can be folded into a mousse, sprinkled on a plate or placed on tuile cookies before they are baked. Additionally, the kernels can be dusted with a bit of sea salt and/or chilli powder, which will give them a full plate profile.

In its ground form, corn can be found in tortillas, grits, masa, corn flour, and corn meal. Use corn meal to make a sweet corn polenta. Follow the same procedure as for savory polenta, substituting heavy cream for chicken stock and adding a bit of honey. Once the polenta is thoroughly cooked, spread it out on a sheet pan. Once it is chilled, cut it into desired sizes. Grill the polenta and brûlée just before service. This can be used as an entrée item or as a tasty base to anchor your ice cream or sorbet.

Partner with

Fruits: blackberries, cherries, lemons, limes, mangoes, nectarines, oranges, passion fruit, peaches, pineapple, plums, raspberries

Vegetables: bell peppers, carrots, cucumbers, garlic, onions, tomatoes

Dairy: Asiago cheese, cream cheese, goat cheese, mascarpone cheese, Parmesan cheese, sour cream, yogurt

Sweeteners: brown sugar, caramel, honey, raw sugars

Nuts: coconut, pine nuts

Dried fruits: cherries

Liquors: beer, red wine, tequila

Baking spices: allspice, cinnamon, mace, nutmeg, vanilla

Culinary spices: basil, chilli peppers (fresh and dried), Chinese five spice, cilantro, dill, marjoram, oregano, peppercorns, rosemary, sage, star anise, tamarind, tarragon

Pantry ingredients: corn meal, olive oil, tortillas

This plate explores corn's various textures. It starts with a corn tortilla broth. The broth is made by simmering corn tortillas in water with

FIGURE 7.3

Corn tasting plate: shooter of corn tortilla broth, sweet and spicy berry tamale, fresh fruit salsa, candied corn, and grilled corn sorbet. (From back to front)
Illustration by Reginald S. Abalos.

some sugar and a small pinch of salt. The mixture is strained and the result is a sweet water full of corn flavor. The tamale is made in the traditional culinary manner with fruit replacing the spicy meat filling. The fruit is a mixture of berries that have been cooked down to a jam-like consistency. The mixture is flavored with a bit of ancho chilli powder and a small amount of fresh jalapenos. The result is a sweet marmalade-like filling with a base note of heat. This works well when surrounded by the sweet but somewhat bland flavor of the masa filling. The salsa consists of fresh berries and pineapple with a bit of mint and a sprinkle of tequila. The candied corn is sprinkled on the plate. The grilled corn sorbet begins with grilled corn kernels that are infused into a simple syrup mixture. The mixture is then puréed, strained, and churned into a sorbet.

The plate has no fatty components. The lack of fat makes it easy for the corn to stand strong as the plate's middle note. The variations on corn flavor, tortilla, tamale, candied, and grilled work well here with no one component overwhelming the others.

 cucumbers

Cucumbers impart a delicate, crisp, clean flavor to plated desserts. This flavor is the perfect example of a "watercolor" type of flavor—light and grassy. Members of the squash family, cucumbers are related to many of the summer melons such as honeydew, cantaloupe, and watermelon.

The light, grassy crispness of cucumber's flavor is its strength. The delicate freshness of cucumbers is destroyed when cooked, so this is rarely done. Thinly shave slices of raw cucumber on a mandolin. Use the slices to line a terrine mold and then fill the mold with either a mousse or a gelee. Cucumbers can also be juiced. Use the juice as the base of a sorbet or the beginnings of a refreshing dessert consommé. Cucumber's crisp, green, clean flavor harmonizes well with other clean flavors. It is lost, however, in the presence of too much fat.

Partner with

Fruits: cantaloupe, honeydew, lemons, limes, lychees, oranges, watermelon

Vegetables: bell peppers, carrots, corn, daikon, garlic, onions, tomatoes

Dairy: buttermilk, crème fraîche, goat cheese, ricotta, sour cream, yogurt

Sweeteners: honey

Nuts: almonds, cashews, coconut

Dried fruits: apricots

Liquors: sake, light white wine

Beverages: green tea

Baking spices: mint

Culinary spices: chilli peppers (fresh), dill, garlic, ginger (fresh), lemon grass, peppercorns, star anise

Pantry ingredients: mirin, sweet soy sauce

This plate celebrates the fresh, clean character of cucumber flavor. Only fresh cucumbers are used, in raw slices and juiced. The sour tang of the Greek yogurt and buttermilk complement the refreshing notes in cucumber and in the dill of the tuile cookie. The various textures of the cucumber guarantee that its flavor will be a strong middle note on the plate.

The terrine mold is lined with paper-thin slices of fresh cucumber. The mousse is made with Greek yogurt, which is much thicker and tastier than its American counterpart. The honey has been reduced slightly before being added to the mousse. Cucumber juice has been stabilized into a

chapter 7 vegetables

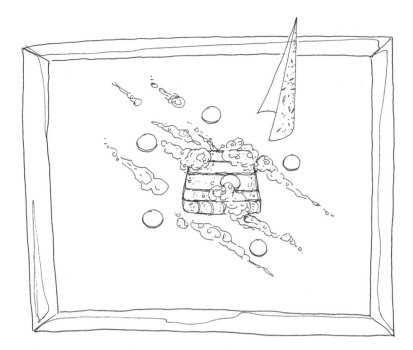

FIGURE 7.4

Cucumber terrine with honey Greek yogurt mousse accompanied by cucumber foam, buttermilk cucumber gelee, and dill tuile cookie. Illustration by Reginald S. Abalos.

foam and there is a sprinkling of small cubes of gelée made with buttermilk and fresh cucumber pieces.

 # fennel

Fennel is a member of the carrot family. Like carrots, fennel is served both raw and cooked. Raw fennel's strong anise character comes from the chemical anethole. This is the same chemical found in star anise and anise seeds. Fennel's strong anise taste is tempered, however, with a bit of citrus sparkle. Raw fennel is often thinly sliced and used in salads. Roasting fennel changes its character. It loses some of its citrus notes and the anise flavor takes on an earthier quality. Roasted fennel holds up well to other heavy flavors and to components containing fat.

Fennel can be transformed into a light anise-like candy when it is made into chips. Simply slice the fennel vertically on the mandolin, preserving the flame-like shape of the bulb. Simmer lightly in simple syrup and continue as for fruit chips. The chips lend both great flavor and visual impact to plated desserts.

Partner with

· ·

Fruits: lemons, oranges, peaches, pears, plums, raspberries, strawberries

Vegetables: beets, carrots, corn, daikon, garlic, onions, pumpkin, squash (butternut), tomatoes

Dairy: crème fraîche, goat cheese, mascarpone cheese, Parmesan cheese, ricotta cheese, sour cream

Sweeteners: brown sugar, honey, raw sugars

Nuts: almonds, pine nuts

Liquors: medium heavy white wine

Beverages: black tea

Chocolate: milk, white

Baking spices: anise seed, vanilla

Culinary spices: caraway seed, Chinese five spice, dill, fennel seed, peppercorns, star anise, tarragon

Pantry ingredients: balsamic vinegar, cornmeal

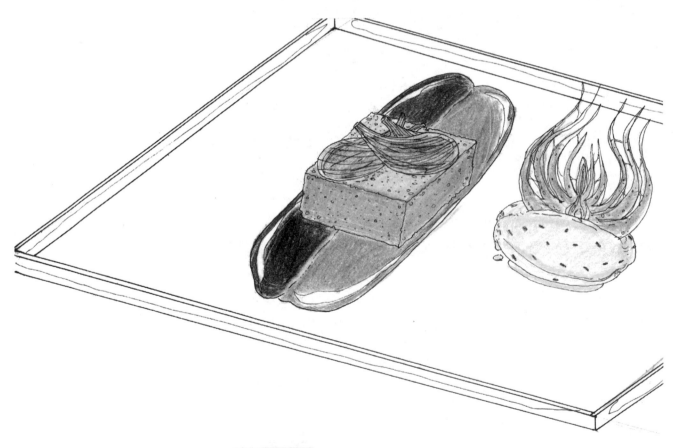

FIGURE 7.5

Honey-braised fennel on top of a vanilla pound cake, served with red wine orange and honey reduction sauces partnered with an orange and fennel seed ice cream and a fennel flame. Illustration by Reginald S. Abalos.

chapter 7   vegetables

The different flavors of fennel make up the core of this dish. The fennel is presented with sweet, heavy notes when braised, in the stronger form of fennel seed and in its raw crispy state as a fennel chip (fennel flame).

Whether braised, raw, or in a seed, the anise essence of fennel is complemented by the fresh vanilla bean pound cake, the full-bodied red wine and orange reduction sauce, and the tart richness of the orange and fennel seed ice cream.

 garlic

The overall pungent bite of garlic is best subdued before incorporating it into pastry work. Thus, garlic should be roasted before use. Although it is a member of the onion family, garlic has more fructose and less water than onion. Garlic's relatively high fructose content means that its sugars will begin to caramelize fairly quickly. Roasting garlic, therefore, requires less time than roasting an onion.

To roast garlic, rub the entire head of garlic with a bit of oil. Wrap loosely with foil and place in a 350°F (175°C) for approximately 30 minutes. Once the garlic has cooled, merely press each bulb to extract the roasted garlic pulp.

Garlic works best in plated desserts when it is accompanied with fat. French-style roasted garlic ice cream, for example, is a wonderful use of the pungency and power of garlic. The fat of the heavy cream and egg yolks help to take the edge off of garlic's sharpness. In terms of plated desserts, garlic works best when used as a backup rather than as a lead singer.

Partner with

Vegetables: beets, bell peppers, carrots, corn, squash (acorn and butternut), sweet potatoes, tomatoes

Dairy: Asiago cheese, goat cheese, mascarpone cheese, Parmesan cheese, ricotta, sour cream

Sweeteners: honey, brown sugar, raw sugars

Nuts: macadamia nuts, pine nuts

Dried fruits: figs

Liquors: red wine, white wine

Chocolate: dark, milk, white

Baking spices: anise seed, vanilla

Culinary spices: basil, cilantro, coriander, cumin, dill, mustard seed, oregano, peppercorns, sage, tarragon, thyme

Pantry ingredients: balsamic vinegar, cornmeal, olive oil

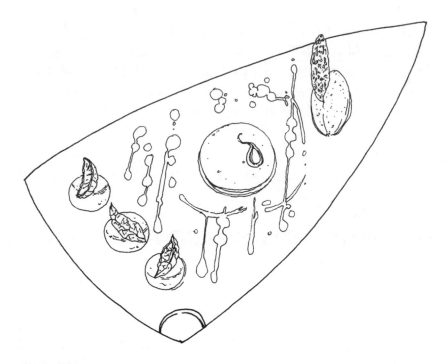

FIGURE 7.6

Trio of Italian ices: fresh tomato sorbet, roasted garlic ice cream, basil sherbet.
Served with balsamic vinegar reduction and a Parmesan cheese chip.
Illustration by Reginald S. Abalos.

    This plate is geared toward an adventurous consumer. The frozen components start with the clear flavor of fresh tomato in a sorbet with no fat, the basil sherbet incorporates a bit of sour cream, which accentuates the cooling properties of basil. The roasted garlic ice cream contains heavy cream, which will smooth out the edges of the garlic's flavor. All three ices go well with the sour/sweet balsamic reduction and the salty Parmesan chip. This is meant to be a mini dessert, one or two teaspoons of each ice is plenty.

    Parmesan chip: Simply grate the Parmesan cheese and spread on a Silpat-lined sheet pan in the desired shape. Bake at 350°F (175°C) until light golden brown. The chips can be shaped immediately upon removal from the oven.

red onion

Red onions are well known in the culinary world for their delicate, sweet flavor. Because red onions lack the harsh pungency of other onion family members, they are most often used raw. Their subtle bite makes them the perfect addition to the pastry world. Caramelizing the onions will increase their sweetness. Use red onions as the base for an onion marmalade; you will find that very little, if any, sugar needs to be added.

Partner with

Fruits: apples, cherries, oranges, peaches, pears

Vegetables: bell peppers, cucumbers, squash (acorn and butternut), sweet potatoes, tomatoes

Dairy: Asiago cheese, buttermilk, cheddar cheese, crème fraîche, goat cheese, mascarpone cheese, Parmesan cheese, sour cream

Sweeteners: brown sugar, honey, molasses, raw sugar

Nuts: pecans, pine nuts, walnuts

Dried fruits: apricots, dates, figs, raisins

Liquors: red wine, white wine

Baking spices: anise seed, cloves, ginger (dried), mace, nutmeg, vanilla

Culinary spices: basil, Chinese five spice, cilantro, oregano, peppercorns, rosemary, sage, star anise, tarragon

Pantry ingredients: balsamic vinegar, olive oil

The onions are on this plate solely as a complement to the richness of the vanilla bean crème brûlée. Cooked down together with the Anjou pears, a small spoonful of the marmalade on the side of the brûlée will suffice. Alternatively, the marmalade could be served on a small separate

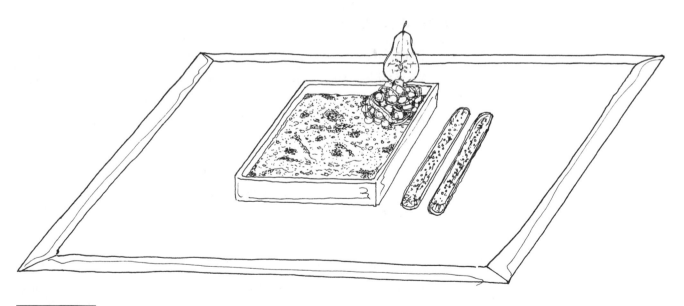

FIGURE 7.7

Vanilla bean crème brûlée accompanied with a red onion and Anjou pear marmalade. Served with maple sugar cookies and a pear chip. Illustration by Reginald S. Abalos.

dish together with the maple sugar cookies and pear chip. The customer is directed to dip the cookies and pear chip into the marmalade in between bites of the brûlée.

 vidalia onions

Vidalia onions are native to a few specific counties in Georgia. Their unique sweetness is due to the high sulfur content found in the ground in which they are grown. They can be a wonderful component to a plated dessert, especially when roasted.

The idea behind slow-roasting onions is to allow the natural sugars in the onion to be released. Once these sugars have risen to the surface they will then caramelize, which intensifies their natural sweetness. The result transforms onions into an entirely different taste sensation. The harsh almost jagged heat of a raw onion is then replaced with smooth, deep, earthy, sweet notes. Take your time when caramelizing onions. Start with a bit of olive oil in the pan (1 or 2 tablespoons will do the trick) and high heat. Add the thinly sliced onions with a pinch of salt and stir fairly frequently until they begin to wilt. As they continue to cook they will stick to the bottom of the pan, make sure that when you stir the onions you scrape up all of this fond. The onions will brown and their structure will begin to collapse, turning into a soft, pulpy mass.

Partner with

Fruits: apples, mangoes, passion fruit, peaches, pears, plums, pineapple

Vegetables: beets, bell peppers, carrots, corn, fennel, garlic, squash (acorn and butternut), sweet potatoes, tomatoes

Dairy: Asiago cheese, buttermilk, cheddar cheese, crème fraîche, goat cheese, mascarpone cheese, sour cream, yogurt

Sweeteners: brown sugar, honey, maple syrup, molasses, raw sugars

Nuts: almonds, peanuts, pecans, pine nuts

Dried fruits: apricots, cherries, dates, figs, raisins

Liquors: beer, red wine, white wine

Baking spices: anise seed, cloves, ginger (dried), vanilla

Culinary spices: basil, chillis (fresh and dried), Chinese five spice, cilantro, coriander, cumin, curry powder, dill, ginger, lemon grass, marjoram, mustard seed, oregano, peppercorns, rosemary, saffron, sage, star anise, tamarind, tarragon, thyme

Pantry ingredients: balsamic vinegar, olive oil, sesame oil, sweet soy

FIGURE 7.8

Orange scented goat cheese cheesecake, with mango–Vidalia onion jam and apricot fig chutney. Served with black pepper sugar cookies and red wine sorbet. Illustration by Reginald S. Abalos.

This plate mirrors many of the components found in a more traditional cheese platter: goat cheese, chutney, a savory marmalade, crackers, and a glass of wine. In this instance, the familiar components have been slightly altered for use on a plated dessert. The orange zest in the cheesecake helps to cut through its richness. The sweet/sour and savory jam and the sweet/sour chutney both pair well with the stark acidity of the goat cheese. The cheesecake is made without a crust, as it is meant to be spread on the sugar cookies. The cookies supply the plate with a crispy texture and a welcome spicy sweetness. The sorbet cleanses and refreshes the palate similar to having a sip of wine.

sweet bell peppers

Bell peppers are the largest member of the pepper family. The size of a pepper is usually an indication of its heat level, so it is not surprising that bell peppers are also the sweetest of the pepper family. (See Chilli section for more information.) They rank between 0 and 600 on the Scoville scale. The bell pepper is so sweet that it is often used in its raw state. The flavor is extremely clean with a clear, grassy note. When roasted that grassy flavor is replaced by a deep sweetness. Roasting the pepper on a grill adds a smoky back note as well.

Partner with

Fruits: apricots, cantaloupe, honeydew, lemons, limes, mangoes, oranges, peaches, pineapple, raspberries, strawberries, tangerines

Vegetables: corn, cucumbers, fennel, garlic, pumpkin, squash (acorn and butternut), sweet potatoes

Dairy: Asiago cheese, buttermilk, cheddar cheese, cream cheese, crème fraîche, goat cheese, Parmesan cheese, ricotta, sour cream, yogurt

Sweeteners: caramel, honey

Nuts: almonds, coconut, macadamia nuts, peanuts

Dried fruits: apricots

Liquors: red wine, tequila, white wine

Beverages: green tea

Baking spices: anise seed

Culinary spices: basil, chillis (fresh and dried), cilantro, marjoram, oregano, rosemary, sage, tarragon, thyme

Pantry ingredients: balsamic vinegar, olive oil

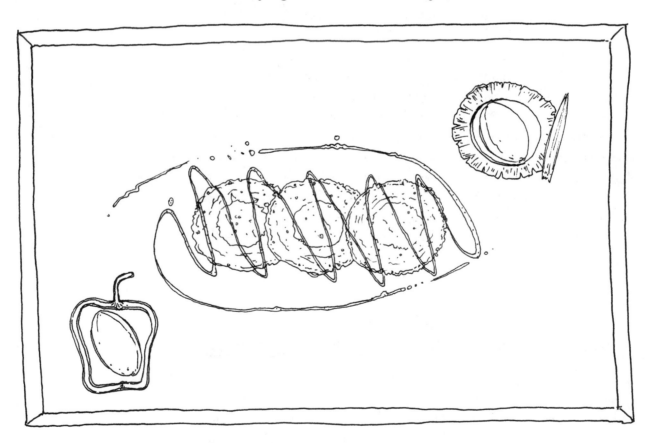

FIGURE 7.9

Pancakes, syrup, and ice cream: warm Johnnie cakes drizzled with cilantro syrup accompanied by red bell pepper sorbet and pineapple sherbet. Illustration by Reginald S. Abalos.

chapter 7   vegetables

Johnnie cakes are a New England tradition, similar to a cornmeal-based pancake. Here they appear with a cilantro syrup, which is merely a cilantro clear sauce. The crisp bell pepper flavor is introduced with a scoop of red bell pepper sorbet made with a base of puréed and strained raw bell peppers. The pineapple sherbet is accented with the addition of small-diced green bell pepper, which is folded in after the sherbet has been spun. The warm corn and cilantro serve as the perfect complement to the raw bell pepper flavor.

 # winter squashes: acorn squash, butternut squash, pumpkin

Winter squashes, which include acorn, butternut, and pumpkin, have long been an important part of American cuisine. It is estimated that these squash were first domesticated in the Americas circa 5000 BC. Winter squashes are used in a very different manner than their cousins, the summer squashes. Summer squashes, such as cucumbers, cantaloupes, and honeydews, are best eaten raw, while winter squashes require cooking. They hold up to long stewing and roasting.

Cooking winter squash brings out its inherent sweetness. The starch granules that make up the squash are hard when raw but begin to swell and soften as they are cooked. Squash is traditionally used in savory as well as pastry dishes. Each November we all enjoy a squash dessert in the form of pumpkin pie.

The three squashes included in this section offer examples of the wide range of flavors found in winter squashes. Acorn squash has an earthy note. It goes well with earthy, heavy spices such as curry powder and cumin. Butternut squash is lighter in flavor and complements fresh flavors such as orange, lime, and fresh ginger. Pumpkin is, perhaps, the blandest of the three squash and for that reason is often used in American sweets such as pies, cakes, muffins, and quick breads. Pumpkin is so popular as a dessert ingredient that there is a premixed pumpkin pie spice available at most food stores. Instead of this traditional mix, try using star anise, Chinese five spice, black peppercorns, curry powder, or fresh ginger in your next pumpkin pie.

When working with winter squash, don't forget to save and use their seeds. Rinse the seeds and then dredge them in sugar, salt, or spice. Roast in a 350°F (175°C) oven until they are a light golden brown. The roasted seeds can then be sprinkled onto a plate, incorporated into a nut brittle, or ground into a flavorful powder.

Partner with (for all three squash)

Fruits: apples, blackberries, cherries, cranberries, lemons, limes, mangoes, oranges, passion fruit, pears, plums

Vegetables: bell peppers, carrots, chillis (fresh and dried), corn, fennel, garlic, onions, sweet potatoes, tomatoes

Dairy: Asiago cheese, crème fraîche, cream cheese, goat cheese, mascarpone cheese, Parmesan cheese, ricotta cheese, yogurt

Sweeteners: brown sugar, honey, maple syrup, molasses, raw sugars

Nuts: almonds, cashews, coconut, hazelnuts, macadamia nuts, peanuts, pecans, pine nuts, pistachios, walnuts

Dried fruits: apricots, cherries, cranberries, dates, figs, raisins

Liquors: beer, bourbon, port, red wine, rye whiskey, scotch whiskey, sherry, white wine

Beverages: black tea, coffee

Chocolate: dark, milk, white

Baking spices: allspice, cinnamon, cloves, ginger (dried), mace, nutmeg, vanilla

Culinary spices: basil, chillis (fresh and dried), Chinese five spice, cilantro, coriander, cumin, curry powder, galangal, ginger (fresh), lavender, marjoram, mustard seed, oregano, rosemary, saffron, sage, star anise, tamarind, tarragon, thyme

Pantry ingredients: balsamic vinegar, olive oil, sesame oil, sweet soy sauce

This dessert is based on a perennial favorite, pumpkin pie. In this version the pumpkin pie filling is made with freshly roasted pumpkin. Chinese five spice, fresh ginger, vanilla bean, and maple syrup are added to the pumpkin as it cooks. The mixture is then puréed and traditional pumpkin pie filling ingredients are added. Instead of using a regular pastry pie shell, the crust for these tartlettes is made of layers of phyllo dough and ground walnuts. The individual tarts are served with a bourbon ice cream. The apple cider is simply reduced down with the addition of fresh ginger and some maple syrup. The tartness of the apple cider and the heat of the ginger will help to cut through some of the starchiness of the roasted pumpkin. The garnish is a paper-thin brittle made with roasted pumpkin seeds and walnuts.

The flavors of this dessert remain fairly consistent with the classic American pumpkin pie. The use of freshly roasted, as opposed to canned, pumpkin along with the addition of Chinese five spice and fresh ginger add a woodsy, warm depth of flavor missing in the traditional pie. The phyllo crust, reduction sauce, and brittle all add a modern twist to an otherwise very familiar dessert.

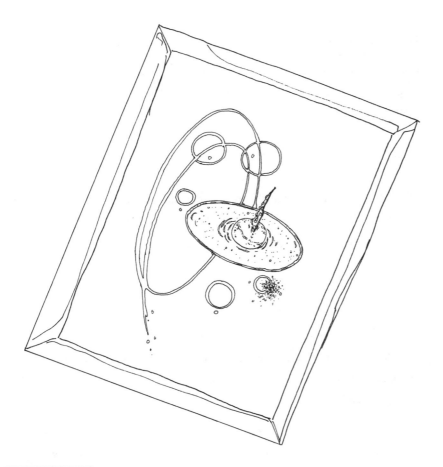

FIGURE 7.10

Pumpkin pie tartlette served with bourbon ice cream, seeded brittle, and a spicy apple cider reduction. Illustration by Reginald S. Abalos.

 sweet potatoes

The sweet potato is a native of South America. It was brought by Columbus to Europe. A few hundred years later, the sweet potato had made its way to China. Today it enjoys enormous popularity in China, making it the second most important vegetable in the world. Like winter squashes, the sweet potato is extremely adaptable. The sweet potato can be cooked, boiled, roasted, or stewed. There are many varieties of sweet potatoes but most sweeten tremendously when cooked. Roasting allows the natural sugars to intensify through caramelization. When roasting try using sweeteners other than granulated sugar. Maple syrup, molasses, honey, and raw sugars, along with a pinch of salt and pepper, will add a depth of richness to the end product.

Partner with

Fruits: apples, apricots, blackberries, blueberries, cherries, cranberries, figs, kumquats, lemons, limes, mangoes, nectarines, oranges, papayas, passion fruit, peaches, pears, pineapple, plums, prickly pears, raspberries, strawberries

Vegetables: beets, carrots, corn, fennel, garlic, onions, squash (acorn, butternut, pumpkin), tomatoes

Dairy: Asiago cheese, buttermilk, cheddar cheese, goat cheese, mascarpone cheese, Parmesan cheese, ricotta cheese, sour cream, yogurt

Sweeteners: brown sugar, caramel, honey, maple syrup, molasses, raw sugar

Nuts: almonds, cashews, coconut, hazelnuts, macadamia nuts, peanuts, pecans, pine nuts, pistachios, walnuts

Dried fruits: apricots, cherries, cranberries, dates, figs, raisins

Liquors: bourbon, dark rum, port, red wine, rye whiskey, scotch whiskey, sherry, tequila, white wine

Beverages: black tea, coffee

Chocolate: dark, milk, white

Baking spices: allspice, cinnamon, cloves, ginger, mace, nutmeg, vanilla

Culinary spices: basil, cardamom, chillis (fresh and dried), Chinese five spice, cilantro, coriander, cumin, curry, dill, galangal, ginger, lavender, lemon grass, marjoram, mustard seed, oregano, peppercorns, rosemary, sage, sesame seeds, star anise, tamarind, tarragon, thyme, wasabi

Pantry ingredients: balsamic vinegar, sesame oil, sweet soy sauce

This plate incorporates many traditional American dessert flavors: sweet potato, walnuts, and oatmeal. In this case the sweet potato has been roasted with honey, salt, and pepper and drizzled with just a touch of olive oil. Although the potato's natural sweetness will be evident, there is also an underlying savory note. The mousse has an inlay of diced sweet potatoes, which have been roasted plain and then caramelized on the stovetop with a dusting or two of granulated sugar. Thus, the entrée has two slightly different variations of a roasted sweet potato, one sweeter than the other.

The sauce is simply a reduction of maple syrup with a touch of curry powder. Oatmeal lace cookies are a variation on the classic almond lace cookie, with raw oatmeal added to the batter in place of the nuts. The sorbet is made with a base of simple syrup infused with toasted walnuts. Toast the walnuts a bit lighter than you would other nuts. Their skins can easily make the mixture too astringent. A sorbet is used here to contrast with the starch and fat of the mousse.

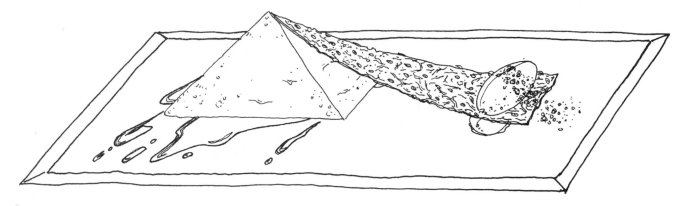

FIGURE 7.11

Sweet potato mousse served with a toasted walnut sorbet, curry maple reduction, and an oatmeal lace cookie. Illustration by Reginald S. Abalos.

tomatoes

Tomatoes form the foundation of many diverse cuisines throughout the world. The way in which each culture manipulates and uses tomatoes offers wonderful insight into their individual cuisines.

When working with tomatoes, remember that they are an agricultural product and as such their quality will differ from month to month and from region to region. Use vine-ripened tomatoes whenever possible, as the artificially ripened tomatoes available year-round are relatively flavorless.

Tomatoes are actually a fruit and, like the fruit in a fruit coulis, their flavor will be enhanced by the addition of both sweet and sour. A pinch of sugar and a bit of orange zest or a touch of balsamic vinegar will help to intensify the flavor of tomato.

Raw tomatoes have a clean, green note, which is lost once the fruit is cooked. Once cooked, the tomato's essence becomes deeper and more robust.

Partner with

Fruits: blackberries, blueberries, kumquats, lemons, limes, mangoes, oranges, peaches, pineapple, tangerines, watermelon

Vegetables: bell peppers, chillis (fresh and dried), corn, cucumbers, fennel, garlic, onions, squash (butternut)

Dairy: Asiago cheese, buttermilk, cheddar cheese, cream cheese, crème fraîche, mascarpone cheese, Parmesan cheese, ricotta cheese, sour cream, yogurt

Sweeteners: brown sugar, caramel, honey, raw sugar

Nuts: almonds, cashews, pine nuts

Dried fruits: apricots, cherries

Liquors: port, red wine, white wine

Baking spices: mint, nutmeg

Culinary spices: basil, chillis (fresh and dried), cilantro, coriander, cumin, curry powder, dill, marjoram, mustard seed, oregano, peppercorns, rosemary, sage, tarragon, thyme

Pantry ingredients: balsamic vinegar, olive oil

This plate offers a tasting plate of tomatoes' many flavors. It incorporates raw tomato, roasted tomato, and crispy tomato chips. It also utilizes the various flavors of the tomato in varying textures. This ensures that the tomato will have a strong presence in the top, middle, and base notes of the plate.

For the gelée the tomato is roasted and added to some simple syrup and gelatin. The resulting gelée is chilled in small dome molds. A salsa is made with tomato, mango, orange, and a bit of cilantro. In this preparation the tomato is left raw. The salsa is tossed with a touch of lime juice

A tomato sampler offering sweet tomato gelée accompanied by a fresh salsa, tomato chip, and a light tomato sorbet. Illustration by Reginald S. Abalos.

and tequila. The tomato chips are made by placing the thinly sliced tomatoes on a Silpat-lined sheet pan in a 300°F (150°C) oven. Don't simmer the slices first in simple syrup as they are too fragile and will disintegrate. Juiced and strained raw tomatoes form the base of the tomato sorbet. A touch of orange zest in the base helps to accentuate the tomato flavor. The essence here is just a delicate tomato whisper. This sampler plate offers a sweet look at the many possibilities and variations of tomatoes in desserts.

herbs and spices

 The goal of this chapter is to expand the pastry chef's spice shelf. The use of herbs and spices is nothing new for pastry chefs. They have been used in bakeshops for centuries. Many of the herbs and spices included in this chapter, however, are those traditionally found on the culinary spice rack. Incorporating these spices into plated desserts opens up an exciting new range of flavor possibilities. Their inclusion will help you to develop full and satisfying flavor and plate profiles.

basil

A member of the mint family, basil shares many of mint's cooling menthol properties. Fresh basil has a wonderful fresh, almost piney quality to it. Its fresh leaves are incredibly pungent. Basil's menthol qualities will add a light trigeminal response or base note to a plated dessert. The trigeminal response is most evident when it is used in a product containing little or no fat. Consider a strawberry–basil sorbet; it is sweet with a middle note of strawberry and basil and a base note of sourness from the berries as well as a bit of cooling from the menthol properties of basil. Compare this to a strawberry–basil French ice cream in which the fat takes center stage, masking most of basil's fresh essence.

There are, however, instances when the cooling nature of basil, as well as its clear, grassy, somewhat piney flavor will help to cut through the richness of a fatty entrée item. Consider a buttermilk–basil panna cotta. In this instance the minty nature of basil helps to cut through the fatty richness of the panna cotta. The result is a dessert that is more refreshing than heavy or cloying.

Fresh basil's pungency makes it perfect for use in infusions. Simply add some leaves into the scalding dairy to form the base of a French-style ice cream, Bavarian cream, pastry cream, or panna cotta. Basil leaves infused in simple syrup can work well for a basil sorbet or sherbet. When infusing basil make sure to strain the leaves out of the base before churning (in the case of ice cream or sorbet) or continuing on with the recipe (as for a panna cotta, for instance). Once heat is applied to the basil leaves they become brown and usually unappealing. Fresh basil can also be used as the base for herb clear sauces. Blanch the leaves before processing them with the corn syrup. This will insure that they will retain their bright green color. Basil leaves can also be fried and used as a flavorful garnish.

Basil is perhaps most commonly associated with the cuisine of the Mediterranean, specifically Italy. Thus, ingredients from the Italian flavor profile will always work well with basil. Certainly one of the most well-known uses for fresh basil is pesto. The traditional pesto incorporates fresh basil, salt, pine nuts, Parmesan or other grated hard cheese, and olive oil. Garlic can also be added. A variation of this classic sauce can be adapted for use in the pastry world. Process the basil with some honey or simple syrup, and add some citrus (lemon works well here) and pine nuts. The applications for this sauce are limitless. If a less sweet sauce is desired, traditional pesto (minus the garlic) can also be used. Try to stay away from combining heavy earthy flavors and basil; they do not complement each other well.

Basil is also seen in Asian cuisine. Often, the basil is chiffonaded and added to the dish just before service. In this way, it retains its crisp, clear, grassy notes. The coolness of basil offers a wonderful contrast to the heat of some Asian cuisines. It is also used in the curries of Asia.

Basil is believed to have originated in India and is often placed around Hindu holy areas. It is placed in the hands of the dead to ensure a swift and safe journey to the spirit world.

Partner with

Fruits: apricots, cantaloupe, cherries, honeydew, lemons, limes, mangoes, oranges, papayas, passion fruit, peaches, pineapple, plums, raspberries, strawberries, watermelon

Vegetables: corn, garlic, onions, squash, tomatoes

Dairy: Asiago cheese, buttermilk, crème fraîche, Parmesan cheese

Sweeteners: brown sugar, caramel, honey, raw sugars

Nuts: almonds, coconuts, peanuts, pine nuts

Liquors: mirin, red wine, sake, white wine

Chocolate: milk, white

Baking spices: mint, vanilla

Baking spices: curry powder, galangal, ginger, marjoram, oregano, parsley, peppercorns, rosemary, sage, sea salt, Thai chillis, thyme

Pantry ingredients: balsamic vinegar, cornmeal, sweet soy sauce

FIGURE 8.1

Corn cream ice cream, served with basil pesto, balsamic reduction, pine nut brittle, and fresh strawberries. Illustration by Reginald S. Abalos.

basil

This dessert celebrates basil's relationship to Italian cuisine. The entrée is a rich, somewhat heavy French ice cream with corn cream used in place of the traditional heavy cream. The corn cream is made by infusing heavy cream with fresh corn cobs and kernels. It will take a while for the sweetness of the corn to fully infuse into the cream, so be patient. Roast the corn before infusing it into the cream for increased flavor. This will add a wonderful subtle smoky note to the ice cream. The pesto is not overly sweet, consisting of fresh basil leaves, pine nuts, a touch of Parmesan cheese, and a small amount of corn syrup. The addition of the Parmesan adds a much-needed salty note. Balsamic vinegar and strawberries are a classic combination. The addition of strawberries on this plate adds a new texture and a crisp sour/sweet flavor that works well with the richness of the ice cream.

The fat of the dish is found solely in the ice cream. This allows the essence of the other flavors to really shine through. The pungency of the pesto insures that the basil flavors will resound even when accompanied by a French-style ice cream.

Some hints for making brittles: (1) use roasted nuts to ensure maximum flavor, and (2) place a Silpat-lined sheet pan in the oven while the caramel is cooking. When the caramel has reached the desired temperature, remove the sheet pan from the oven. Stir the roasted nuts into the caramel and pour immediately onto the hot Silpat. The heat of the Silpat allows the caramel to be spread into a thin layer without seizing up. The Silpat can be easily lifted to allow the caramel to flow in the thinnest layer possible. A thin brittle is both visually attractive and easier for the customer to consume.

cardamom

A native of south India, cardamom grows on a shrub. The cardamom pods are the dried fruit of this perennial herb. Individual cardamom pods are green with a papery outer skin. Between 30 and 35 tiny black seeds are packed inside of each pod. The oblong pods are picked before they are completely ripened and are then cured by drying. The harvesting of the pods is all done by hand; this contributes to cardamom's high price. It is the third most costly spice in the world, following saffron and vanilla.

White cardamom is simply bleached green cardamom. This process mellows out and dampens some of the spice's depth of flavor. The processing also increases the spice's price almost threefold. Black cardamom is not true cardamom. It has a smoky roasted flavor to it and is used primarily in Asian cooking.

The flavor of cardamom is complex. Foremost, it has a floral nature that can easily overpower a dish if used with a heavy hand. It also has a touch of lemon and eucalyptus, which can be quite refreshing. In fact, cardamom is used in some Asian countries as a breath freshener. Chewing a cardamom pod after a meal is also believed to aid in digestion.

Cardamom's strong floral nature allows it to stand up brilliantly in the face of other strong flavors. Coffee and chocolate are just two examples of the wonderfully strong backgrounds against which cardamom can be used. It also does well with strong earthy notes. The squash family (acorn, butternut, and pumpkin) works well with cardamom. Molasses, honey, brown sugar, and maple syrup are good choices of sweeteners to use with cardamom.

The flowery notes of cardamom work well when contrasted with the sharp, crisp flavors of fruits such as pears and apples. The floral nature of the cardamom should be a delicate back note to your plated dessert. The consumer should be left with a pleasant, perfume like humming as they swallow each bite. Try roasting apples with a touch of fresh apple cider, cardamom and brown sugar or poaching pears in red wine, honey and cardamom. In both instances the cardamom offers the dessert a delicate base note.

Cardamom is most associated with the eastern parts of the world. It is used with great frequency in countries such as Turkey and India. It is, perhaps, most associated with chais and curries as well as with Turkish coffee. Consider the deeply sweet confections of India as well as their abundant use of dried fruits and nuts. All of these ingredients will work well with cardamom.

When adding cardamom to a dish the pods can be used whole or crushed. Dry sautéeing will release more of the spice's flavor. Although more costly, try to use cardamom pods rather than ground cardamom. The difference in flavor between the two products is considerable. Grind the cardamom directly before use, as the flavor will decrease the longer the spice is exposed to air.

Partner with
. . . .

Fruits: apples, apricots, bananas, cherries, kumquats, lemons, oranges, peaches, pears, plums, raspberries, strawberries

Vegetables: beets, carrots, squash (acorn and butternut), sweet potatoes

Dairy: buttermilk, crème fraîche, mascarpone cheese, sour cream, yogurt

Sweeteners: brown sugar, caramel, honey, maple syrup, raw sugars

Nuts: almonds, chestnuts, hazelnuts, pecans, pistachios, walnuts

Dried fruits: apricots, black mission figs, calamyrna figs, cherries, raisins

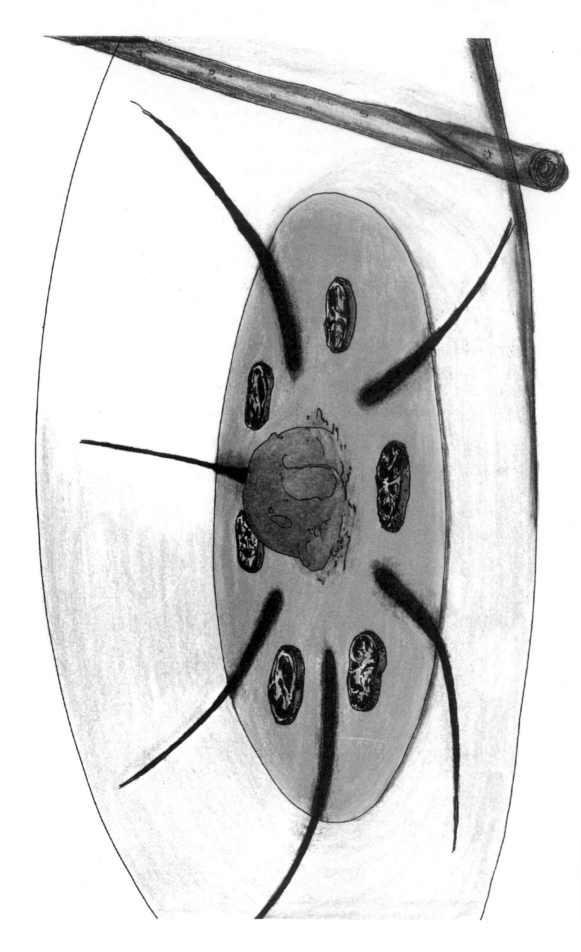

FIGURE 8.2

Orange consommé with preserved kumquats and a drizzle of black tea syrup. The consommé is garnished with a shredded phyllo, honey, and pistachio "cigarette" and served with a coffee–cardamom granite. Illustration by Reginald S. Abalos.

Liquors: bourbon, hearty red wine, Scotch whisky

Beverages: black tea, coffee

Chocolate: dark, milk, white

Baking spices: cinnamon, cloves, ginger (dried), mace, nutmeg, vanilla

Culinary spices: galangal, ginger (fresh), mint, peppercorns, star anise

The idea for this dessert originated in the Middle Eastern use of cardamom. There cardamom is often served with coffee or a strong black tea—thus, the use of a sweet black tea syrup and coffee–cardamom granite. The shredded phyllo, honey, and pistachio "cigarette" is reminiscent of the honey and nut phyllo pastries often seen in that part of the world. The orange consommé and preserved kumquats were chosen to be light and refreshing contrasts to the other heavy and sweet components on the plate. The lack of fat in the plate allows the flowery essence of the cardamom to shine brightly.

chillis

Chilli peppers form the backbone for a number of diverse cuisines. The foods of Mexico, Spain, Hungary, and some parts of Asia are all defined, to a great degree, by their individual use of peppers. The various spellings associated with chilli peppers are often confusing. The native Mayan word was chilli. This changed to chile in Spain and chili in America. To make matters more complicated, chilli is used to refer to a ground powder, a stew, and the peppers themselves. With an eye on consistency, I will refer to pungent peppers by their original Mayan name of chilli.

In the midst of the many spellings and diverse definitions, the root or common denominator is, of course, the chilli pepper. The chilli pepper is actually the fruit of a small shrub native to South America. Chillis are a true American original and are presently the most widely cultivated spice in the world. The majority of chilli peppers are grown and consumed in Mexico.

The heat from chillis comes from the chemical capsaicin; thus, products made with chillis will include a base note of trigeminal response. The heat from capsaicin is made up of approximately five separate chemical components. The initial heat hits the consumer at the back of the palate, while the slower acting chemicals take a bit longer to be felt on the tongue and the midpalate. The Scoville scale is used to register the heat of a chilli with a bell pepper registering 0 and habaneros at the other extreme, registering anywhere from 80,000 to 150,000 Scoville units.

The heat of the chillis lies in its white membrane, not its seeds. Thus, the closer that membrane is to the flesh of the pepper, the stronger its trigeminal response. The smaller the pepper, the hotter it will be when consumed. Picture the shape of a bell pepper, lots of space between the flesh and its membrane. Now picture a Thai chilli pepper, no larger than your little finger. Its tiny shape means that its flesh and membrane are packed closely together. The result is an extremely hot pepper.

A pepper's heat is distinct and separate from its flavor. When working with peppers focus on each pepper's unique flavor and taste. It is the flavors of the peppers that must be the middle note, not their heat. Consider the plate profile graphics in Chapter 3. Too much heat, too large of a base note will soon push all of the plate's remaining flavors out of the balloon. The flavors of the peppers must be in the forefront, with the heat from the capsaicin providing a faint humming as a base note.

Remember the painted room syndrome? You may want to have a colleague taste your preparation for correct heat level, since the more you taste the dish, the more you will become immune to its pungency. Also be aware of your individual flavor box. If you are someone who enjoys and often eats spicy, hot food then use a light hand in your chilli preparation. Your customer who may not have as great a tolerance for large amounts of capsaicin as you do. The customer will also be eating a greater quantity of the product than the chef will in the course of tasting.

A *hint:* Capsaicin is barely soluble in water, thus gulping down a large glass of water to quench the fire in your mouth will not help. In fact, the water merely washes the oil throughout your mouth, thereby increasing the burning sensation. Instead, a spoonful of plain rice or a bite of bread or tortilla will help to calm the pepper's bite.

There are many reasons why consumers enjoy eating chilli-laden food. The heat of the chilli tells the brain to produce endorphins and endorphins produce a feeling of pleasure or euphoria. Additionally the heat of the chillis also causes blood to rush to the surface of the consumer's skin. This results in a cooling sensation. This is one reason why the cuisines of so many hot climates utilize chillis.

When purchasing a commercially processed chilli powder, make sure that it is somewhat moist and lumpy. These are both indications that the volatile oils of the chilli are still present. Most chilli powders start to lose potency and flavor after approximately six months, so plan and purchase the spice accordingly.

Dried Chilli Peppers

Ancho

The ancho pepper is a dried and smoked poblano pepper. It is perhaps the most commonly used chilli in Mexico. Ancho is the Spanish word for wide and that aptly describes this pepper with its broad shoulders. It is the sweetest of all the dried chillis and carries with it wonderful smoky coffee notes, along with the flavor of heavy dried fruit, such as raisins. Although these chillis are dried, they should be flexible and unbroken when purchased. Their suppleness is a sign of their freshness.

It is best to roast and rehydrate dried chillis before working with them. Roast the chillis by placing them on a sheet pan in low oven 300°F (150°C) for approximately 4–5 minutes. Alternatively, they can be dry roasted in a sauté pan on the stove. Roast just until the chilli becomes crisp and balloons up. Be careful not to overroast as the result will introduce an undesirable bitter note to your end product. Once they are roasted, the chillis can be rehydrated in water. For use in desserts, using hot coffee helps to underscore the inherent smoky notes in the chillis' flavor. Place the peppers in a heat-resistant container and cover with the hot coffee. Weigh down the chillis, as they will float to the surface. Continue to let the chillis soak until they are soft and completely rehydrated.

After the chillis are rehydrated, take them out of the coffee (discard the coffee) and remove their stems and seeds. This can be easily accomplished under running water. Next place the chillis in a robot coupe or food processor. Begin to process the chillis while slowly adding fresh coffee. The resulting mixtures should be thicker than water but thin enough to push through a chinoise mousseline. When the mixture has reached the correct consistency, strain it through a chinoise mousseline. The skin will remain in the chinoise and the resulting mixture will be completely lump free.

This rust-colored chilli flavoring compound will keep in the refrigerator for many weeks. It is somewhat akin to vanilla extract in that it smells fantastic but tastes horrible until combined with additional ingredients. Using this compound allows the chef to closely control the amount of heat and flavor he/she is adding to any one particular dessert. Remember when flavoring with chillis that less is more. The flavors will grow as the mixture sits. A chocolate chilli mousse that does not taste that hot today will be doubly hot tomorrow.

Partner with

Fruits: apricots, bananas, blackberries, cherries, guavas, lemons, limes, oranges, mangoes, passion fruit, peaches, pineapple, raspberries, strawberries

Vegetables: bell peppers, corn, cucumbers, garlic, onions, squash (acorn, butternut, pumpkin), sweet potatoes, tomatoes

Dairy: buttermilk, cheddar cheese, crème fraîche, goat cheese, sour cream, yogurt

Sweeteners: brown sugar, caramel, honey, maple syrup

Nuts: almonds, coconut, pine nuts

Dried fruits: apricots, cherries, raisins, strawberries

Liquors: beer, bourbon, rum, tequila

Beverages: coffee

Chocolate: dark, milk, white

Baking spices: cinnamon, cloves, ginger (dried), mint, nutmeg, vanilla

Culinary spices: chillis (fresh), cilantro, cumin, ginger (fresh), peppercorns, star anise, tamarind

Pantry ingredients: cornmeal, olive oil

This dessert reflects a bit of chocolate's history. Originally the Mayans made a drink from roasted and ground cocoa beans. The ground beans were mixed with ancho chillis, vanilla, and ground corn. All of these elements are evident on this plate. The chocolate cake with its liquid center revisits the centuries old Mayan drink. The vanilla of that original beverage, the ancho, and the corn are also evident in the various components of the plate. The salsa offers a cooling component to the plate as well as a fresh note that will cut through some of the heaviness of the chocolate and ice cream. Using a salsa rather than a fruit coulis also places the dish into a Mexican context. The tortilla sunburst is a visual reference to the warmth of the Mayan lands.

FIGURE 8.3

Chocolate molten cake served on a vanilla bean caramel sauce, accompanied by ancho chilli ice cream. The plate is finished with a fresh mango salsa and a crispy sweet and spicy tortilla sunburst. Illustration by Reginald S. Abalos.

A note about working with tortillas: Both flour and corn tortillas work well as crispy garnishes. Cut the tortillas into desired shapes and fry. This will result in a crispy yet somewhat free-form shape, as the tortilla will balloon once it hits the hot oil. For a sharply outlined and flatter form like the tortilla sunburst, cut the shape from the tortilla. Brush both sides of the tortilla lightly with water and dust with desired seasonings. For the above dish the tortilla is dusted with a mixture of granulated sugar and ancho chilli powder. Place the tortilla on a Silpat-lined sheet pan. Place in a 350°F (175°C) oven, turning every 5–6 minutes until golden brown. If a completely flat form is sought, cover the tortillas with an additional Silpat throughout the baking process. Store tightly wrapped at room temperature.

Chipotle

The chipotle pepper is a dried and smoked jalapeño. It is smaller than the ancho and thus ranks higher on the Scoville scale. The chipotle will impart more heat to your dish, so use accordingly. Its flavors are a bit deeper and more complex than those of the ancho, with a wonderful back note of chocolate and a hint of smoky tobacco flavor. These smoked, dried peppers go well with heavy, earthy flavors.

Before use, the peppers should be roasted and rehydrated as for the ancho chilli peppers.

Partner with
· · · · · · · · · · · · · · · · ·

Fruits: apricots, bananas, blackberries, cherries, guavas, kiwi, lemons, limes, mangoes, oranges, papayas, passion fruit, peaches, persimmons, pineapple, plums, rhubarb, raspberries, strawberries

Vegetables: carrots, corn, fennel, squash (acorn, butternut, and pumpkin), sweet potatoes, tomatoes

Dairy: buttermilk, cheddar cheese, crème fraîche, goat cheese, sour cream, yogurt

Sweeteners: brown sugar, caramel, honey, maple syrup

Nuts: almonds, cashews, coconut, macadamia nuts, peanuts, pecans, walnuts

Dried fruits: apricots, cherries, raisins

Liquors: beer, bourbon, Scotch whisky, tequila

Beverages: coffee

Chocolate: dark, milk, white

Baking spices: cinnamon, cloves, ginger (dried), mace, nutmeg, star anise, vanilla

Culinary spices: basil, chillis (fresh), Chinese five spice, cilantro, cumin, ginger (fresh), oregano, peppercorns, star anise, tamarind

Pantry ingredients: cornmeal, olive oil

The chilli cheesecake has small-diced caramelized acorn squash folded into the batter. The chipotle helps to cut through the fattiness of the cheesecake as does the bourbon glaze and chocolate sauce. Likewise, the richness of the cheesecake and the starchiness of the squash hold up well to the smoky heat of the chipotle pepper. The chocolate sauce is made with no fat, just cocoa powder, water, and sugar. The result is a deep, bitter chocolate, which serves as a foil for the heat of the chilli. The strong base note of the chocolate helps to counterbalance the strong trigeminal response of the chipotle chilli. The brittle is made as for a nut brittle with the addition of acorn squash seeds that have first been roasted with some chipotle powder. The sherbet starts with a simple syrup infused with roasted walnuts and is finished with a bit of bourbon.

Be careful when working with walnuts. Their skin is incredibly astringent, especially if the nuts are roasted for too long. Take them out of the oven early and let carryover heat continue to cook them to the desired color.

FIGURE 8.4

Chilli cheesecake with a bourbon glaze, accompanied by a chocolate sauce, spicy seed brittle, and a walnut bourbon sherbet. Illustration by Reginald S. Abalos.

Fresh Chilli Peppers

Habanero Peppers

Habaneros are the hottest member of the chilli pepper clan. They are also, not coincidentally, one of the smallest. Habaneros can rank anywhere from 80,000 to 150,000 on the Scoville scale.

When using habaneros in plated desserts limit the amount of time the pepper is in contact with the other ingredients on the plate. For instance, in the following dish the pepper is folded into the salsa at the last moment. This prevents the habenero from overpowering the other flavors in the dish. Remember that less is more; the heat of the pepper should be a base note. Although the heat of the chilli will accumulate on the palate with each bite, it should never become so strong that it becomes the middle note of the plate. Using the habenero in tandem with fatty elements will help to tame its heat.

In the 1980s salsa beat out ketchup to become America's number one condiment. This plate is a sweet tribute to salsa. The Bavarian cream has a strong mango flavor and is served on top of a small cornmeal short dough cookie. The salsa is both fruity and spicy, a combination of strawberries, mango, habaneros, and cilantro. The habanero is folded into the mixture just before service. The tequila sorbet reinforces the plate's connection to Mexican cuisine and is refreshing after the richness of the Bavarian cream and the heat of the salsa. The coconut lace contributes a relatively neutral backdrop for the flavorful salsa.

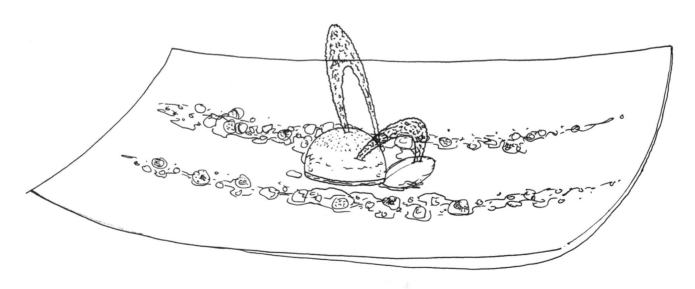

FIGURE 8.5

Mango Bavarian cream with a corn short dough cookie. Served with a fruity piquant salsa, tequila sorbet, and coconut lace cookie. Illustration by Reginald S. Abalos.

Jalapeño Peppers

Jalapeños are rated at between 2500 and 10,000 on the Scoville scale. Hotter than a bell pepper, the heat of a jalapeño is not too overwhelming. The popularity of jalapeño poppers is a tribute to the relatively mild heat of a jalapeño pepper. Poppers consist of a stuffed, breaded, and fried jalapeño that is eaten in its entirety. Raw jalapeños have a clean, grassy flavor that becomes much sweeter if the pepper is roasted.

When using hot chilli peppers on a plated dessert it is important that they are an accent, not the primary flavor. In this dish the jalapeño is smoothed out by the fat and sourness of the sour cream. The rich strawberry ice cream and the astringent, bitter chocolate sorbet offer intense flavors that work well with the jalapeño's heat. The caramelized crunchy corn tortilla layers give the plate its structural integrity and add wonderful texture. A bit of clear jalapeño sauce is drizzled onto the classic caramel sauce. This adds a bit of a zing and reinforces the jalapeño flavor on the plate. A classic caramel sauce is used here because of its fatty richness that helps to smooth out the jalapeño's heat.

Poblano Peppers

Poblanos rate a 1000–1500 on the Scoville scale. Their relative sweetness makes them popular for use in dishes where the entire pepper is consumed, such as chilli rellenos. In this dish the pepper is filled with a cheese

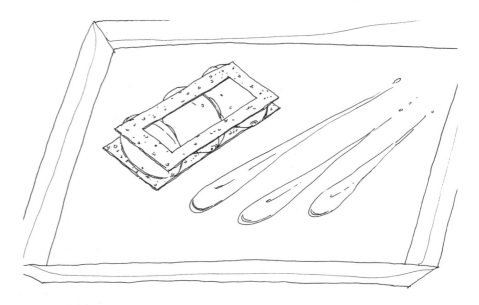

FIGURE 8.6

Napoleon of Mexican ices: crispy sweet tortillas form the layers for this napoleon. The ices consist of a jalapeño–sour cream sherbet, strawberry ice cream, and chocolate sorbet. A classic caramel sauce and a jalapeño clear sauce accompany the napoleon. Illustration by Reginald S. Abalos.

chapter 8   herbs and spices

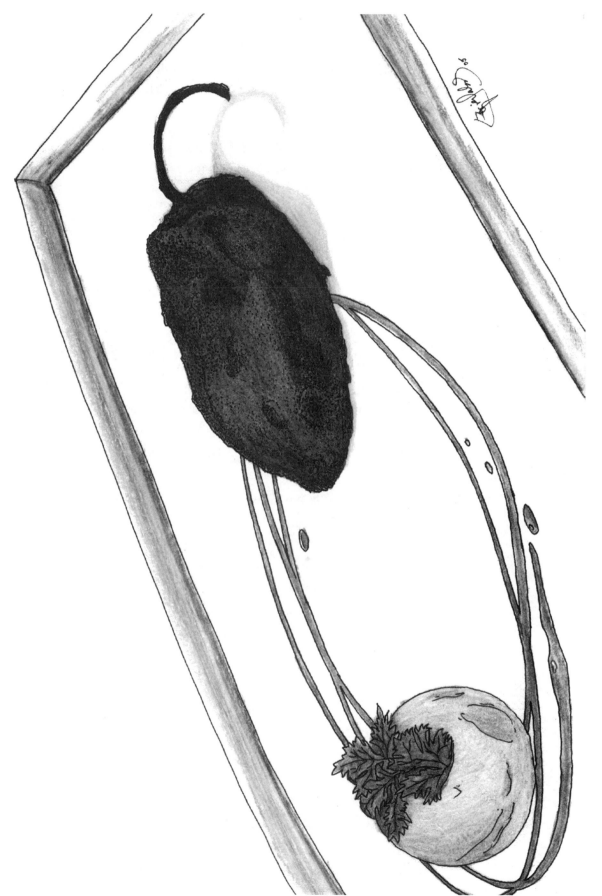

FIGURE 8.7

Chilli relleno stuffed with a sweetened cream cheese, served with cilantro sorbet and a tequila honey reduction. Illustration by Reginald S. Abalos.

mixture, dredged in flour and egg, and then fried. The following plated dessert is a variation of this popular culinary dish.

Try to find small poblano chillis for this dish. A large pepper will be overwhelming when served as a dessert. The filling for the relleno is a lightly sweetened cream cheese. Add some dried mangoes and cherries to the mixture and then fill the chilli. Wrap the chillis tightly in plastic wrap and refrigerate until the filling becomes firm (about one hour). Dredge the peppers in flour and then egg before frying.

The combination of frying the chilli and filling it with a fatty cheese helps to smooth out the heat of the poblano. It is important, however, that the guest is not left with only the flavor and sensation of fat on their palate. The addition of the cilantro sorbet and the tequila honey sauce help to cut through the fat of the fried pepper. Base notes are added to the dish through the cooling of the cilantro and the alcohol burn from the tequila.

Partner with (for all three of the above chillis)

Fruits: apples, blackberries, blueberries, cherries, guavas, kiwi, lemons, limes, mangoes, oranges, papayas, passion fruit, peaches, pears, pineapple, plums, prickly pears, raspberries, strawberries

Vegetables: bell peppers, carrots, corn, cucumbers, garlic, onions, squash, sweet potatoes

Dairy: buttermilk, cheddar cheese, goat cheese, mascarpone cheese, sour cream, yogurt

Sweeteners: brown sugar, caramel, honey, raw sugars

Nuts: coconut, macadamia nuts, peanuts, pine nuts

Dried fruits: apricots, cherries

Liquors: beer, rum, tequila

Chocolate: dark, milk, white

Baking spices: cinnamon, mace, mint, vanilla

Culinary spices: chillis (dried), cilantro, cumin, curry powder, dill, ginger (fresh), mustard seed, oregano, peppercorns, tamarind

Pantry ingredients: cornmeal, olive oil

chinese five spice

Chinese five spice is a combination of five spices. The blend consists of star anise, fennel seeds, cinnamon, cloves, and Sichuan or black peppercorns. It offers the best of Asian flavors with its hot, spicy, and sweet flavors. Chinese five spice has a smoky warm flavor with a bit of bite from the peppers and cloves. This heat is complimented by the cooling notes found in the star anise and fennel seeds. The trigeminal response from the anise offers a cooling base note, which is the perfect accompaniment to heavier flavors. In short, the spice blend has a beautifully rounded full plate profile. Using Chinese five spice instead of the more traditional pumpkin or gingerbread spice blends will give your finished product a deeper, more well-rounded flavor.

Most often associated with Asian cuisine, Chinese five spice is traditionally used in dishes that are cooked for a fairly long time. These include the barbecue sauce for Chinese spare ribs as well as many pork or duck dishes.

Partner with

Fruits: apples, apricots, bananas, blackberries, cherries, cranberries, kumquats, mangoes, nectarines, oranges, peaches, pears, pineapple, plums, raspberries, rhubarb, strawberries

Vegetables: beets, carrots, corn, squash, sweet potatoes, tomatoes

Dairy: buttermilk, cheddar cheese, crème fraîche, mascarpone cheese

Sweeteners: brown sugar, caramel, honey, maple syrup, molasses

Nuts: almonds, cashews, coconut, hazelnuts, macadamia nuts, peanuts, pecans, pine nuts, walnuts

Dried fruits: apricots, cranberries, figs, raisins

Liquors: bourbon, red wine, sherry, whiskey, white wine

Beverages: black tea, coffee

Chocolate: dark, milk, white

Baking spices: cinnamon, cloves, ginger (dried), mace, nutmeg, star anise, vanilla

Culinary spices: cumin, galangal, ginger (fresh), mustard, peppercorns, tamarind

Pantry ingredients: cornmeal

Rather than construct a dish that echoes the Asian roots of Chinese five spice, this plate reinvents a traditional American dessert that is familiar to many customers. The dish revolves around gingerbread cake, a classic fall treat. In this version the gingerbread cake is made with a combination of Chinese five spice, dried ginger, and just a touch of dry mustard powder. After the cake is baked and cooled, it is crumbled and stirred into some warm caramelized sugar. Add just enough caramel to the crumbs so that they stick together. The resulting mixture is placed into small, flat flexipan molds and baked for 5–7 minutes at 350°F (175°C). The

FIGURE 8.8

Asian ice cream sandwich: Chinese five spice ice cream sandwiched between gingerbread cake pastilles topped with a compote of fall fruits and served with a red wine reduction along with sweet and spicy walnuts. Illustration by Reginald S. Abalos.

result is a wonderful "pastille" of caramelized gingerbread cake. It is a crunchy variation of the more traditional gingerbread cake. The pastilles are used as the top and bottom of the ice cream sandwich. The ice cream is a traditional French-style ice cream made with an infusion of Chinese five spice. The sandwich is topped with a compote of apples, cranberries, oranges, brown sugar, and fresh ginger. The compote is spooned over the top of the sandwich. This ensures that the guest will get a bit of fruit with each bite of the ice cream sandwich. The long cooking time needed for a compote is reminiscent of the spice's traditional use in Asian cuisine. It is the dish's only nod to the spice blend's roots. The nuts are roasted, lightly coated with egg whites, and dredged with a mixture of sugar and Chinese five spice. The dessert offers flavors that are familiar to most customers while the Chinese five spice gives those same flavors a deep, rich plate profile.

cilantro

Cilantro is a member of the parsley family. Its seed, coriander, will be discussed separately. Cilantro is also known as Chinese parsley and is an integral part of both Asian and Latin cuisines. It has a light lemony flavor with an intense anise base note. Those who do not like cilantro complain of its soapy nature. Use caution, for cooking cilantro can intensify this soapy taste.

Cilantro is a diverse spice. It can accompany both heavy, as well as light and clean flavors. The cooling properties of its anise base notes make it the perfect match for the heat of chilli peppers or curry. It is a traditional addition to fiery salsas for this very reason. In Asian cooking cilantro's roots are often ground into a spicy paste. Both its stems and leaves impart a great deal of flavor when used in infusions.

Partner with

Fruits: bananas, cantaloupe, cherries, guavas, honeydew, lemons, limes, mangoes, nectarines, oranges, papayas, passion fruit, peaches, pineapple, plums, raspberries, strawberries, watermelon

Vegetables: bell pepper, corn, cucumbers, onion, squash, tomatoes

Dairy: buttermilk, crème fraîche, sour cream, yogurt

Sweeteners: caramel, honey, raw sugars

Nuts: almonds, coconut, macadamia nuts, peanuts, pine nuts

Dried fruits: apricots

Liquors: tequila

Beverages: mirin, red wines (dry), sake, white wine

Baking spices: mint

Culinary spices: chillis (fresh and dried), cumin, curry powder, jalapeños, mustard seed, peppercorns

Pantry ingredients: cornmeal

This dessert is truly modern American cuisine. It gives a nod to cilantro's country of origin and then goes off on its own. The combination of jalapeño and cilantro is fairly traditional. The mousse with its chilli pepper base note is coupled with a cilantro clear sauce. Using a clear sauce lets cilantro's flavor come through loudly. The cooling anise base of the cilantro works well with the mousse. The frozen nature of the sorbet amplifies cilantro's inherent cooling qualities. The red bell pepper coulis offers a sweet yet savory edge to the dish and its grassy notes echo the green notes of the cilantro. The bell pepper coulis has a touch of lemon added to

Strawberry and jalapeño mousse, served with a cilantro clear sauce and a red bell pepper coulis. Garnished with coconut tuile and cilantro sherbet.
Illustration by Reginald S. Abalos.

it, which compliments the sour notes found in the strawberry mousse. The coconut tuile is the sole crispy piece on the plate. It is the only component that requires any amount of chewing. Thus, the flavors of the tuile will resonate on the palate for quite a while. In this way, the relatively neutral flavor of the coconut works to cleanse the palate between bites.

 coriander

Coriander is the seed of the cilantro plant although their flavors are not at all similar. Coriander's pungent aroma is linked to the Greek word for bedbug. As the plant grows, its smell is comparable to that of a sheet full of bedbugs. This smell thankfully dissipates by the time the seeds are dried and the longer they are kept, the more fragrant they become.

Coriander has a citrusy tang with a flowery sharpness that resonates in the palate. It is often used in pickling and curries where it lends an earthy quality with a hint of orange sparkle.

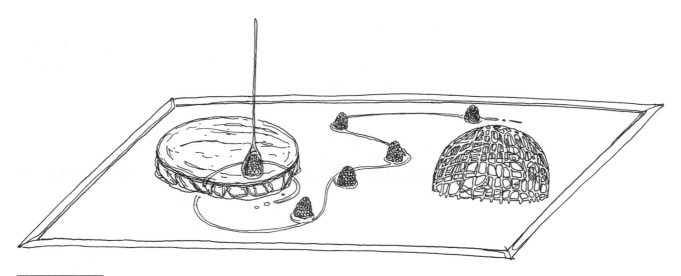

Peach tarte tatin accompanied by an orange–coriander reduction, fresh raspberries and coriander ice cream in a cage made of honey. Illustration by Reginald S. Abalos.

Partner with

Fruits: apples, bananas, kumquats, lemons, mangoes, nectarines, oranges, peaches, pears, raspberries, strawberries

Vegetables: bell peppers, carrots, corn, cucumbers, onions, squash (acorn, butternut, and pumpkin), sweet potatoes, tomatoes

Dairy: buttermilk, cheddar cheese, crème fraîche, goat cheese, sour cream

Sweeteners: brown sugar, caramel, honey, raw sugar

Nuts: almonds, cashews, coconuts, macadamia nuts, peanuts, pecans, pistachios, walnuts

Dried fruits: apricots, calamyrna figs, cherries, mission figs

Chocolate: dark, milk, white

Baking spices: allspice, cinnamon, ginger (dried), mace, nutmeg

Culinary spices: cumin, mustard seed, peppercorns

Coriander is best as an accompaniment, not, necessarily, as a lead singer. Therefore, the peach tarte tatin takes center stage on this plate. The peaches are sweet with caramelization. The sour and savory orange coriander reduction is the perfect accompaniment. The orange complements the coriander and contrasts nicely with the sweetness of the peaches. The raspberries serve the same purpose with the coriander ice cream. The fatty nature of the ice cream is a welcome counterpart to the leanness of the tatin.

The cage is made from a mixture of honey and fondant. Use 1 part honey and 2 parts fondant by weight. Place in a saucepot on high heat and stir occasionally. Once the desired color has been reached, the mixture is ready to use for garnish work.

 cumin

An ancient spice, mentioned in the Bible and in works of Hippocrates, cumin is yet another member of the extended parsley family. Its aroma and flavor are perhaps most associated with Mexican cuisine. The heavy, roasted warm notes of cumin work especially well when mixed with other strong, earthy flavors. Cumin's flavor is brought out when the seeds are dry roasted before being ground.

Cumin is not only used in Mexican cooking. It also forms an integral part of garam masal along with coriander seeds, cardamom, black peppercorns, cloves, mace, bay leaf, and cinnamon. As such it is an important part of Indian cuisine. Cumin's presence in any cuisine is unmistakable; it adds a wonderfully smoky base note to any dish it is in.

Partner with

Fruits: apples, bananas, cranberries, guavas, lemons, limes, mangoes, oranges, peaches, pears, pineapple, raspberries, strawberries

Vegetables: beets, corn, garlic, onions, pumpkin, squash (acorn and butternut), sweet potatoes, tomatoes

Dairy: buttermilk, cheddar cheese, crème fraîche, mascarpone cheese, sour cream, yogurt

Sweeteners: brown sugar, caramel, honey, molasses, raw sugar

Nuts: almonds, Brazil nuts, coconut, peanuts, pecans, walnuts

Dried fruits: apricots, cherries

Liquors: beer, bourbon, dark rum, whisky

Beverages: black tea, coffee

Chocolate: dark, milk

Baking spices: cardamom, cinnamon, mace, nutmeg, vanilla

Baking spices: chillis (fresh and dried), Chinese five spice, cilantro, coriander, curry powder, peppercorns, star anise

Pantry ingredients: cornmeal

Cumin's connection to Mexican cuisine is obvious in this dish. The smokiness of the cumin harmonizes well with the cinnamon-filled Mexican

FIGURE 8.11

Beggar's purse filled with roasted pineapple accompanied by a Mexican chocolate semifreddo. Served with a dark rum caramel sauce and cumin-scented pineapple chips. Illustration by Reginald S. Abalos.

chocolate as well as with the dark rum. The pineapple offers a tart, slightly sour, contrast to the earthiness of the cumin. It is roasted with brown sugar and a bit of cumin, then wrapped inside of a phyllo beggar's purse and flash baked (baked at an extremely high temperature for a short period of time) until the phyllo becomes golden. The pineapple chips are first simmered in simple syrup for 2–3 minutes and then dusted with a touch of cumin before they are baked. Use the finest sieve available to insure that the cumin does not overpower the pineapple flavor. Bake at 325°F (160°C) for 30 minutes or until dried. The sauce is a clear caramel sauce finished off with dark rum instead of heavy cream. This allows the vanilla notes of the dark rum to shine. The only fat on the dish is in the semifreddo.

curry powder

Curry is a diverse term. It can refer to a spice mixture, a cooking process, or a particular dish. In India the spices included in a curry powder blend often change according to geographical region. Traditionally, the mixture is blended a la minute, while one is cooking. The notion of a ready-made or already mixed curry powder began in England. Brits returning from India wanted to duplicate the curries they had eaten there and in the subcontinent and, thus, developed an easy to use blend of spices. Such blends often contain coriander seeds, mustard seeds, turmeric, fenugreek seeds, cumin seed, red chilli flakes, ginger, cinnamon, black peppercorns, and cardamom seeds. For the greatest depth of flavor the individual spices should be dry sautéed before being ground. It is best to fry each spice separately as each will roast at a different rate. Curry differs from garam masala. Unlike curry powder, garam masala has no turmeric or chillis.

The earthy heat of curry works well when contrasted with other cooling elements. Ingredients such as citrus, cilantro, mint, and yogurt all work as beautiful foils for the warmth and heat of curry powder.

Curry can also refer to a savory dish that is served with a hot and spicy sauce. Traditionally the sauce was served with rice. The British variation of this dish is a stew with a small amount of rice in it.

Partner with

Fruits: apples, apricots, bananas, blackberries, blueberries, cherries, lemons, limes, mangoes, oranges, peaches, pears, pineapple, raspberries, strawberries

Vegetables: beets, cucumbers, garlic, onions, pumpkin, squash (acorn and butternut), sweet potatoes

Dairy: buttermilk, cheddar cheese, crème fraîche, mascarpone cheese, yogurt

Sweeteners: brown sugar, caramel, honey, raw sugar

Nuts: almonds, coconut, macadamia nuts, pecans, pistachios, walnuts

Dried fruits: apricots, calamyrna figs, cherries, cranberries, dates, mission figs, raisins

Liquors: beer

Beverages: black tea, coffee

Chocolate: dark, milk, white

Baking spices: cardamom, cinnamon, ginger (dried), mace, mint, nutmeg, vanilla

Culinary spices: Chinese five spice, cilantro, coriander, cumin, ginger (fresh), peppercorns

The earthy heat of curry makes it the perfect accompaniment for the sour tartness of fresh fruit. The lemon curd, fresh berries, and sorbet all offer a refreshing note to the curry sugar cookie crust and mango–curry swirl in the sorbet. The chocolate garnish has been dusted with curry. The bitterness of the caramel and of the dark chocolate will help to balance out

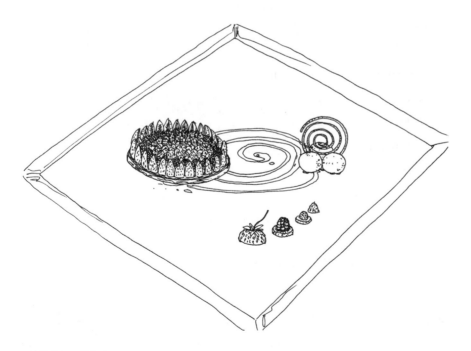

FIGURE 8.12

Fresh berry tartlet filled with lemon curd on a curry sugar cookie crust, partnered with caramel raspberry sauce, chocolate spiral and berry sorbet with a mango-curry swirl. Illustration by Reginald S. Abalos.

curry's big base note. The result is a plate that is refreshing with just a hint of savory earthiness.

dill

· ·

Another member of the parsley family, dill is closely related to fennel. Although dill lacks fennel's intense anise flavor, it does contribute cooling properties to plated desserts. Both the leaves and seeds of dill are used in cooking. Dill leaves (fronds) have a clear, crisp, grassy flavor not found in the seeds. Due to their delicate nature, add the fronds at the end of the cooking process. Their light, clean flavor make dill the perfect complement to other clean flavors on the plate. Dill can, however, work as a contrasting element to a plate with other heavier flavors. The seeds are best utilized when a more intense flavor is required. Use the seeds for infusions and hot preparations.

Partner with

· ·

Fruits: apricots, lemons, limes, mangoes, oranges, nectarines, peaches

Vegetables: beets, bell peppers, carrots, corn, cucumbers, root vegetables (roasted), squash, tomatoes

Dairy: buttermilk, cheddar cheese, crème fraîche, goat cheese, Parmesan cheese, sour cream, yogurt

Sweeteners: caramel, honey

Nuts: almonds, coconut

Dried fruits: apricots

Liquors: red wine, white wine

Beverages: carrot juice, green tea

Chocolate: white

Culinary spices: cilantro, coriander, mint, mustard (dry), peppercorns, sesame seed

Pantry ingredients: cornmeal

Dill's relationship with carrot is exploited in this dish. Both carrots and dill offer wonderfully clean, crisp, grassy notes. The panna cotta is made with buttermilk. Its low fat content as well as its sourness will ensure that dill's clean notes are not lost. The carrot foam is aerated carrot juice. The bubbles add a nice textural contrast to the plate both visually and on the palate. A bit of sweetness is introduced with the white wine reduction sauce. It is made of white wine with a bit of honey and dill, which is then

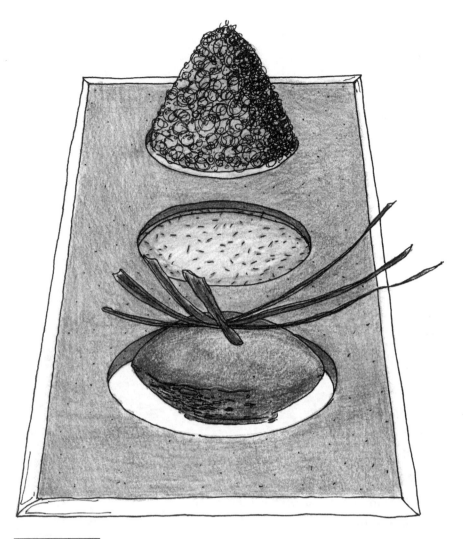

Carrot–dill panna cotta served with carrot foam and a white wine dill reduction sauce. Garnished with carrot chips and an orange sorbet. Illustration by Reginald S. Abalos.

reduced down. The orange sorbet offers a pungent sour note and the carrot chips bring a crispness to both the palate and plate.

 galangal

Galangal is a member of the ginger family. Like ginger, galangal is a rhizome, or root, with fibrous flesh. Its relationship to ginger is evident in its appearance as well as in its flavor. The outside of galangal is somewhat waxy with clearly marked rings. It is more yellow in color than ginger. While the inner flesh is fibrous like ginger, it is slightly lighter in color. Galangal has an aroma reminiscent of camphor.

Galangal has a light clean flavor with distinct citrus overtones. The often intense heat of ginger is not found in galangal. In fact, galangal's name is taken from the Arabic word for "mild ginger". Galangal's flavor is more of a watercolor as opposed to the strong flavor of ginger which is more reminiscent of an oil painting. Galangal's lighter, more delicate flavor has both advantages and disadvantages. The primary disadvantage is that its fragile essence is easily lost when combined with fatty ingredients.

Peel and crush galangal before using it in a dish. The root is harder and firmer than ginger so you may need to slice it before attempting the crushing. Crushing ruptures the individual cells, releasing more flavor. (See Ginger section for more information on working with galangal.)

Galangal is primarily used in Thai cuisine as a complement to lighter flavors and a cooling crisp contrast to the heat of Thai chillis.

Partner with

Fruits: apricots, cherries, lemons, limes, lychees, mangoes, oranges, peaches

Vegetables: carrots, cucumbers, squash (acorn, butternut, and pumpkin), sweet potatoes

Dairy: buttermilk, yogurt

Sweeteners: caramel, honey

Nuts: almonds, cashews, coconut, peanuts

Dried fruits: apricots

Liquors: mirin, sake, white wine

Beverages: black tea, green tea

Chocolate: white

Baking spices: ginger (dried), nutmeg

Baking spices: chillis (fresh and dried), cilantro, kefir lime leaves, lemon grass, tamarind

Pantry ingredients: rice noodles, sweet soy sauce

Using a consommé as an entrée item allows the light watercolor natures of both lemon grass and galangal to shine. Steamed dumplings filled with a sweet adzuki bean paste are a traditional Asian dessert. Their presence on this plate underlies galangal's relationship to that cuisine. The sorbets are presented in small scoops; each offers a sampling of intense lime, mango, and galangal flavor. The consommé is to be eaten between each bite of sorbet, cleansing the palate with a wash of lemon grass and galangal. The coconut curls and a sprinkling of small-diced mango and lychee supply textural and visual interest.

FIGURE 8.14

Galangal and lemon grass consommé with steamed adzuki bean dumplings. A trio of sorbets: lime, mango, and galangal, accompany the consommé along with fresh fruit and coconut curls. Illustration by Reginald S. Abalos.

 # ginger

Ginger is a rhizome (or root) covered with a brown papery skin. Under the skin, ginger is extremely fibrous and can range in color from a deep tan to a dull yellow. There is little or no comparison between fresh and dried ginger in terms of flavor. Fresh ginger has a fresh, tangy, almost citrus flavor, which is often accompanied by a large base note of heat. Dried ginger, on the other hand, has an earthy quality to it and lacks both the heat and the pungency of fresh ginger. It tastes a bit like a somewhat musty, watered down version of fresh ginger.

When using fresh ginger look for pieces that are moist and firm to the touch. Be wary of the tremendous heat that often accompanies ginger's fresh flavor. As with chilli peppers, the trigeminal response (in this instance triggered by the oil gingerols) should be clearly defined as a base note, and not interfere with the top or middle notes of the plate. Too much heat will overpower the other notes of the plate profile.

Ginger's heat will vary according to its freshness. The only way to truly judge the amount of heat in any specific piece of ginger is by tasting it. Does the heat hit you all at once, even before the actual flavor of the spice comes through, or do you get to enjoy some ginger flavor before the heat kicks in? If there is too much heat in the ginger, it should be blanched, often more than once, before continuing with the recipe.

Slice the ginger into the desired size and place it in a chinoise mousseline. (This way you won't have to fish the individual pieces of ginger out of the boiling water.) Once the water is boiling, place the chinoise into the pot and count to thirty. Then immediately plunge the chinoise into ice water. Taste the ginger. If it is still too hot, repeat the process. Make sure to use fresh boiling water each time. The water is being used to leech the heat from the ginger. Continuing to blanch the ginger in the same boiling water is a bit like bathing in dirty water. Taste the ginger after each blanching and when the heat is at a point where it will work for your particular recipe, stop. Beware of the painted room syndrome. The more fresh ginger you taste, the more acclimated to its heat you will become. It is often a good idea to ask a colleague to taste the ginger as well.

After it has been blanched, the ginger can be candied. Simmer the ginger in simple syrup until the fibers have broken down and are completely infused with the sugar mixture. Tasting the ginger is the only way to check on its progress. Once the ginger's sweetness is where you want it, it can be used directly out of the syrup, in which case it will be shiny and glossy-looking on your plate, or it can be dredged in granulated sugar for a more crystallized appearance. The crystallized ginger can be stored at room temperature for weeks. Make sure to wrap the ginger tightly to protect it from humidity.

The ginger can also be made into chips. Slice the ginger lengthwise on a meat (or deli) slicer and continue as you would for fruit chips (see the Appendix). If a deli slicer is not available, an extremely sharp mandolin can be used. The resulting abstract-looking chip can work well on a plate where the remaining components have very sharp edges. The chip has a bit of sweetness, wonderful flavor, a bit of heat, and some crunch. Additionally, the resulting simple syrup can be used as a base for a sorbet or sherbet. Chips should be stored at room temperature, tightly wrapped, with silica gel if possible, to prevent them from becoming soggy.

Cultivated in Asia for thousands of years, the exact origins of ginger are unclear. Traditionally, pickled ginger (gari) is served with sushi or sashimi to cleanse the palate. Ginger is also believed to possess calming digestive properties. Both of these attributes can be utilized by the chef when designing a ginger-based plated dessert. Use the tangy, clean bite of ginger to help cut through the fatty richness found in so many desserts. This can be done either through candied ginger, ginger chips, or a fresh ginger infusion. The use of fresh ginger will help to draw attention to the middle note(s) of the dish by cleansing the consumer's palate with each bite.

Partner with

Fruits: apples, apricots, bananas, blackberries, blueberries, cherries, cranberries, lemons, limes, lychees, mangoes, nectarines, orange, passion fruit, peaches, pears, pineapple, plums, raspberries, strawberries

Vegetables: beets, bell peppers, carrots, cucumbers, garlic, onions, squash (acorn, butternut, and pumpkin), sweet potatoes

Dairy: buttermilk, crème fraîche, mascarpone, sour cream, yogurt

Sweeteners: brown sugar, caramel, honey, maple syrup, molasses, raw sugars

Nuts: almonds, cashews, coconut, hazelnuts, lychee, macadamia nuts, pecans, pine nuts, walnuts

Dried fruits: apricots, calamyrna figs, cherries, cranberries, mission figs

Liquors: red wine, white wine

Beverages: black tea, green tea

Chocolate: dark, milk, white

Baking spices: allspice, cardamom, cinnamon, cloves, ginger (dried), mace, nutmeg

Culinary spices: coriander, curry powder, lemon grass, mustard (dried), peppercorns, star anise, tamarind

Pantry ingredients: mirin, rice noodles, sesame oil, soy sauce, sweet soy sauce

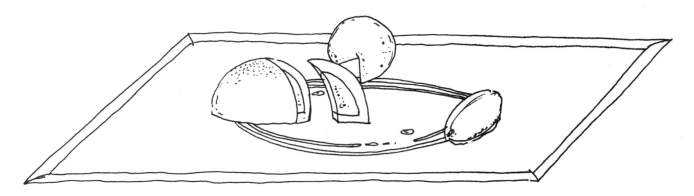

FIGURE 8.15

Chocolate sabayon mousse with a roasted banana–ginger insert served with a ginger clear sauce and bitter caramel. Accompanied by spicy tuile and caramel sherbet. Illustration by Reginald S. Abalos.

Chocolate sabayon mousse is rich and creamy and full of strong flavors. The insert consists of bananas that have been roasted in the oven with some fresh ginger. The fruit is then stabilized with just a touch of gelatin, placed in a mold, and refrigerated. Use a mold that is just slightly smaller than the mold in which the mousse is going to be made. Make sure that the gel is set before beginning the mousse.

Partially fill each mold with the mousse; each should be approximately 50% full. Insert the banana-ginger gelée into the center of each mold. Add more mousse if needed in order to completely fill each mold. Using a metal spatula, flatten the mousse tops and place molds in the freezer until the mousse is completely set. For service, cut a wedge out of each mousse so that the guest can see the gelée in the center.

The chocolate, ginger, and bitter caramel all contribute strong base notes to this dish which offset the richness of the chocolate sabayon mousse. The sweetness of the ginger clear sauce and of the caramel sherbet also help to balance the dish's overall plate profile.

 lavender

Lavender's relationship to the mint family is clear once it is tasted. A slight menthol note accompanies its floral essence. Native to the Mediterranean region, lavender is traditionally included in the classic herbes de Provence. This spice blend consists of chervil, marjoram, tarragon, basil, thyme, and lavender. Any of these herbs work well with lavender. When lavender is used alone, however, care must be taken. Lavender's floral flavor does not necessarily mean that it is delicate. In the culinary world it stands up well to strong presences such as lamb. In the pastry world it can be a wonderful accompaniment to the strong flavors of black tea, coffee, and bitter chocolate.

Too much lavender in a product often prompts thoughts of bath soap and aromatherapy. Lavender should always be a harmonizing flavor, not the primary middle note of the dish. Fresh lavender has a much smoother overall quality than the relatively harsh floral flavor of most dried lavender buds. Grinding dried buds with granulated sugar makes it possible to easily incorporate lavender into baked goods.

Partner with

Fruits: apricots, blueberries, cherries, kumquats, lemons, limes, mandarin oranges, nectarines, oranges, peaches, plums, raspberries, strawberries

Vegetables: beets, carrots, fennel, pumpkin, squash (acorn, butternut, and pumpkin), sweet potatoes

Dairy: buttermilk, crème fraîche, goat cheese, mascarpone cheese, sour cream, yogurt

Sweeteners: brown sugar, caramel, honey, raw sugars

Nuts: almonds, macadamia nuts, pistachios

Dried fruits: apricots, cherries

Liquors: port, robust red wines

Beverages: black tea, coffee

Chocolate: dark, milk, white

Baking spices: cinnamon, ginger (dried), mint, nutmeg, vanilla

Culinary Spices: anise seed, basil, cardamom, ginger (fresh), marjoram, oregano, peppercorns, tarragon, thyme

This plate is a perfect example of the adage "less is sometimes more." Lavender crème brûlée is a beautifully rich entrée. It needs nothing more than the addition of a few fresh raspberries to cut through some of the fat. The madeleines offer a textural contrast to the dish. The addition of just a touch of lavender to the cookies ensures that the herb's flavor will sing throughout the dessert. The use of the traditionally French crème brûlée and madeleines underscore lavender's relationship with that country.

FIGURE 8.16

Lavender crème brûlée accompanied by lavender honey madeleines and fresh raspberries. Illustration by Reginald S. Abalos.

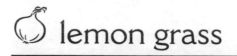 lemon grass

Lemon grass is a perennial grass common to the tropics of Southeast Asia. It grows in long shoots and although all parts of the shoot are fantastically aromatic, only the lower portion is tender enough to be eaten. The tougher parts of the stalk can be used for infusions.

Lemon grass and lemon zest are not interchangeable. Lemon grass has a much more delicate citrus flavor and aroma, with a bit of a floral, sometimes lightly soapy base note. To compare lemon grass to lemon zest is to compare a watercolor to an oil painting. One is not necessarily better than the other; they are simply two separate entities. Lemon grass has a smooth, round aroma and flavor with none of the sharp acidity associated with fresh lemons. Because of its delicate nature, lemon grass works best on plates with little or no fat. Too much fat will cover up the floral nature of this herb.

When using lemon grass remove the outer leaves and cut off the stringy roots at the very bottom of the stalk. Slice the bulb portion crosswise into thin pieces. Crush each piece with the side of a cleaver or French knife. This ruptures the individual cells in the plant, releasing more flavor. In traditional Thai cooking, the lemon grass is then pounded into a pulp, which is the base of many spice pastes. The lemon taste of lemon grass can have a cooling effect on many of the hot dishes associated with Thai cuisine.

Partner with

Fruits: cantaloupe, guavas, honeydew, limes, lychees, mangoes, papayas, passion fruit, pineapple, rhubarb

Vegetables: bell peppers, cucumbers, Vidalia onion

Dairy: buttermilk, sour cream, yogurt

Sweeteners: honey

Nuts: almonds, cashews, coconut, peanuts

Liquors: sake, white wine

Beverages: black tea, green tea

Chocolate: white

Baking spices: cinnamon, nutmeg

Culinary spices: Chinese five spice, cilantro, galangal, ginger, sea salt, star anise

Pantry ingredients: mirin, rice, rice noodles, sweet soy sauce, tofu

Bubble tea is frequently found in parts of Asia. It is a sweetened tea with large pearls of tapioca in it. The tea is slurped up through an oversize straw. Pieces of that idea are found in this lemon grass-tasting plate.

FIGURE 8.17

A bubble tea of cilantro consommé and lemon grass-infused large pearl tapioca. Accompanied by cilantro and mango gelées, coconut tuile, and coconut-lemon grass sherbet. Illustration by Reginald S. Abalos.

The consommé is served in a tube-like glass with an oversized straw; on the bottom of the glass are the large tapioca pearls that have been infused with lemon grass while they were cooking. The mango and cilantro gelées are strong enough that they can be picked up with the fingers and simply popped into the mouth. The last taste is a small quenelle of coconut and lemon grass sherbet served in a small coconut tuile bowl. The plate is designed to be whimsical, yet it also makes clear connections between lemon grass and its country of origin. There is very little fat on the plate; this allows the watercolor nature of the flavor of lemon grass to come through.

marjoram

Marjoram is native to the Mediterranean region and is a member of the mint family. Think of marjoram as oregano's shy cousin. Marjoram has the same green, floral, somewhat woody flavors of oregano with none of its penetrating strength. Due to its delicate nature, it is best to add marjoram at the end of the cooking process. Use fresh marjoram whenever possible.

Marjoram's fresh flavor makes it a natural accompaniment for fresh vegetables and fruits. It is often lost when used with heavier, earthy flavors. It is best to turn to marjoram's gregarious cousin, oregano when using heavy or fatty flavors.

Partner with

Fruits: blackberries, blueberries, lemons, limes, mangoes, oranges, papayas, peaches, pineapple, plums, raspberries, strawberries

Vegetables: beets, bell peppers, carrots, garlic, red onions, squash (acorn, butternut, and pumpkin), tomatoes, Vidalia onions

Dairy: Asiago cheese, buttermilk, cheddar cheese, Parmesan cheese, yogurt

Sweeteners: honey

Nuts: almonds, pine nuts

Dried fruits: apricots, golden raisins

Liquors: red wine, white wine

Chocolate: milk, white

Culinary spices: basil, lavender, mint, oregano, peppercorns, rosemary, sage, tarragon, thyme

Pantry ingredients: balsamic, cornmeal, olive oil

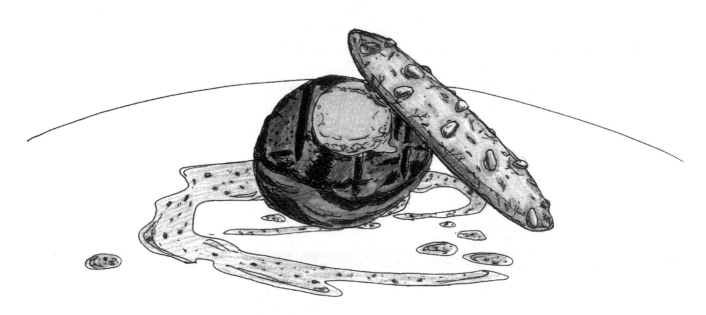

FIGURE 8.18

Grilled peaches accompanied by a marjoram clear sauce, pine nut sugar cookies, and a honey frozen yogurt. Illustration by Reginald S. Abalos.

The simplicity of this dish allows the relatively reticent marjoram to take center stage. The peaches are grilled with no additional sweeteners added. The pine nut sugar cookies serve as a connection to marjoram's country of origin. The slight bitterness of the honey frozen yogurt balances out the sweetness of the peaches. In order to increase the depth of honey's flavor, reduce it down slightly before adding it to the rest of the frozen yogurt ingredients. Although the only fat on the plate is the frozen yogurt, its sour notes help marjoram's flavor to shine through. The use of the marjoram clear sauce also guarantees that the herb's presence will not be overwhelmed by the plate's other components. Overall this is a light and refreshing dessert that allows the essence of marjoram's flavor to be enjoyed.

mustard seed

Mustard seeds are members of the cabbage family. Like its cousins, wasabi and horseradish, mustard has a pungent aroma as well as a strong bite. All of these spices affect the consumer through the nasal as well as through the oral passage. Consequently, a whiff of jalapeño does not startle the consumer, as does a large whiff of dry mustard or wasabi. However, mustard's heat does not linger on the palate as does the burn from a jalapeño.

Mustard seeds are used in many different types of cuisines throughout the world, both as a preservative and as a condiment. Today most Americans associate mustard with the condiment. The flavor associated with the condiment comes from ground mustard seed. Interestingly, this powder does not begin to release its heat until mixed with a liquid. Room temperature water works best while highly acidic liquids will inhibit mustard's flavor release. Use caution when working with mustard seed so that its heat does not overwhelm its wonderfully earthy, spicy, and warm flavor.

For plated desserts, whole mustard seed offers a wonderfully full, earthy middle note. The whole seeds can be toasted, as they often are in Indian dishes. The result is a lessening of the mustard's pungency and the introduction of a slightly bitter, nutty note. Use the seeds in infusions and when roasting, braising, or stewing.

Mustard goes well with other heavy, earthy flavors; its pungency will not be lost. It can also be used with fatty items on the plate.

Partner with

Fruits: apples, cherries, lemons, oranges, peaches, pears, pineapple, plums

Vegetables: bell peppers, beets, corn, squash (acorn, butternut, and pumpkin), sweet potatoes, tomatoes

Dairy: cheddar cheese, crème fraîche, mascarpone cheese, sour cream, yogurt

Sweeteners: brown sugar, caramel, honey, maple syrup, raw sugars

Nuts: almonds, macadamia nuts, peanuts, pecans, walnuts

Dried fruits: apricots, figs, prunes, raisins

Liquors: beer, bourbon, red wine

Chocolate: dark

Baking spices: allspice, cinnamon, ginger (dried), mace, nutmeg

Culinary spices: Chinese five spice, coriander, cumin, ginger (fresh), peppercorns, saffron, star anise

This plate is a variation of slow-braising meat and then serving it with a sauce made of pan drippings or fond. In this case the fruit is slowly roasted with mustard seed and some brown sugar. The fruit is then removed from the pan and some classic caramel sauce is added to the drippings and then reduced. The resulting sauce has a strong middle note containing all of the flavors of the roasted fruits. The orange sorbet adds an acidic note to the plate, which contrasts with the sweetly caramelized roasted fruit. The phyllo purse is filled with pistachios, almonds, a bit of honey, ground mustard seed, orange and lemon zest, and some dried cherries. This serves as a textural contrast as well as another introduction to mustard seed.

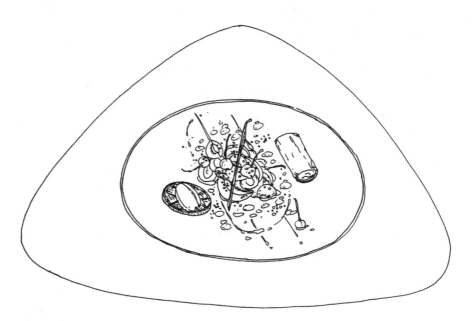

FIGURE 8.19

Stone fruit (plums, peaches, and cherries) slow roasted with mustard seed and served with a pan reduction sauce, orange sorbet, and a fruit and nut-filled phyllo "cigarette." Illustration by Reginald S. Abalos.

Overall, the mustard seed supplies an earthy back note to what might otherwise be an almost too sweet plate.

 oregano

Oregano is another member of the mint family. It has a strong woody, clean, and somewhat grassy flavor and aroma. Its presence on a dish is unmistakable. Although it is the spice that most Americans associate with Italian food, its use in America is fairly new. It was not until post World War II and the rise of pizza in America that oregano first became known here.

Oregano's strong voice holds up well to the other strong flavors of Italian cooking, such as garlic, heavy tomato sauces, and various meats. Unlike its quiet cousin marjoram, oregano's strong demeanor makes it a perfect accompaniment for fatty items as well as for items that are braised and stewed.

Partner with

Fruits: blackberries, cherries, lemons, limes, oranges, peaches, pears, pineapple, plums, raspberries, strawberries

Vegetables: bell peppers, beets, carrots, garlic, onions, squash (acorn, butternut, and pumpkin)

Dairy: Asiago cheese, buttermilk, cheddar cheese, goat cheese, mascarpone cheese, Parmesan cheese

Sweeteners: caramel, honey, maple

Nuts: almonds, hazelnuts, pine nuts, walnuts

Dried fruits: apricot, cherries

Liquors: red and white wines

Beverages: black tea

Chocolate: milk, dark

Baking spices: cinnamon, mint, nutmeg, vanilla

Culinary Spices: basil, coriander, marjoram, mustard seed, peppercorns, rosemary, sage, tarragon, thyme

Pantry ingredients: balsamic vinegar, cornmeal, olive oil

This plate's use of polenta, Parmesan cheese, tomato and infused olive oil place it firmly within an Italian environment. The polenta is made with honey and braised cherries, both of which help to increase the pudding's sweetness. The sweetness serves as a terrific backdrop for the savory components of the dish, the black pepper clear sauce, oregano olive oil and

FIGURE 8.20

Polenta pudding with braised cherries accompanied by a black pepper clear sauce and oregano oil. Garnished with Parmesan tuile and tomato sorbet. Illustration by Reginald S. Abalos.

tomato sorbet. The Parmesan tuile is small, leaving just a bit of saltiness in its wake. The tomato sorbet is made with fresh tomatoes and a touch of lemon, giving the dish a crisp, clean wash of savory flavor with just a hint of sweetness.

peppercorns

The omnipresence of the black peppercorn on the nightly dinner table belies its majestic origins. Known as the "king of spices," there was a time when peppercorns were worth more than their weight in gold. This is the spice that spurred on the spice trade and the resulting exploration and colonization of the new world. In the mid-1500s black pepper's price set the standard for European business in general.

Native to southwest India, peppercorns grow on a perennial vine. The vine takes approximately eight years to reach maturity, and its berries grow in a spike-like fashion. As the berry matures, its pungency increases. Its flavor is at its height while the berry is still green. Black peppercorns are picked from these mature, yet still unripe berries. It is at this stage that their aromatics are the most dense. The peppercorns are quickly blanched, which cleans the fruit and begins an enzymatic process that will eventually turn the berries black. They are then dried either by machine or in the sun. Black peppercorns have a wonderful earthy quality to them as well as a bit of heat, especially when freshly ground. When too much is used, the heat is noticeable in the front of the throat and the back of the palate.

Green peppercorns are harvested before they are fully ripened. The berries are preserved through dehydration or by placing them in a brine solution. The flavors of green peppercorns vary according to the method of preservation.

White peppercorns have been left on the vine until they are completely ripened. They are harvested and soaked, the husk is then peeled away and the inner white kernel is left to dry. White pepper does not have the same round smoothness of black peppercorns. The flavor is more abrupt, almost dusty; it hits the consumer in the back of the throat almost instantly. White peppercorns are often used in lightly colored foods in which the specks of black peppercorn are not desirable.

Despite their name, pink peppercorns are not true peppercorns at all. They are, instead, the fruit of the Brazilian pepper tree. Their flavor is vaguely reminiscent of black peppercorns in that they have a somewhat dusty heat. Pink peppercorns differ from black peppercorns, however, in their accompanying sweet, fruit notes.

Partner with (for all 3 peppercorns)

Fruits: apples, apricots, bananas, blackberries, blueberries, cantaloupe, cherries, cranberries, fresh figs, honeydew, kiwi, lemons, limes, mangoes, oranges, papayas, peaches, pears, plums, pineapple, raspberries, rhubarb, strawberries, watermelon

Vegetables: beets, bell peppers, corn, cucumbers, fennel, garlic, onions, pumpkin, sweet potatoes, squash (acorn, butternut, and pumpkin), tomatoes

Dairy: Asiago cheese, cheddar cheese, crème fraîche, goat cheese, mascarpone cheese, Parmesan cheese, sour cream

Sweeteners: brown sugar, caramel, honey, raw sugars

Nuts: almonds, cashews, hazelnuts, macadamia nuts, peanuts, pine nuts, pistachios, walnuts

Dried fruits: apricots, cherries, cranberries, raisins

Liquors: bourbon, whisky, red and white wine

Chocolate: dark, milk, white

Baking spices: cinnamon, ginger (dried), mace, nutmeg, vanilla

Culinary spices: basil, cardamom, chillis (fresh and dried), Chinese five spice, coriander, cumin, curry, dill, galangal, ginger (fresh), lavender, marjoram, mustard (dry), oregano, rosemary, saffron, sage, sesame seeds, tarragon, thyme

Pantry ingredients: balsamic vinegar, cornmeal, olive oil, sesame oil

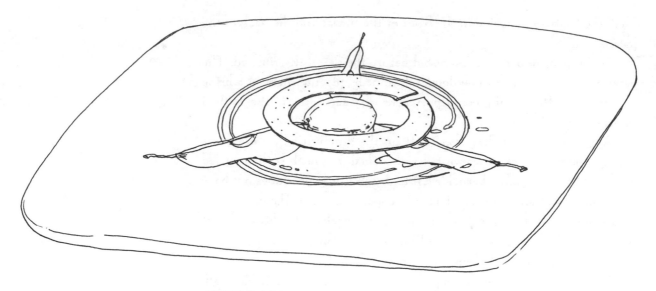

FIGURE 8.21

Pears poached with red wine, honey, and black peppercorns. Served with a pink peppercorn honey mascarpone sherbet, red wine reduction sauce, and black peppercorn tuile. Illustration by Reginald S. Abalos.

Poached pears are certainly not a new dessert. In this version they serve as the stage for the peppercorns. The addition of black peppercorns to the poaching liquid adds a depth of flavor to the pears by supplying a base note. The fat of the plate is found in the mascarpone sherbet and the use of pink peppercorns adds a slightly floral note to the frozen component. The peppery tuile ensures that the palate will have a light taste of pepper with each bite. The pears themselves supply a crisp, slightly sour note, which contrasts well with the sometimes-dusty black peppercorns.

 rosemary

Rosemary is a hardy member of the mint family. It has, in past years, undergone great indignity in its use as a garnish on culinary plates. I am referring, of course, to the ubiquitous sprig of rosemary piercing a pork chop or lamb loin.

Rosemary grows on an evergreen shrub native to the Mediterranean and it is most associated with the flavors of that region. Rosemary has a thick, almost branchlike stem, strong enough to hold up to use as a skewer. Its leaves resemble small pine needles and have a crisp, woodsy aroma. When using fresh rosemary leaves make sure to chop finely or grind in a mortar. Rosemary can also be ground with either sea salt or sugar and then added to baked goods. Although rosemary's leaves hold their shape when dried, they lack some of the distinctive fresh resin flavor of their fresh counterpart.

Rosemary's strong character holds up well to long cooking times and strong accompanying flavors. But this powerful presence can easily overwhelm the other flavors on a plated dessert. Use rosemary with discretion; its menthol base note can offer a cooling sensation to the other flavors on your plate.

Partner with

Fruits: apples, apricots, blackberries, blueberries, cherries, lemons, limes, oranges, peaches, pears, pineapple, plums, raspberries, strawberries

Vegetables: beets, bell pepper, carrots, corn, fennel, garlic, onions, squash (acorn, butternut, and pumpkin), sweet potatoes, tomatoes

Dairy: Asiago cheese, cheddar cheese, crème fraîche, goat cheese, mascarpone, Parmesan cheese, ricotta cheese, sour cream

Sweeteners: brown sugar, caramel, honey, molasses, raw sugar

Nuts: hazelnuts, macadamia nuts, pecans, pine nuts, walnuts

Dried fruits: apricots, cherries, figs, strawberries

Liquors: bourbon, red wine, whiskey, white wine

Chocolate: dark, milk

Baking spices: cinnamon, cloves, ginger (dried), mace, nutmeg, vanilla

Culinary spices: basil, marjoram, oregano, peppercorns, sage, tarragon, thyme

Pantry ingredients: balsamic vinegar, cornmeal, olive oil

FIGURE 8.22

Rosemary crème caramel with a single malt scotch reduction. Served with pecan lace, and roasted apple, garnished with an apple chip. Illustration by Reginald S. Abalos.

The piney resin of rosemary works well here with the slightly sour apple and the earthy scotch. Single-malt scotch is expensive but its smoky burn works well with the buttery crème caramel. A scotch with peat notes in it will work best for this dish. The scotch can be reduced with the caramel from the crème caramel. Invert the crème caramel over a sauté pan; thus none of its caramel "sauce" will be lost. The fat of the crème caramel is perfect for this plate as it rounds out the sometimes-harsh edges of the rosemary. No additional sweeteners are used when roasting the apples; they will sweeten through the roasting process. The light crispness of the pecan lace bowl offers a much needed textural contrast to the plate.

saffron

Saffron is part of the trinity of the world's most expensive spices (with vanilla and cardamom taking up the remaining two slots). Its high price is due to the time and effort required in its cultivation and harvesting. Saffron is a member of the iris family. Each flower offers three stigmas that must be painstakingly harvested by hand. Approximately 250,000 flowers are needed for one pound of saffron. Harvesting those flowers takes almost 200 hours of labor.

Saffron is perhaps most associated with Spanish cuisine. It is used in their rice dishes, most notably paella. Typically thought of for the color it brings to a dish, the dusty muddy earthiness of saffron's flavor is sometimes overlooked. It is the dusty nature of saffron's flavor that makes it so unique. Lightly roasting and then infusing the threads in a liquid will greatly intensify the flavor they bring to any particular dish.

Saffron's earthiness can be the perfect foil for tart fruits such as citrus and cherries as well as for the rich sweetness of dried fruits. The addition of rice to a plate offers a wonderfully neutral background against which saffron's flavor can be most appreciated. Be careful: too much saffron results in a bitter, astringent, and ultimately unappealing flavor.

Partner with

Fruits: apricots, cherries, figs, lemons, oranges, peaches, pears, plums, raspberries, strawberries

Vegetables: carrots, onions, pumpkin, squash (acorn, butternut, and pumpkin)

Dairy: buttermilk, crème fraîche, mascarpone cheese, sour cream, yogurt

Sweeteners: caramel, honey

Nuts: almonds, coconut, pine nuts, pistachios

FIGURE 8.23

Saffron rice pudding topped with broiled fresh figs, and covered with a sherry/honey glaze. Accompanied by a dried cherry tuile and saffron sorbet. Illustration by Reginald S. Abalos.

Dried fruits: apricots, cherries, dates, figs, raisins

Liquors: port, sherry, white wine

Baking spices: cinnamon, ginger (dried), nutmeg, vanilla

Culinary spices: Chinese five spice, peppercorns, sesame seeds, star anise

Pantry ingredients: rice: jasmine and basmati

The rice pudding in this dish is meant to mirror saffron's traditional use in paella. The broiled fresh figs take the place of the seafood used in the classic dish. Saffron's earthy notes work well with this dessert's many sweet components. The saffron sorbet contrasts with the richness of the rice pudding. Its fat-free nature allows saffron's true flavor to shine through. The tuile offers a contrast of both texture and flavor, introducing the plate's only sour note in the form of the dried cherries.

sage

Sage is a member of the mint family. It is an herb strongly identified with Italian cuisine, especially dishes containing poultry. Sage works particularly well with items that are going to be cooked. It also has a long history of use as an infusion and was used as an infused beverage in England before the arrival of tea from China.

The base of sage's flavor is fairly woody, accompanied by a strong camphor presence. Use care, as too much sage can easily overpower the other flavors in your dish. There are some advantages to sage's strong voice. It will hold up well with fatty elements of the dessert. It also works well with heavy earthier flavors, such as acorn squash, sweet potatoes, and pumpkin, to name but a few. Its flavor is also a wonderful accent to the crisp tartness of an apple or pear. Because of the tough nature of its leaves, try to avoid using raw sage as any part of your final plate design.

Partner with

Fruits: apples, cranberries, lemons, oranges, peaches, pears, plums

Vegetables: beets, corn, garlic, onions, pumpkin, squash (acorn, butternut, and pumpkin), sweet potatoes, tomatoes

Dairy: Asiago cheese, cheddar cheese, crème fraîche, goat cheese, mascarpone cheese, Parmesan cheese, ricotta cheese, sour cream

Sweeteners: brown sugar, honey, maple syrup, molasses

Nuts: hazelnuts, pecans, pine nuts, walnuts

Dried fruits: apricots, cherries, figs, dates, raisins

Liquors: beer, bourbon, red wine, white wine

Chocolate: dark, milk, white

Baking spices: cinnamon, ginger (dried), mace, nutmeg, vanilla

Culinary spices: marjoram, mustard seed, oregano, peppercorns, rosemary, tarragon, thyme

Pantry ingredients: balsamic vinegar, cornmeal, olive oil

This plate begins with sage's connection to Italian cuisine but adds some modern notes. The texture of the polenta cake is between that of a pound cake and corn bread. Its texture closely resembles the moist crumb of a pound cake, with the strong corn flavor of corn bread. The plums have been slowly cooked until they are almost completely broken down. Their

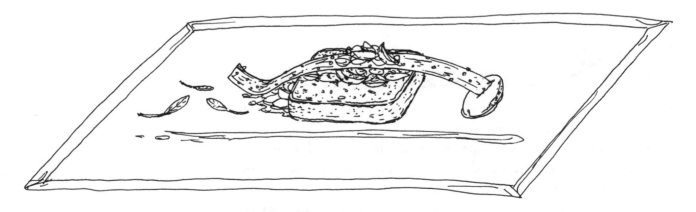

FIGURE 8.24

Sage polenta cake covered with plum compote and served with classic caramel sauce. Accented with cranberry sorbet and a walnut sugar wave. Illustration by Reginald S. Abalos.

almost jam-like sweetness will hold up well against the presence of sage. The caramel sauce supplies the only fat on the plate, a mildly bitter richness. The heavy nature of the entrée item is contrasted with the tart astringency of the cranberry sorbet. The sorbet guarantees that the sage will not overwhelm the plate. The walnut wave is made in the same manner as powdered caramel (see the Appendix).

sesame seeds

Sesame seeds have long been associated with the cuisines of Africa, Asia, and the Middle East. The term "open sesame" may come from the fact that the sesame pods, which house the sesame seeds, have a tendency to split open when ripe, scattering the seeds everywhere. Thus, the pods are harvested when they are not quite ripe to prevent the loss of the crop to the ground. There are three primary varieties of sesame seeds, black, white, and brown. No matter which variety is chosen, the seeds should be roasted before use. Because of their small size, dry roasting in a sauté pan works well. Be careful as the seeds contain approximately 50% oil and will, therefore, easily burn. Roasted sesame seeds have a wonderfully buttery, nutty flavor.

Sesame seeds are traditionally used in tahini paste, a thick paste made from either roasted or unroasted sesame seeds. Tahini paste is a frequent ingredient in many mideastern dishes such as hummus. Halvah is perhaps the best-known sesame confection. It is a mixture of honey and toasted sesame seeds.

Partner with

Fruits: blackberries, lemons, limes, lychees, mangoes, oranges, plums, raspberries, strawberries

Vegetables: carrots, cucumbers, squash (acorn, butternut, and pumpkin), sweet potatoes

Dairy: buttermilk, crème fraîche, sour cream, yogurt

Sweeteners: brown sugar, caramel, honey, raw sugar

Nuts: almonds, pistachios

Dried fruits: apricots, cherries, dates, figs, raisins

Liquors: red wine

Beverages: black tea, coffee

Chocolate: milk, white

Baking spices: cinnamon, ginger (dried), nutmeg, vanilla

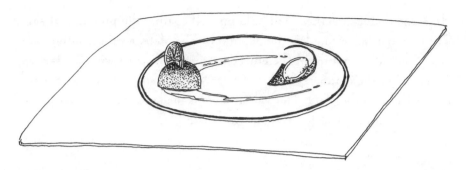

FIGURE 8.25

Black sesame seed crème fraîche panna cotta served with an orange cherry reduction, orange chip, sesame lace, and a morello cherry sorbet. Illustration by Reginald S. Abalos.

> **Culinary spices:** Chinese five spice, coriander, galangal, ginger (fresh), lemon grass, star anise, tamarind
> **Pantry ingredients:** rice noodles, sesame oil

The presence of crème fraîche, coupled with roasted sesame seeds, means that the panna cotta in this dish is fairly rich and fatty. The tartness of the reduction and sorbet present the plate profile with much needed sour notes. The sesame lace is lace dough with the addition of white sesame seeds. The dessert is a study of contrasts with elements of sweet and sour, rich and lean, as well as creamy and crunchy.

star anise

Star anise grows on a native Chinese pine tree. The tree takes approximately 6 years to reach maturity, but continues to bear fruit for up to 100 years! Its name clearly derives from its shape, an eight-pronged star. The shell that encases the star anise seed forms the points of the star. The flavor of star anise comes from this casing.

The Chinese consider a whole star anise to bestow good luck. It is often given to newly wed couples as a symbol of a harmonious marriage. Just like the points of the star, which join in the center, the individual characteristics of the bride and groom join in the unity of marriage.

Although usually recognized as one of the elements of Chinese five spice, star anise has a wonderfully full flavor all by itself. It contains anethole, the same essential oil found in anise. This gives star anise a strong cooling base note. The strength of star anise makes it a perfect choice for dishes that are going to be cooked for a long time. Star anise flavor is slightly floral and well rounded; it does not have the sharp edges often associated with other forms of anise.

Partner with

Fruits: apples, blackberries, cantaloupe, fresh figs, honeydew, lemons, limes, lychees, oranges, peaches, pears, pineapple, plums, raspberries, strawberries

Vegetables: beets, carrots, fennel, squash (acorn, butternut, and pumpkin), sweet potatoes

Dairy: buttermilk, crème fraîche, mascarpone cheese

Sweeteners: brown sugar, honey, maple syrup, raw sugar

Nuts: almonds, cashews, coconut, macadamia nuts, peanuts, pecans, pine nuts, walnuts

Dried fruits: apricots, cherries, dates, figs

Liquors: bourbon, mirin, port, sake, scotch whisky

Beverages: black tea, coffee

Chocolate: dark, milk, white

Baking spices: allspice, cinnamon, cloves, ginger, mace, vanilla

Culinary spices: cardamom, chillis (dried), Chinese five spice, coriander, cumin, curry powder, galangal, ginger (fresh), mustard seed, peppercorns, rosemary, sesame seeds, tamarind

Pantry ingredients: rice noodles, sesame oil, sweet soy sauce

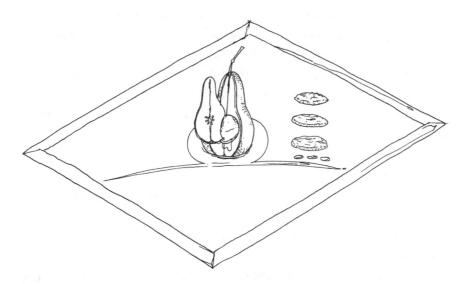

FIGURE 8.26

Star anise and maple-roasted pears with spicy French ice cream. Served with maple-star anise spice cookies, a ginger maple reduction sauce, and pear chips. Illustration by Reginald S. Abalos.

The pears are roasted with maple syrup and star anise. The resulting pan fond is used as the base for the reduction sauce along with the addition of fresh ginger. Star anise is used again in the spicy French ice cream along with some cinnamon. The maple of the pears is echoed in the spice cookies. These are a variation of classic 1-2-3 or short dough in which the granulated sugar has been replaced with maple sugar. Overall the dish has a bit of spicy bite. This is prevented from overwhelming the dish by the crisp sweetness of the pears and the richness of the French ice cream. This would be an excellent dish to present on a fall menu.

 tamarind

As one of the ingredients in Worcestershire sauce, probably most everyone has come into contact with tamarind at least once. Tamarind by itself, however, is a completely different matter. Tamarind refers to the pulp that encases the seeds of the tamarind pod. It is a member of the bean family. With a papery, fibrous skin outside, the sticky pulp surrounds several rather large seeds within each pod, or bean. In the pulp lies the heart of tamarind's overwhelmingly sour flavor. That sourness is at the base of many refreshing beverages enjoyed in tropical climates. Tamarind is used in many cuisines, including those from the Caribbean islands and as well as in Asia.

Working with whole tamarind pods is extremely time-consuming and requires a bit of diligence. If possible, try to purchase the tamarind in block form. In this form the pulp has been separated from the skin, although there are still the seeds and lots of fibers with which to contend. Cook the pulp down with some water. Doing this over a double boiler will avoid an overly cooked flavor, which ruins the otherwise refreshing characteristics of tamarind. Once the mixture has thinned out, strain it to get rid of the seeds and any residual fibers.

Alternatively, one can take some of the pulp and simply allow it to soak in some warm water (about 1 tablespoon of pulp to 2/3 cup water). Let it soak for a few minutes, giving it an occasional stir. Strain and use the remaining juice.

Avoid using tamarind nectars, compounds, and concentrates. While certainly convenient, their processing adds a cooked, almost musty flavor to the tamarind. Tamarind's strength is its tart clean flavor. This is lost in the cooking process.

If you ever have the opportunity, try tamarind candy from either the Caribbean or Asia. It comes in many forms; my favorite is simply tamarind pulp with some sugar and chilli powder. It is rolled into a ball and dredged in a mixture of salt and sugar. Each bite carries with it a perfect plate profile, a bit of salt, sweet, sour, and heat. An acquired taste, but delicious!

Tamarind's strongly assertive nature makes it a perfect accompaniment for heavy, earthy flavors. It can also work well with lighter flavors when diluted, presenting a refreshing note to the plated dessert.

Partner with

Fruits: bananas, blackberries, blueberries, cantaloupe, cherries, guava, honeydew, lychees, mangoes, oranges, papayas, passion fruit, peaches, pineapple, plums, raspberries, strawberries

Vegetables: carrots, cucumbers, squash (acorn, butternut, and pumpkin), sweet potatoes

Dairy: crème fraîche, mascarpone cheese, sour cream, yogurt

Sweeteners: brown sugar, honey, raw sugar

Nuts: almonds, cashews, coconut, macadamia nuts

Dried fruits: apricots, figs

Beverages: black tea

Baking spices: cinnamon, ginger (dried), nutmeg, vanilla

Culinary spices: Chinese five spice, chilli peppers (dried), galangal, ginger (fresh), lemon grass, star anise

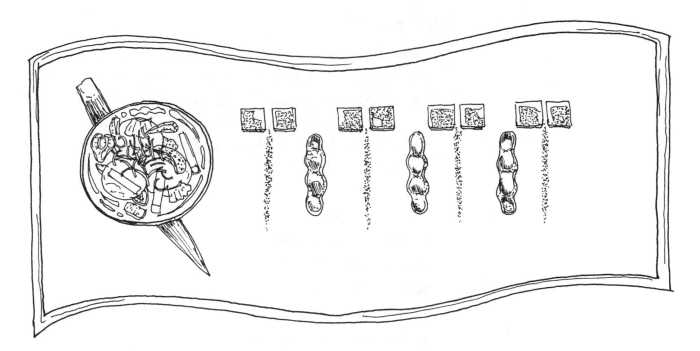

FIGURE 8.27

Tamarind sampler: tamarind gelées served with fresh pineapples, mango, and strawberries. Vanilla sorbet, chocolate sauce, and freshly toasted coconut round off the plate. Illustration by Reginald S. Abalos.

This plate reflects the many variations of tamarind candy. The tamarind pulp has been made into small cubes of gelée. Some of the cubes are dredged in salt, some in sugar, some in chilli powder, and some in all three. The intention is to have the customer try each gelée followed by a taste of the plate's other components. The only fat on the plate is found in the chocolate sauce and fresh coconut. The vanilla sorbet and fresh fruit mellow the tartness of the tamarind. This is a refreshingly light dessert, which would work well after a spicy meal.

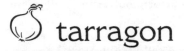 tarragon

A member of the daisy family, tarragon has a delicate anise flavor. Its clear anise flavor has a slightly peppery back note. Do not cook tarragon for too long or it will become bitter. It is best to add the herb at the end of the cooking process.

Tarragon is a member of fines herbes, along with chervil, parsley, and chives. Russian tarragon can grow wild and has a harsh, relatively flat flavor. French tarragon, however, has delicate thin leaves, and a mild, delicate anise flavor.

Partner with

Fruits: apples, blueberries, cherries, lemons, limes, mangoes, nectarines, oranges, passion fruit, peaches, pears, plums, raspberries, strawberries

Vegetables: carrots, corn, fennel, squash (acorn, butternut, and pumpkin), sweet potatoes, tomatoes

Dairy: Asiago cheese, cheddar cheese, crème fraîche, goat cheese, mascarpone, ricotta cheese

Sweeteners: brown sugar, honey, raw sugar

Nuts: almonds, cashews, macadamia nuts

Dried fruits: apricots, cherries

Liquors: red and white wines

Beverages: black tea, coffee

Chocolate: dark, milk, white

Baking spices: anise seed, nutmeg, star anise, vanilla

Culinary spices: basil, chervil, chives, marjoram, oregano, parsley, peppercorns, rosemary, sage

Pantry ingredients: balsamic vinegar, cornmeal, olive oil

FIGURE 8.28

Cherry financier served with a brown butter/tarragon caramel sauce, caramel garnish, and a tarragon–lemon sherbet. Illustration by Reginald S. Abalos.

For something so easy to make, brown butter's flavor is amazingly complex. Simmering the butter allows the water to evaporate. The milk solids drop to the bottom and their lactose starts to caramelize. The result is butter full of nutty flavor with a hint of vanilla. The flavor of brown butter is what makes a financier cake so wonderful. This plate uses brown butter not only in the cake but also as part of the caramel sauce. To make the caramel sauce, infuse the butter with tarragon as it simmers. Once the butter is brown, remove the tarragon leaves and proceed as for a classic caramel sauce. The richness and fat of a traditional caramel sauce is needed on this plate; it helps the tarragon flavor to linger on the palate.

The tarragon and lemon sherbet accentuates the green notes of fresh tarragon. The sourness of the lemon coupled with the anise of the tarragon work well together. The caramel garnish is made from caramel powder. Cook caramel to desired color and pour onto a Silpat-lined sheet pan. Cool. Break pieces into a robot coupe and process to a powder. The powder can then be sprinkled on a Silpat-lined sheet pan, heated briefly in a 350°F oven and pulled into a desired shape. The visual random look of this garnish works well with the plate's other clean-cut components.

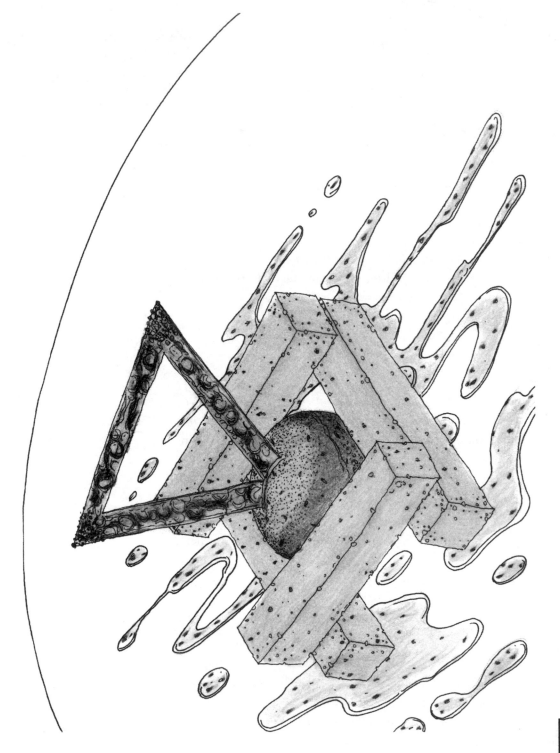

chapter 8   herbs and spices

FIGURE 8.29

Orange pound cake and herbes de Provence ice cream. Complemented with fleur de sel lace and a thyme clear sauce. Illustration by Reginald S. Abalos.

 thyme

Thyme is a member of the mint family. Its essential oil is similar to that found in oregano. In thyme, however, that same woody, grassy flavor is found in a softer form. Thyme is a regular component of bouquet garni and herbes de Provence.

Its small leaves and delicate flavor make thyme the perfect herb to use raw. Its flavor is best when added at the end of the cooking process.

Partner with

Fruits: apples, blackberries, blueberries, cherries, cranberries, grapefruit, lemons, limes, oranges, peaches, pears, plums, raspberries, strawberries

Vegetables: beets, carrots, corn, cucumbers, fennel, garlic, onions, squash (acorn, butternut, and pumpkin), sweet potatoes, tomatoes

Dairy: cheddar cheese, crème fraîche, goat cheese, mascarpone cheese, sour cream, yogurt

Sweeteners: honey, raw sugars

Nuts: almonds, hazelnuts, pine nuts

Dried fruits: apricots, cherries

Liquors: red wine, white wine

Chocolate: milk, white

Baking spices: nutmeg, vanilla

Culinary spices: lavender, marjoram, peppercorns, oregano, rosemary, sage, tarragon

Pantry ingredients: balsamic vinegar, cornmeal, olive oil

The plate is a simple one. Its flavors draw an explicit connection between thyme and France. The herbes de Provence ice cream supplies a rich, fatty element to the plate while also introducing thyme. The thyme clear sauce complements the slightly tart pound cake and the fat of the ice cream. There is a bit of fleur de sel in the lace cookies, just enough to add a light top note to the dish.

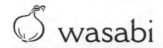 wasabi

A member of the cabbage family, fresh wasabi is rarely seen outside of Japan due to difficulty in its cultivation. Wasabi grows naturally along cool mountain streams with a temperature that remains constantly between 51 and 57°F throughout the year. Thus, the wasabi most often seen and tasted in America comes from a powder or a paste. When using the dried powder, make sure to allow enough time for it to become fully rehydrated before use.

Wasabi has the same tangy, rough flavor we associate with horseradish. In wasabi, this roughness is accompanied by a tremendous amount of heat. It has a fantastic back note and is the perfect accompaniment for fatty items. Alternatively, wasabi also works well when matched with something rather bland, such as rice. Consider sushi, a dish that contrasts the heat of wasabi with rice's neutral flavor. This same pairing can be successfully incorporated into a plated dessert. When using wasabi make sure that it is a harmonizing note, rather than the lead singer.

Partner with

Fruits: guavas, lemons, limes, lychee, mangoes, oranges, passion fruit, peaches, plums, raspberries, strawberries

Vegetables: pumpkin, squash (acorn, butternut, and pumpkin), sweet potatoes

Dairy: crème fraîche

Sweeteners: honey, raw sugars

Nuts: almonds, cashews, coconut and coconut milk, macadamia nuts, peanuts, pistachios

FIGURE 8.30

Fruity egg rolls with chocolate and caramel mango dipping sauces. Served with a side of wasabi ice cream. Illustration by Reginald S. Abalos.

Dried fruits: apricots, cherries

Liquors: mirin, sake

Beverages: black tea, green tea

Chocolate: dark, milk, white

Baking spices: ginger (dried), mace, nutmeg, vanilla

Culinary spices: cilantro, galangal, ginger (fresh), pickled ginger

Pantry ingredients: rice, soy sauce, sweet soy sauce, tofu

This plate is a play on the more traditional culinary egg rolls. Guests are prompted to use their hands to eat the egg rolls, dipping them into the two sauces. The wasabi ice cream is used as a palate cleanser.

There is a lot of fat in this dish. The egg rolls are fried and the French-style ice cream starts with an anglaise base. That fat will prevent the harsh bite and heat of wasabi from overwhelming the plate. The sauces are designed to complement the fruit in the egg roll. Their bitter (chocolate, caramel) and sour (mango) notes will also help to cut through the fat in the plate's other components.

dairy

Dairy products are integral to the structure of baked goods and pastry items. The dairy products in this chapter were chosen for the flavor they contribute to plated desserts. Their inclusion in a plated dessert will help to build a full plate profile.

 buttermilk

True buttermilk is a by-product of the butter-making process. After the butter has been churned, the remaining milk begins to ferment. The resulting buttermilk continues to ferment. It thickens and develops a tangy, sour flavor. "Cultured buttermilk" is a product found in most stores. When making cultured buttermilk, the fermentation process is sped up through the addition of lactic acid bacteria. The bacteria thickens the milk and contributes a light sour flavor. This is not true buttermilk.

Substituting buttermilk for whole milk can result in a product with a wonderfully tangy acidity. A panna cotta made with buttermilk, for instance, can help to develop a base note that might otherwise be missing from that dessert.

Partner with

Fruits: apples, apricots, blackberries, blueberries, cantaloupe, cherries, cranberries, fresh figs, grapefruit, honeydew, lemons, limes, lychees, nectarines, oranges, passion fruit, peaches, pears, pineapple, plums, raspberries, rhubarb, strawberries, watermelon

Vegetables: beets, carrots, corn, cucumbers, fennel, garlic, onions, bell peppers, squash (acorn, butternut, and pumpkin), sweet potatoes, tomatoes

Dairy: cream cheese, crème fraîche, sour cream

Sweeteners: brown sugar, caramel, honey, maple syrup, molasses, raw sugar

Nuts: almonds, cashews, chestnuts, coconut, hazelnuts, macadamia nuts, peanuts, pecans, pine nuts, pistachios, walnuts

Dried fruits: apricots, cherries, dates, figs, raisins

Liquors: bourbon, port, rye whiskey, scotch whiskey, sherry

Beverages: black tea, green tea

Chocolate: dark

Baking spices: cinnamon, cloves, ginger (dried), mace, mint, nutmeg, vanilla

Culinary spices: basil, cardamom, chillis (fresh and dried), Chinese five spice, cilantro, coriander, cumin, curry powder, dill, galangal, ginger (fresh), lavender, lemon grass, marjoram, mustard seed, oregano, peppercorns, rosemary, sage, sesame seeds, star anise, tamarind, thyme

Pantry ingredients: cornmeal

This plate celebrates the tangy acidity of buttermilk. The dessert incorporates different degrees of sourness, from the lemon curd, strawberry, and

FIGURE 9.1

Lemon curd bread pudding, served with strawberry–buttermilk sherbet and a rhubarb coulis accompanied by lavender-scented sugar cookies. Illustration by Reginald S. Abalos.

rhubarb and finally from the buttermilk itself. Cook the rhubarb for the coulis with a bit of orange and lemon zest and a touch of honey. The sour notes of the plate are complemented by the sweet richness of the bread pudding and the light floral flavor of the lavender sugar cookies.

 asiago cheese

Cheese is, for the most part, simply a way of preserving and storing milk. It requires milk, fermentation, and the addition of rennet enzymes, which curdle the milk. In the simplest terms, the milk is soured and curdled. The watery whey is drained off, and the remaining curds are salted, cut, and pressed into some kind of mold. The result takes on thousands of variations throughout the world.

Cheese flavors range from the mild to the downright stinky. They can be smooth and rich as butter or hard, crumbly, and salty. Try as many different cheeses as possible. Their deep, complex, and often powerful flavors can be surprisingly apt additions to some plated desserts.

Asiago cheese is most associated with Italian cooking. It is relatively mild with a bit of salt and a layer of buttery richness. Its nutty, butterscotch notes make it a good match for desserts. Asiago cheese can be used by itself or in combination with other cheeses. It adds a nutty note of flavor when used with mozzarella cheese. On the other hand, its inclusion with Parmesan cheese will help to tone down that cheese's saltiness.

Partner with

Fruits: apples, blackberries, blueberries, cherries, figs, kumquats, lemons, limes, nectarines, oranges, peaches, pears, plums, raspberries, strawberries

Vegetables: beets, carrots, corn, fennel, garlic, onions, squash (acorn, butternut, and pumpkin), sweet potatoes, tomatoes

Dairy: crème fraîche, Parmesan cheese, ricotta cheese, sour cream

Sweeteners: brown sugar, caramel, honey, raw sugars

Nuts: almonds, hazelnuts, pine nuts, pistachios

Dried fruits: apricots, cherries, dates, figs, raisins

Liquors: port, red wine, white wine

Chocolate: dark

Baking spices: caraway seeds, mace, nutmeg, vanilla

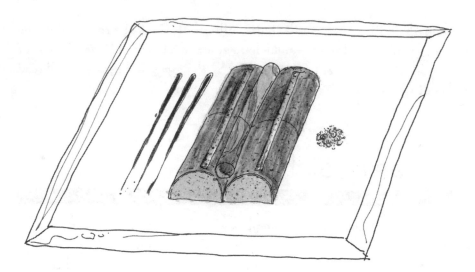

FIGURE 9.2

Olive oil and basil cake with lemon–strawberry swirled sherbet, garnished with Asiago cheese "cracker" and balsamic reduction. Illustration by Reginald S. Abalos.

Culinary spices: basil, chillis (fresh), cilantro, coriander, dill, marjoram, mustard seed, oregano, peppercorns, rosemary, sage, tarragon, thyme

Pantry ingredients: balsamic vinegar, cornmeal, olive oil

The flavors of Italy are clearly evident in this dish. The addition of olive oil to the cake makes it rich and moist while adding a slightly grassy flavor. The basil echoes olive oil's savory murmur with a cooling base note. Lemon and strawberry sherbets are swirled together to accent both the cake and the tang of the balsamic reduction. To make the Asiago "cracker," grate the cheese into the desired shape onto a Silpat-lined sheet pan. Bake until lightly golden brown and quickly form into desired shapes. The Asiago brings a crunch to the plate, but more importantly its nutty notes partner well with the entrée item.

cheddar cheese

Cheddars can range from the mild and creamy to the sharp and crumbly. The milder cheddars work well with fresh crisp fruits such as pears and apples. The sharp zest of an aged cheddar can be partnered with heavy earthy flavors. Experiment with cheddars from different American regions as well as those made in Great Britain. The variety of flavors available will surprise you.

Partner with

Fruits: apples, blackberries, cherries, lemons, limes, oranges, peaches, pears, plums, raspberries, strawberries

Vegetables: bell peppers, corn, garlic, onions, squash (acorn, butternut, and pumpkin), sweet potatoes, tomatoes

Dairy: buttermilk, crème fraîche, sour cream

Sweeteners: brown sugar, caramel, honey, maple syrup, molasses, raw sugars

Nuts: almonds, hazelnuts, macadamia nuts, peanuts, pecans, pistachios, walnuts

Dried fruits: apricots, cherries, dates, figs, raisins

Liquors: beer, bourbon, red wine, rye whiskey, scotch whiskey, tequila, white wine

Beverages: black tea

Chocolate: dark

Baking spices: cinnamon, cloves, ginger (dried), mace, nutmeg, vanilla

Culinary spices: basil, chillis (fresh and dried), Chinese five spice, cilantro, coriander, cumin, curry powder, dill, marjoram, mustard seed, oregano, peppercorns, rosemary, sage, sesame seeds, star anise, tarragon, thyme

Pantry ingredients: balsamic vinegar, cornmeal

Wisconsin apple pie with chipotle ice cream, caramel sauce, and cheddar cheese web

Apple pie in Wisconsin is often topped with a slice of cheddar cheese. This plate is a variation of that theme. The apple pie is made in individual tarts. Grated aged cheddar cheese has been added to the piecrust. The earthiness of the chipotle ice cream combines well with the sharp tang of the cheese. The tartness of the apples offsets the richness of the caramel sauce. The cheese web is made from grated cheddar that has been randomly placed onto a Silpat-lined sheet pan. The cheese pieces are widely spaced so that when baked they will form a loose type of web. The web is placed over a soup ladle immediately after it is removed from the oven. The resulting cup is placed over the scoop of chipotle ice cream. This insures that the customer will get a bite of cheese with each taste of ice cream.

goat cheese

There are hundreds of types of goat cheese. What they all have in common is their distinct flavor. Goat cheese has an indefinable something that consumers either love or hate. Its distinct flavor includes some tangy acidity. Overall, goat cheese does not have the buttery richness associated with some harder cheeses. It melts well when added to a sauce or sautéed item at the end of the cooking process. Less is definitely more here. The addition of too much goat cheese can be a bit jarring on a plated dessert. It works best when the other elements of the plate are not overly sweet.

Partner with

. . . .

Fruits: apples, blackberries, blueberries, cherries, figs, lemons, limes, oranges, peaches, pears, plums, raspberries, rhubarb, strawberries

Vegetables: bell peppers, beets, carrots, corn, cucumbers, fennel, garlic, onions, pumpkin, squash (acorn, butternut, and pumpkin), sweet potatoes, tomatoes

Dairy: crème fraîche, sour cream, yogurt

Sweeteners: brown sugar, caramel, honey, maple syrup, raw sugar

Nuts: almonds, hazelnuts, pecans, pine nuts, pistachios, walnuts

Dried fruits: apricots, cherries, dates, figs, raisins

Liquors: port, red wine, sherry, white wine

Chocolate: dark

Baking spices: caraway, mace, vanilla

Culinary spices: basil, cardamom, chillis (fresh and dried), Chinese five spice, cilantro, coriander, cumin, curry powder, dill, ginger (fresh), lavender, marjoram, mustard seed, oregano, peppercorns, rosemary, saffron, sage, star anise, tarragon, thyme

Pantry ingredients: balsamic vinegar, cornmeal, olive oil

Broiled fresh figs with honeyed goat cheese, served with port reduction and saffron sorbet. Dark honey truffles to follow.

The touch of sweetness that the honey adds to the goat cheese makes it the perfect combination to complement the fresh figs. The port reduction adds a velvety richness contrasted with the slightly astringent and dusty saffron sorbet. A sorbet is used here rather than an ice cream so that the only fatty component on the plate is the tart goat cheese. The plate is designed so that the honey flavor of the goat cheese filling is mirrored in the chocolate truffles. Make the truffles with a chocolate containing at least 70% cocoa liquor. For both the goat cheese filling and the truffle base reduce the honey before adding to the rest of the ingredients. In this way the honey's flavor will be intensified and able to stand up against the strong flavors of the goat cheese and dark chocolate.

# mascarpone cheese

Think of mascarpone cheese as cream cheese minus the salt, and with more fat. Unlike cream cheese, mascarpone cheese is made with cream instead of with milk. The result is a thick, luxurious cheese with a butterfat content that rivals butter itself. It is smoother and easier to spread than cream cheese. While its rich nature makes it a wonderful addition to dishes like tiramisu, exercise caution when using the cheese on a plated dessert. Partner mascarpone with bitter or sour elements, which help to cut through the cheese's buttery character.

Partner with

Fruits: apples, apricots, bananas, blackberries, blueberries, cherries, cranberries, guavas, lemons, limes, mangoes, nectarines, oranges, peaches, pears, pineapple, plums, quinces, raspberries, rhubarb, strawberries

Vegetables: bell peppers, beets, carrots, corn, fennel, garlic, onions, squash (acorn, butternut, and pumpkin), sweet potatoes, tomatoes

Dairy: crème fraîche, sour cream

Sweeteners: brown sugar, caramel, honey, maple syrup, molasses, raw sugars

Nuts: almonds, cashews, hazelnuts, peanuts, pecans, pine nuts, pistachios, walnuts

Dried fruits: apricots, cherries, dates, figs, raisins

Liquors: bourbon, port, red wine, scotch whiskey, sherry, white wine

Beverages: black tea, coffee

Chocolate: dark, milk

Baking spices: allspice, cinnamon, cloves, ginger (dried), mace, mint, nutmeg, vanilla

Culinary spices: basil, cardamom, chillis (fresh and dried), Chinese five spice, cilantro, coriander, cumin, curry powder, dill, ginger (fresh), lavender, marjoram, mustard seed, oregano, peppercorns, rosemary, saffron, sage, star anise, tamarind, tarragon, thyme

Pantry ingredients: balsamic vinegar, cornmeal

This plate uses the thick, creamy, rich qualities of the mascarpone cheese. The cheese is sweetened with a bit of molasses and flavored with some

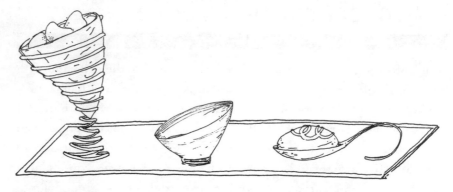

FIGURE 9.3

Chips and dip: spicy/sweet mascarpone dip with acorn squash, sweet potato, and gingersnap chips partnered with bourbon reduction and fresh ginger sherbet. Illustration by Reginald S. Abalos.

Chinese five spice. The earthy qualities of the molasses and of the spice blend work well with the richness of the cheese. That same earthiness is echoed in the root vegetable and gingersnap "chips." The vegetable chips are sprinkled with a dusting of sugar and salt and then baked. The gingersnap "chips" are, in fact, small, thin gingersnap cookies. The bourbon reduction is a full-bodied complement to the chips and spice, while the ginger sherbet cleanses the palate with its refreshing zing.

chapter 10

pantry ingredients

Open the pantry doors and peruse the shelves with new eyes. Start looking at the familiar products in terms of the flavors they can contribute to your desserts. Experiment with the ingredients included in this chapter. Once you are comfortable with their inclusion in your desserts, you will undoubtedly find additional ingredients to add to your growing pastry pantry.

olive oil

Once the sole provenance of Mediterranean cuisine, olive oil's healthy properties have recently made it extremely popular in America as well. Almost 90% of the world's olives are used in the manufacture of olive oil. The primary producers are Mediterranean countries. The olives used are approximately 7 months old. They have reached their maximum oil content and are on the cusp of changing color from green to black. The olives (pits included) are cleaned, roughly ground and pressed. The oil that results from this first cold press is extra virgin and of the highest quality. Each subsequent pressing produces oils of diminishing quality.

Olive oil is unique among oils in that it is fat with crisp, grassy notes. Cooking can alter the flavor of olive oil so a high-grade olive oil should not be used in the cooking process but, rather, drizzled at the end to finish off the dish directly before service.

Partner with

Fruits: blackberries, figs, kumquats, lemons, nectarines, oranges, peaches, plums, raspberries, strawberries

Vegetables: bell peppers, beets, carrots, corn, cucumbers, fennel, garlic, onions, squash (acorn, butternut, and pumpkin), sweet potatoes, tomatoes

Dairy: Asiago cheese, cream cheese, goat cheese, Parmesan cheese

Sweeteners: brown sugar, caramel, honey, raw sugar

Nuts: almonds, pine nuts, pistachios

Dried fruits: apricots, cherries, raisins

Liquors: beer, red wine, white wine

Chocolate: milk, white

Baking spices: anise seed, caraway seed, ginger (dried), nutmeg, vanilla

Culinary spices: basil, cilantro, coriander, dill, ginger (fresh), marjoram, mustard seed, oregano, peppercorns, rosemary, sage, tarragon, thyme

Pantry ingredients: balsamic vinegar

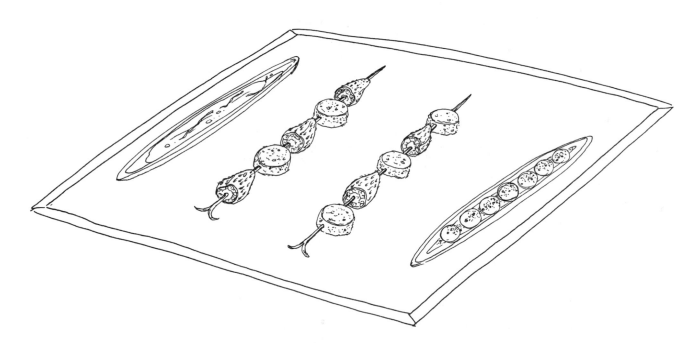

FIGURE 10.1

Kabobs of grilled strawberries and lemon basil pound cake. Served with an olive oil–yogurt dipping sauce and a balsamic reduction. Accompanied by olive dusted white chocolate sorbet. Illustration by Reginald S. Abalos.

Olive oil is a fat; as such its inclusion in a plated dessert should not seem odd. In this plate the olive oil is added to Greek yogurt to make a dipping sauce. The result has the creamy texture of a mayonnaise with a wonderful acidic tang. The warm strawberries and caramelized pieces of pound cake, along with the balsamic reduction, help to cut through the fat of the oil–yogurt sauce. White chocolate sorbet (instead of an ice cream) is used here due to its rather low fat content. The olive powder is made by finely puréeing pitted kalamata olives. After puréeing, drain the olives in a colander, allowing time for the oil to separate from the fruit. Spread the olives onto a Silpat-lined sheet pan and let dry overnight. The mixture can then be crumbled by hand and contributes a wonderfully salty olive flavor when sprinkled on top of the sorbet. In this way the flavor of olives is experienced in two different textures: the oil and the powder.

sesame oil

Sesame seeds are small; it takes almost 8000 individual seeds to make up an ounce of sesame oil. Over half of each seed's weight is made up of oil. This oil is extracted to make sesame oil. Before extraction the seeds are darkly roasted (for about 20 minutes). Sesame oil is extremely pungent, with a rich, nutty flavor. Less is more here; use great care when incorporating sesame oil into a plated dessert for it can easily overwhelm the dish's other flavors.

Partner with

Fruits: apples, blackberries, cantaloupe, cherries, honeydew, lemons, limes, lychees, mangoes, oranges, passion fruit, peaches, pears, plums, raspberries, strawberries, tangerines, watermelon

Vegetables: bell peppers, carrots, cucumbers, garlic, onions, squash (acorn, butternut, and pumpkin), sweet potatoes, tomatoes

Dairy: buttermilk, crème fraîche, mascarpone cheese, ricotta cheese, sour cream, yogurt

Sweeteners: brown sugar, caramel, honey, raw sugars

Nuts: almonds, cashews, coconut, macadamia nuts, peanuts

Dried fruits: apricots, cherries, raisins

Liquors: beer

Beverages: black tea, green tea, coffee

Chocolate: dark, milk, white

FIGURE 10.2

Fruit tempura with sesame and sweet soy dipping sauces, accompanied by a lychee nut sorbet and short dough chopsticks. Illustration by Reginald S. Abalos.

Baking spices: cinnamon, cloves, ginger (dried), nutmeg, vanilla

Culinary spices: cardamom, Chinese five spice, coriander, galangal, ginger (fresh), lemon grass, peppercorns, sesame seeds, wasabi

Pantry ingredients: mirin, rice noodles, soy sauce, sweet soy sauce

For this dessert pick fruit that is on the tart side. The fruit also needs to be physically strong so that it won't fall apart when fried. Some good choices for this dish are pineapple, mango, and passion fruit. Prepare the fruit using a classic culinary recipe for tempura batter. The fruit should be just barely covered. The sesame oil and sweet soy require no preparation; they can be used "as is." Both sauces are pungent and only a small quantity of each is required. The sauces serve to accentuate the natural flavors of the fruit. The chopsticks are made out of 1-2-3 dough. Roll out the dough about $\frac{1}{4}$-inch thick, then cut into chopsticks. Place on a sheet pan and bake in a 350°F (175°C) oven. Once they are cool, the base of the sticks can be decorated with chocolate piping. The result is a plate that both visually and in terms of taste reminds the consumer of sesame oil's Asian roots.

balsamic vinegar

Balsamic vinegar is associated with Mediterranean cuisines. Traditional balsamic vinegars are aged for a minimum of 12 years. The manufacture involves a long and slow evaporation process in wooden barrels. It can take as much as seventy pounds of grapes to produce just one cup of balsamic vinegar.

The quality of balsamic can vary greatly. When using a true aged Aceto Balsamica, very little is needed. An aged balsamic is an awe-inspiring combination of sweet, sour, and a myriad of other complex flavors, delivered in a thick, velvety smooth liquid. Some balsamic vinegars are sold complete with an eyedropper; they are so flavorful that a drop is all that is needed to complete the dish. While the flavor of an Aceto Balsamico is incomparable, its price can be prohibitive. There is a wide range of less potent, and consequently, less expensive balsamics readily available. Reducing these vinegars before use is always a good idea. Reduction will help to concentrate their flavor.

Partner with

Fruits: cherries, kumquats, mangoes, nectarines, oranges, peaches, plums, raspberries, strawberries

Vegetables: beets, carrots, corn, cucumbers, onions, squash (acorn, butternut, and pumpkin), sweet potatoes, and tomatoes

Dairy: Asiago cheese, cheddar cheese, goat cheese, mascarpone cheese, Parmesan cheese

Sweeteners: brown sugar, caramel, honey, raw sugars

Nuts: almonds, cashews, chestnuts, hazelnuts, pine nuts, pistachios

Dried fruits: apricots, cherries, figs, raisins

Liquors: port, red wine, white wine

Beverages: black tea, coffee

Chocolate: dark, milk, white

Baking spices: cinnamon, cloves, ginger (dried), mace, nutmeg, vanilla

Culinary spices: basil, coriander, dill, marjoram, oregano, peppercorns, rosemary, sage, star anise, tarragon, thyme

Pantry ingredients: cornmeal, olive oil

This plate can be served at the end of the meal or with the presentation of the check. The balsamic caramels are a soft caramel candy with the addition of a drop of Aceto Balsamic vinegar placed on top directly before service. The fleur de sel truffles should be made with an intensely dark

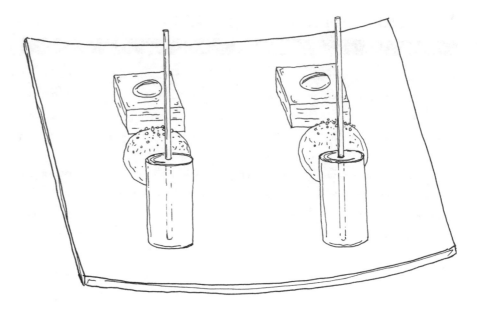

FIGURE 10.3

"Savory candy dish": balsamic caramels, fleur de sel truffles, and basil lollipops.
Illustration by Reginald S. Abalos.

chocolate (at least 70% cacao). The basil lollipop is made with a basil-infused sugar syrup. Strain the basil out and after the sugar has been poured into desired shapes, top with a small sprig of fresh basil. The candy dish is a flavorful and playful way to end a meal.

sea salt/fleur de sel

The difference between salts, specifically fleur de sel or flower of salt, and other types of salt lies in the manner in which they are produced. Mass-produced salts use artificial means of extracting salt either from the sea or from deeply buried salt deposits. The salt is then refined and anti-caking ingredients are added. The result is a relatively harsh and flat salty flavor.

Sea salt, however, is produced through natural evaporation. Seawater is placed in shallow containers and allowed to evaporate. The crystals that remain on the top are carefully scraped away. This is fleur de sel. The crystals that fall to the bottom are gray sea salt. Gray sea salt has a mineral tinge that is not found in the delicate flavor of fleur de sel. Fleur de sel's flavor is developed through changes in the weather and atmosphere, thus it will vary from region to region and from year to year. Because of its relatively fragile flavor, fleur de sel should be added at the end of the cooking process.

Partner with

. . . .

Fruits: apples, blackberries, cherries, lemons, limes, mangoes, nectarines, oranges, passion fruit, peaches, pears, pineapple, plums, raspberries, strawberries

Vegetables: beets, bell peppers, carrots, corn, cucumbers, fennel, garlic, onions, squash (acorn, butternut, and pumpkin), sweet potatoes, tomatoes

Dairy: buttermilk, cheddar cheese, crème fraîche, mascarpone cheese, ricotta cheese

Sweeteners: brown sugar, caramel, honey, maple syrup, molasses, raw sugars

Nuts: almonds, cashews, coconut, hazelnuts, macadamia nuts, peanuts, pecans, pine nuts, pistachios, walnuts

Dried fruits: apricots, cherries, figs, raisins

Liquors: red wine, tequila, whiskey, white wine

Beverages: green tea

Chocolate: dark, milk, white

Baking spices: cinnamon, cloves, ginger (dried), mace, fresh mint, nutmeg, vanilla

Culinary spices: basil, cardamom, chillis (fresh and dried), Chinese five spice, cilantro, coriander, cumin, curry powder, dill, galangal, ginger (fresh), lavender, lemon grass, marjoram, mustard seed, oregano, peppercorns, rosemary, saffron, sage, sesame seeds, star anise, tamarind, tarragon, thyme, wasabi

Pantry ingredients: balsamic vinegar, olive oil, sesame oil

The combination of sweet and salty has long been a favorite; consider the always popular chocolate covered pretzels. Many artisan chocolate shops are now selling salty caramels, often covered in a chocolate shell. This plate is a celebration of the salt and sweet relationship. It centers around a salty caramel mousse, covered with chocolate ganache. It is a plated dessert reinterpretation of a chocolate-covered salty caramel. The sour tang of a balsamic reduction balances out the saltiness as do the refreshingly sweet fresh strawberries. The tempered chocolate garnish adds a bit a chocolate crunch and some visual height to the plate as well.

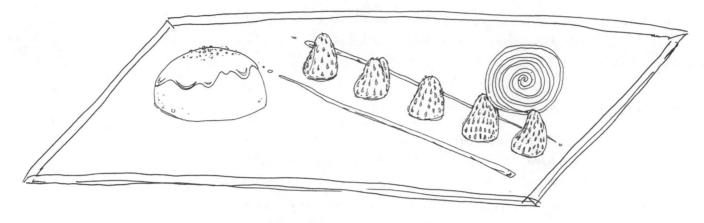

FIGURE 10.4

Salty caramel mousse with chocolate glaze accompanied by balsamic reduction and fresh strawberries and garnished with a chocolate. Illustration by Reginald S. Abalos.

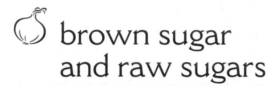 brown sugar and raw sugars

To understand brown sugar, you must understand sugar production. The majority of sugar used in America is produced from sugar cane. The cane is harvested and crushed. The resulting juice is collected and then boiled. This evaporates the juice's water, concentrating its sugar. Lime is added to the mixture to clarify the liquid. The mix is heated and reduced down even further. Seed crystals are added and the mix is placed into a centrifuge and spun. The liquid contains impurities, items of various densities. By spinning it in a centrifuge (much like a gigantic salad spinner), the liquid and crystals are separated. Molasses and raw sugars are the result. (See Molasses, page 170.) The raw sugar must be refined further to be sold as granulated sugar. Further refining whitens the sugar and strips it of its original flavor. Raw sugars, on the other hand, have nuances of flavor that are a result of the reduction process. These flavors can range from butter-scotch, to toasted nuts, to caramel, to name just a few possibilities.

There are a myriad of raw sugars readily available to consumers. Demerara, turbinado, and muscavodo are perhaps the best known. Other raw sugars such as jaggery (popular in India), piloncillo (used in Mexico), and Chinese rock sugar are all worth a try as well.

Brown sugar was originally a by-product of the sugar making process. That is, unfortunately, no longer the case, thanks to modern technology, brown sugar now consists of granulated sugar covered with a layer of dark syrup from one of the earlier stages of sugar production.

The refined granulated sugar crystals are either spray painted with a thin layer of molasses or dissolved in a syrup mixture and then recrystallized. The result is a sugar with a slight molasses note but without the depth of flavor found in some raw sugars.

Partner with

Fruits: apples, apricots, bananas, blackberries, blueberries, cantaloupe, cherries, cranberries, figs (fresh), honeydew, kiwi, lemons, limes, mangoes, nectarines, oranges, papayas, passion fruit, peaches, pears, pineapple, plums, prickly pear, raspberries, rhubarb, strawberries, watermelon

Vegetables: bell peppers, beets, carrots, corn, cucumbers, fennel, garlic, onions, squash (acorn, butternut, and pumpkin), sweet potatoes, tomatoes

Dairy: buttermilk, crème fraîche, goat cheese, mascarpone cheese, ricotta cheese, sour cream, yogurt

Sweeteners: honey, maple syrup, molasses

Nuts: almonds, cashews, chestnuts, hazelnuts, macadamia nuts, peanuts, pecans, pine nuts, pistachios, walnuts

Dried fruits: apricots, cherries, dates, figs, raisins

Liquors: bourbon, red wine, rum, rye whiskey, scotch whiskey, white wine

Beverages: black tea, green tea, coffee

Chocolate: dark, milk, white

Baking spices: allspice, cinnamon, cloves, ginger (dried), mace, mint, nutmeg, vanilla

Culinary spices: basil, cardamom, chillis (fresh and dried), Chinese five spice, cilantro, coriander, cumin, curry powder, dill, galangal, ginger (fresh), lavender, lemon grass, marjoram, mustard seed, oregano, peppercorns, rosemary, saffron, sage, sesame seeds, star anise, tamarind, tarragon, thyme, wasabi

Pantry ingredients: cornmeal, balsamic reduction, sesame oil

Strawberries Romanoff is a classic dessert. Traditionally it consists of fresh strawberries, triple sec or cointreau, brown sugar, and sour cream. In this version the strawberries have been injected with cointreau, hulled, and

FIGURE 10.5

"Strawberries Romanoff": fresh strawberries injected with cointreau served with a brown sugar–sour cream sherbet. Phyllo straws with basil inset and blood orange and brown sugar reduction sauce. Illustration by Reginald S. Abalos.

cut in half. The halves are served on top of a brown sugar–sour cream sherbet. Sheets of phyllo dough have been brushed with brown butter to pick up some of the nuttiness of the brown sugar. Fresh basil leaves have been placed between the sheets and then baked. The phyllo contributes a crunchy texture to the plate and the basil marries well with the strawberries, cointreau, and sour cream. The blood orange and brown sugar reduction sauce adds a wonderful tart note to the plate.

 honey

Honey is a natural product; produced by thousands of bees working together. Over the years humans have done little to improve its already delicious nature. Flowering plants rely upon bees for cross-pollination. The bees, in turn, receive their food from those same flowering plants. Honey is the form in which the nectar, taken from the plants, is stored.

There are an innumerable amount of flowering plants and, therefore, an equally large number of honey flavors. The honey takes on the flavor of the plants around each individual hive. Thyme, lavender, orange blossom, and the ubiquitous clover are just a few examples of popular honey flavors. Due to its inverted nature, honey is not a one-to-one substitute for granulated sugar. However, it offers the chef a wide range of flavor options unavailable in the realm of refined sugars.

The relatively mild clover is perhaps the honey most often found in professional kitchens. Reducing the honey down before use will intensify its otherwise bland flavor. Be careful: the honey will bubble furiously, so use a large saucepan. Simmer until the honey starts to develop a strong aroma. Take off the heat at once, allowing carryover heat to continue the cooking process. Pay attention as burnt honey has an extremely invasive and undesirable bitter flavor.

Partner with

Fruits: apples, apricots, bananas, blackberries, blueberries, cantaloupe, cherries, cranberries, figs (fresh), grapefruit, honeydew, kiwi, kumquats, lemons, limes, lychees, mangoes, nectarines, oranges, papayas, passion fruit, peaches, pears, pineapple, plums, prickly pears, raspberries, rhubarb, strawberries, watermelon

Vegetables: bell peppers, beets, carrots, corn, cucumbers, fennel, garlic, onions, squash (acorn, butternut, and pumpkin), sweet potatoes, tomatoes

Dairy: buttermilk, crème fraîche, goat cheese, mascarpone cheese, ricotta cheese, sour cream, yogurt

Sweeteners: maple syrup, molasses, raw sugars

Nuts: almonds, cashews, chestnuts, coconut, hazelnuts, macadamia nuts, peanuts, pecans, pine nuts, pistachios, walnuts

Dried fruits: apricots, cherries, dates, figs, raisins

Liquors: bourbon, red wine, rum, rye whiskey, scotch whiskey, white wine

Beverages: black tea, green tea, coffee

Chocolate: dark, milk, white

Baking spices: allspice, cinnamon, cloves, ginger (dried), mace, mint, nutmeg, vanilla

Culinary spices: basil, cardamom, chillis (fresh and dried), Chinese five spice, cilantro, coriander, cumin, curry powder, dill, galangal, ginger (fresh), lavender, lemon grass, marjoram, mustard seed, oregano, peppercorns, rosemary, saffron, sage, sesame seeds, star anise, tamarind, tarragon, thyme, wasabi

Pantry ingredients: balsamic reduction, cornmeal, sesame oil

Sopapillas with lavender honey ice cream and an orange blossom honey sauce. Served with fresh berries.

Sopapillas are a traditional Mexican dessert. They are pockets of fried dough served drenched in honey. In this version the sopapillas are quite small. They are partnered with a French ice cream made with a fresh lavender infusion and using lavender honey as its only sweetener. Orange blossom honey, along with some orange zest has been reduced down slightly for the sauce. Fresh strawberries, raspberries, and blackberries offer a tangy contrast to the sweet richness of the rest of the plate.

maple syrup

Maple syrup is produced from the sap of maple trees. It is full of nutty-like, vanilla notes. The production of maple syrup is concentrated primarily in the northeastern region of the United States. This is due to spring weather conditions there. The sap of the maple trees is collected within a short span, starting with the first true thaw and ending when the tree buds start to open. The sap runs best after a severe winter and in areas where there are great swings in temperature between morning and night. The northeastern states meet those criteria.

Today the sap is collected through a system of plastic tubes and centrally located storage tanks. Few sugar houses use the, perhaps more romantic, one bucket to one tree method. After the sap collected it is reduced down. The ratio of sap to finished syrup is approximately forty to one. The longer the sap is reduced the darker it becomes both in terms of color and taste. The more expensive maple syrups are labeled grade A. They are usually less concentrated and have a delicate flavor. Grades B and C are syrups that have been boiled for a longer time and have a slightly harsher note.

Partner with

• •

Fruits: apples, apricots, bananas, blackberries, blueberries, cherries, cranberries, figs, kumquats, lemons, limes, mangoes, nectarines, oranges, papayas, passion fruit, peaches, pears, pineapple, plums, raspberries, rhubarb, strawberries

Vegetables: beets, carrots, corn, fennel, onions, squash (acorn, butternut, and pumpkin), sweet potatoes

Dairy: buttermilk, cheddar cheese, crème fraîche, goat cheese, mascarpone cheese, ricotta cheese, sour cream

Sweeteners: brown sugar, molasses, raw sugar

Nuts: almonds, cashews, hazelnuts, macadamias, peanuts, pecans, walnuts

Dried fruits: apricots, cherries, dates, figs, raisins

Liquors: bourbon, port, red wine, rum, rye whiskey, scotch whiskey

Beverages: black tea, coffee

Chocolate: dark, milk

Baking spices: caraway, cinnamon, cloves, ginger (dried), mace, nutmeg, vanilla

Culinary spices: cardamom, chillis (dried), Chinese five spice, coriander, cumin, curry powder, galangal, ginger, mustard seed, marjoram, oregano, peppercorns, rosemary sage, star anise

Pantry ingredients: balsamic vinegar, cornmeal

Boiling maple syrup and then cooling it very quickly produces maple cream. Place the syrup in an ice bath as it cools and stir vehemently until it reaches 70°F (21°C). Gently rewarm the mix until it becomes smooth and fairly soft. This is the perfect addition to walnut waffles.

The apple–pear compote should still have a bit of bite to it; do not make applesauce. A bit of Chinese five spice and orange zest with the fruit will offset the sweetness of the maple cream. Curry's earthy notes go well with the sweet woodiness of the maple as well as the slight tartness of the pears and apples.

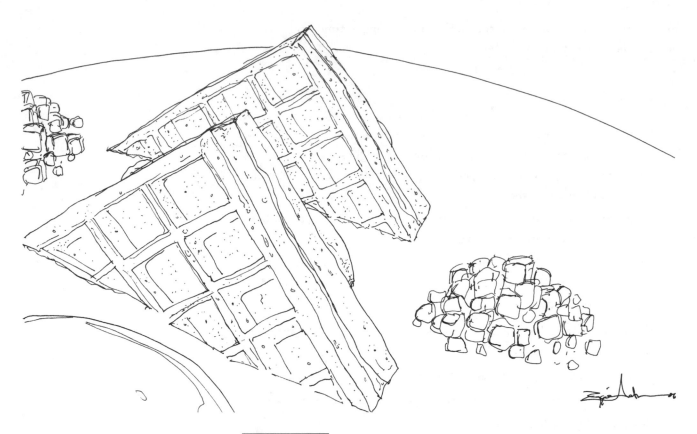

Walnut waffles with maple cream, apple–pear compote, and curry–maple ice cream. Illustration by Reginald S. Abalos.

 molasses

Traditionally molasses is a by-product of the sugar-making process. It is the syrup that remains after all of the sugar crystals have been removed. Because the sugar-refining process takes many steps, there are different grades of molasses. These grades depend on at what point in the refining process the molasses was removed. The light syrup we use in the kitchen is the highest, or first, grade. It is removed early in the sugar-refining process and is, therefore, relatively light in color. It has an almost buttery caramel flavor with a sulfur back note. The second and third grades are progressively darker and considerably less sweet; the sulfur notes are much more pronounced. Blackstrap molasses is third grade and is not usually consumed by humans, although it is sometimes used in the tobacco industry.

Molasses should be considered to be a "heavy" sweetener. When used with light, crisp flavors it can easily overtake the entire plate. For best results, partner molasses with other heavier flavors and spices with deep earthy notes.

Partner with

Fruits: apples, bananas, cherries, figs, grapefruit, lemons, mangoes, oranges, passion fruit, peaches, pears, pineapple, plums

Vegetables: beets, carrots, garlic, onions, squash (acorn, butternut, and pumpkin), sweet potatoes

Dairy: buttermilk, cheddar cheese, crème fraîche, mascarpone cheese

Sweeteners: brown sugar, raw sugars

Nuts: almonds, cashews, chestnuts, hazelnuts, macadamia nuts, peanuts, pecans, pistachios, walnuts

Dried fruits: apricots, cherries, dates, figs

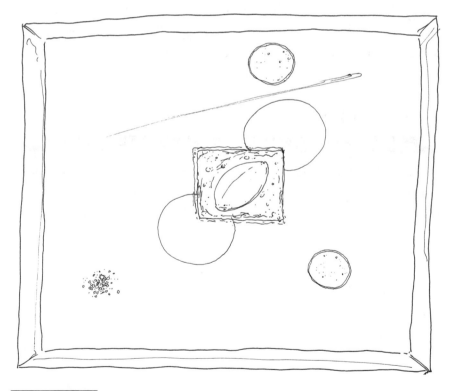

FIGURE 10.7

Sticky toffee pudding with rye whiskey sauce and vanilla bean ice cream accompanied by a spicy molasses cookie. Illustration by Reginald S. Abalos.

Liquors: bourbon, port, red wine, rye whiskey, scotch whiskey

Beverages: black tea, coffee

Chocolate: dark, milk, white

Baking spices: allspice, anise seed, caraway, cinnamon, cloves, ginger (dried), mace, nutmeg, vanilla

Culinary spices: cardamom, dried chillis, Chinese five spice, coriander, cumin, curry powder, galangal, ginger (fresh), mustard, peppercorns, rosemary, sage, star anise, tamarind,

Pantry ingredients: balsamic vinegar, cornmeal

Pudding is the English term for dessert and sticky toffee pudding is a classically English dessert. The sticky toffee pudding used for this dish is more of a cake, not what Americans would consider to be a true pudding. The classic sticky toffee pudding is made with molasses' more refined cousin, treacle. The pudding for this plate is a sweet, gooey combination of molasses, cake, and dried fruit and nuts. The rye whisky sauce offsets the sweetness of the pudding. Using rye rather than Scotch whisky introduces a lightly sharp note to the dish. Sometimes the classic combinations are the best, and I can think of no better addition to the plate than a fresh vanilla bean ice cream. Add a bit of ground mustard seed and coriander to a traditional molasses spice cookie recipe. The resulting savory note will contrast well with the other classical components of the dessert.

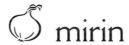 mirin

Mirin is a sweet Japanese cooking alcohol. It is made by combining cooked polished rice, a rice mold which breaks the rice down into sugar, and a distilled spirit from relatively low-grade sake. Mirin has a delicate flavor that combines both fruity and flowery notes. Because it is light in flavor, mirin should be added at the end of the cooking process.

Mirin's fruity nature makes it a natural for plated desserts. It does not need additional sweeteners. It works best as an accompaniment to an entrée item. Use mirin with other clean, clear flavors, as too much fat will overpower its fragile flavor. Mirin, reduced down alone, makes a great sauce.

Partner with

Fruits: apples, blackberries, blueberries, cantaloupe, cherries, guavas, honeydew, lemons, limes, lychees, nectarines, oranges, papayas, passion fruit, peaches, pears, pineapple, raspberries, rhubarb, strawberries, watermelon

Vegetables: bell peppers, carrots, cucumbers, fennel, onions

Dairy: yogurt

Sweeteners: brown sugar, caramel, honey, raw sugar

Nuts: almonds, cashews, coconuts, macadamia nuts, pistachios

Dried fruits: apricots, cherries

Liquors: sake

Beverages: black tea, green tea

Baking spices: cinnamon, ginger (dried), mace, nutmeg, vanilla

Culinary spices: basil, cilantro, Chinese five spice, coriander, galangal, fresh ginger, lemon grass, sesame seeds, star anise, wasabi

Pantry ingredients: sesame oil, sweet soy sauce

 # sweet soy sauce

Soy sauce is made from fermented soybeans. It is used as both a condiment and as an ingredient in Asian cuisine. The making of true soy sauce is a long process. Soybeans are first soaked and then steamed before being mixed with yeast culture and wheat flour. The mixture is then fermented for up to two years before being filtered and bottled. It is the long fermentation process that allows the soy sauce to develop its richness of flavor. There is a wide selection of soy sauces, some light and delicate (similar to the first pressing for virgin olive oil), others thick and full flavored.

Sweet soy sauce is thicker than maple syrup with a black color. It combines sweetness with the salty flavor of fermented soybeans. There is no need to reduce the soy sauce, as it is already incredibly thick. It can be used "as is" directly from the bottle.

Asian dishes are often a combination of salt, sweet, bitter, and sour. Using sweet soy as an accompanying sauce is one way of adding both sweet and salt to your dish. A few drops added to the plate (perhaps in a tie-dye fashion on top of another sauce) are all that is needed to expand upon this very Asian theme.

Partner with

Fruits: apples, apricots, blackberries, blueberries, cantaloupe, cherries, grapefruit, honeydew, lemons, limes, lychees, nectarines, oranges, papayas, passion fruit, peaches, pears, pineapple, plums, raspberries, strawberries

Vegetables: beets, bell peppers, carrots, cucumbers, fennel, garlic, onions, squash (acorn, butternut, and pumpkin), sweet potatoes, tomatoes

Dairy: buttermilk, mascarpone cheese, sour cream, yogurt

Sweeteners: brown sugar, honey, maple syrup, molasses, raw sugars

Nuts: almonds, cashews, coconut, macadamia nuts, peanuts, pistachios

Dried fruits: apricots, cherries, dates, figs, raisins

Liquors: mirin, sake

Beverages: black tea, green tea

Chocolate: dark, milk, white

Baking spices: cinnamon, cloves, ginger (dried), mace, nutmeg, vanilla

Culinary spices: basil, cardamom, Chinese five spice, cilantro, coriander, galangal, ginger (fresh), lemon grass, peppercorns, sesame seeds, tamarind, wasabi

Pantry ingredients: sesame oil

Asian dessert sampler: wontons, steamed rice balls, and steamed dumplings. Accompanied by green and black tea sorbets, sweet soy and mango dipping sauces.

This plate is a variation of appetizers seen in Chinese restaurants. In this case, the wontons are filled with a papaya filling. The steamed rice balls have been infused with lemon grass and hide a lychee nut in their center. The steamed dumplings cover a filling of cashews, cilantro, and pineapple.

The sorbets are all somewhat astringent. Their astringency is a great accompaniment to the amount of starch in the dish's main components. The salty sweet soy and sour mango dipping sauces round out the dessert's plate profile.

works
of flavor

plated
desserts

The previous sections of this book have given you the tools to construct flavorful and thoughtful plated desserts. Part 1 established a vocabulary for discussing and analyzing flavor. Part 2 laid the groundwork for the mechanics of flavor, including cooking techniques, sauce work, and the manipulation of texture. Part 3 analyzed the use of culinary ingredients in the construction of plated desserts. This section takes all of that information and applies it to the development of specific plated desserts.

Each plate in this section has its own distinct personality and each has been included for specific reasons. Some plates follow a specific theme; for example, one is a variation of a classic American dessert, another tells the story of the history of chocolate. Other desserts rely on the characteristics of one or two of their ingredients; one showcases tomatoes and another, herbes de Provence. A few of the plates are whimsical plays on traditional culinary dishes. In some cases the desserts reflect the cuisine of a specific country or of a specific culinary cooking style.

The flavors used in these desserts are varied. On some of the dishes, one flavor loudly takes the front of the stage with the other flavors harmonizing quietly in the background. On others, the flavors work together as if in a repertory theatre group, with no one flavor taking the lead.

For all of their distinct, individual personalities, the plates do have some deep similarities. In all of the plates all of the components of the dishes work together to form full plate and flavor profiles. Each plate has a unique consistency of theme, every item on every plate serves a purpose, and each element makes sense to the plate as a whole. In order

The plates in this section have many components. Do not let the quantity of recipes included for each plate scare you. Most of the components can be done ahead of time and will keep for days when properly stored. Although there are many elements per plate, each individual element will not take a great deal of time to assemble. In all cases the plates can be simplified by using fewer components on the plate.

for you to experiment with these plates, the recipes for each element of each plate have been included, as well as the steps needed to assemble each dish. The creative thought process behind each plate is included as well. Finally, each of the eight plates featured in this chapter has a corresponding photo in the color insert in this book.

chocolate in India

Entrée: chocolate marquise with garam masala served on a coconut cookie shell
Frozen: curry frozen yogurt
Garnish: candied rose petals
Crunch: pistachio brittle
Sauce 1: mint syrup
Sauce 2: honey and orange blossom reduction

The inspiration for this plate is twofold. The primary idea was to design a plated dessert around chocolate. Over the years, America has not lost its love affair with chocolate-based items, especially on a dessert menu. A dessert menu's chocolate items will always be the best sellers; a piece of chocolate cake sells before a fruit tart. There are challenges when working with chocolate. Dark chocolate is a strong deep flavor. Like a loudly banging drum, it can easily overwhelm the other flavors on the plate. Vanilla, orange, raspberry, mint and nuts are some of the traditional accompaniments often used with chocolate. The challenge is to place chocolate in a new environment and to accompany it with new and unexpected harmonizing flavors. This plate was developed to meet that challenge.

The cuisine of India provides chocolate with a new environment and is the second source of inspiration for this plate. Indian cuisine is reflected in the cooking style and the ingredients used for this dish. Many Indian desserts use heavy, sweet sugar syrups and flower essences, and this

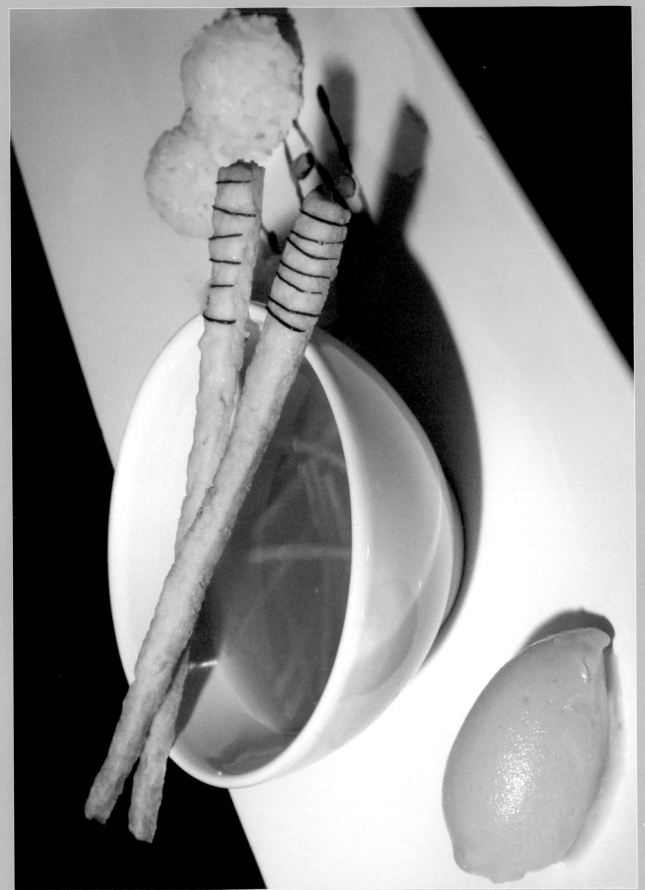

Tomato Trio

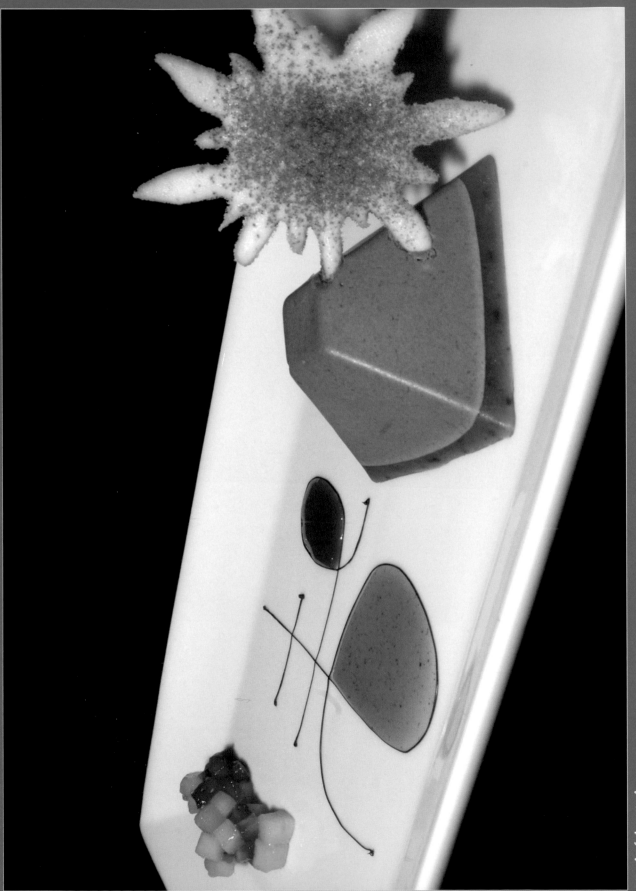

Food of the Gods

Corny Ice Cream Sandwich

is seen in the syrup and reduction sauces, the pistachio brittle and in the use of orange blossom water and rose petals.

The heat of curry is often paired with the cooling sensations of mint and yogurt in Indian dishes. The relationship between hot and cool elements is seen in this plated dessert. Cool frozen yogurt and mint syrup pair with the heat and earthiness of the garam masala and curry powder. Just as they would be for traditional Indian cooking, the spices used in this dessert are dry sautéed. This cooking technique increases the depth of their flavor as well as their overall pungency. The use of coconut and pistachios is also a reflection of Indian cuisine.

The plate works. All of the elements, with the exception of the chocolate marquise, have their roots in traditional Indian desserts and savory dishes. The cooking styles, the pairing of warm and cool elements, the use of syrups and flower essences all work together to form a cohesive whole. Each of the flavors complements chocolate well and together they form a beautifully consistent new environment for chocolate.

Visually the dessert is a plate of contrasts. The focal point is the smooth sphere of the chocolate marquise. The marquise was chosen as the vessel for the chocolate because it is lighter than a flourless chocolate cake and heavier than traditional chocolate mousses. This means that its chocolate essence will be stronger than a chocolate mousse because it takes longer to dissolve on the tongue. Since the marquise is lighter than a flourless chocolate cake the surrounding flavors on the plate will not be overwhelmed by chocolate essence.

The smooth marquise contrasts well with the ragged texture of the coconut shell. The cookie is molded to look like a coconut shell. The visual impact of the candied rose petal is undeniable. When set against the dark backdrop of the chocolate marquise the color of the rose petal really stands out. The fine granules of sugar pick up and refract light, allowing them to glisten a bit like diamonds in the rough. The ragged/smooth contrast is further played out with the shard of pistachio brittle juxtaposed against the curry frozen yogurt. The random flow of the brittle works well against the clean edges of the yogurt. The bright green of the mint syrup picks up the color of the pistachios and the honey and orange blossom reduction reflects the color of the coconut shell.

For a simpler dish, the garam masala-infused chocolate marquise can still be served in a toasted coconut lace shell. A mint-infused frozen yogurt with a honey reduction sauce would work well here.

Plate Profiles
• •

Sweet from the mint clear sauce,
honey, toasted coconut, yogurt,
and chocolate

FIGURE 11.1

Plate profile for Chocolate in India: Top Notes.

Chocolate, curry powder,
garam masala, coconut,
mint, orange blossom,
honey, yogurt, pistachio,
rose petals

FIGURE 11.2

Plate profile for Chocolate in India: Middle Notes.

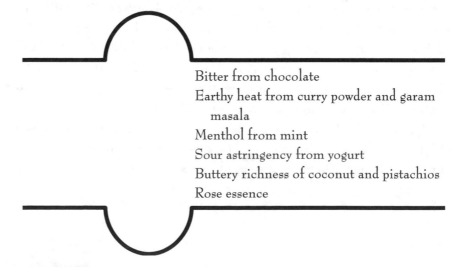

Bitter from chocolate
Earthy heat from curry powder and garam
masala
Menthol from mint
Sour astringency from yogurt
Buttery richness of coconut and pistachios
Rose essence

FIGURE 11.3

Plate profile for Chocolate in India: Base Notes.

Flavor Profile

	SWEET/SOUR/ BITTER/SALT	AROMA	TRIGEMINAL RESPONSE
Entrée: chocolate marquise with garam masala marquise	Sweet: sugar in Bitter: chocolate	N/A	A bit of earthy heat from the garam masala
Coconut shell	Sweet: coconut	N/A	N/A
Curry frozen yogurt	Sweet: frozen yogurt Sour: yogurt	N/A	Heat from the curry
Mint clear sauce	Sweet: corn syrup	N/A	Menthol from the mint
Honey/orange blossom reduction	Sweet: honey Bitter: reduced honey	N/A	N/A
Pistachio brittle	Sweet: brittle Bitter: slightly from the roasted nuts	N/A	N/A
Candied rose petals	Sweet: sugar	N/A	N/A

FIGURE 11.4

Flavor profile for Chocolate of India

Notice that although all portions of the flavor profile diagram are not filled, this plate does have a full plate profile. This dessert reiterates the importance of the relationship between texture and flavor. The various textures of the dish's components allow their flavors to be either shortened or lengthened on the palate. The texture of the entrée item is inherent to the success of this plate. A marquise was chosen solely because of its texture. It is a bit heavier than a mousse, yet lighter than alternatives such as a flourless chocolate cake or a ganache–truffle type of filling. Its texture allows it to be molded easily into small spheres while at the same time melting relatively quickly in the mouth. The crisper texture of the pistachio brittle, the coconut shell, and the rose petals remain on the palate after the marquise has dissipated. The intrinsic strength of flavor found in dark chocolate is, therefore, lessened and the other flavors are allowed to share the stage momentarily. The sauces and frozen yogurt will all join on the palate at the same time, bringing together their contrasting warming and cooling sensations.

chocolate marquise

1½ lb semisweet chocolate

4 ounces unsweetened chocolate

4 ounces (6 each) egg yolks

5 ounces (3 each) whole eggs

1 ounce granulated sugar

4 ounces honey

24 ounces heavy cream

2 tsp garam masala

- Chop the chocolates and melt together on a double boiler. Stir occasionally, scraping the sides and bottom of the bowl.

- In a 5-quart mixer, whip together the yolks, whole eggs, and granulated sugar. Continue to whip on speed 3 until the mixture ribbons. (*Note:* The mixture will turn thick and lighten in color.)

- While the eggs are whipping, place the honey in a saucepan and bring to a boil. Be careful as the boiling honey will bubble up; make sure to use a large enough saucepan. Take the honey off the stove once it reaches a boil. Do not allow it to reduce or it will become bitter.

- Once the egg mixture is at a ribbon state, turn the mixer to speed 1 and slowly and carefully add the honey. Return the mixer to speed 3 and continue to whip until the mixture cools.

- Whip the heavy cream to a medium peak.

- Once the egg and honey mixture has cooled, fold it into the melted chocolate.

- Fold in the whipped cream and refrigerate.

- Allow the marquise to set up in the refrigerator. This will take approximately one hour. Once the marquise is set, scoop out with a hot, slightly wet sorbet or ice cream scoop. This will ensure that the outside of the marquise is smooth and shiny.

- Place the marquise spheres onto a parchment-lined sheet pan. Cover loosely with plastic wrap and return to the refrigerator until needed for service.

coconut tuile

1¼ ounces butter, softened
8 ounces egg whites, room temperature
2 cups grated coconut
10 ounces granulated sugar
1¼ ounces pastry flour

Cream the butter and the sugar, until the mixture is lump free. Scrape the sides and bottom of the bowl often.

Drizzle in the egg whites slowly and continue to mix. Scrape the sides and bottom of the bowl often.

In a separate bowl mix together the coconut and the flour. Add the dry ingredients to the butter–sugar–whites mixture. Stir by hand until just incorporated, about 15 seconds.

Drop the batter by spoonfuls onto a Silpat- or a parchment-lined sheet pan.

Bake for approximately 10–11 minutes at 350°F (180°C), or until the cookies become a light golden brown.

Remove the cookies from the oven and place immediately into desired molds. For the photograph, the cookie was molded into a soup ladle.

The cookies will cool quickly, so work speedily.

Note: Store batter in the refrigerator. Make sure to stir it thoroughly before each use.

mint clear sauce

4 ounces fresh mint leaves
2 ounces light corn syrup

Blanch the mint leaves. Plunge them into boiling water and then place immediately into ice water. Remove the leaves from the ice water and pat them dry with paper towels.

Place the leaves in a small robot coupe or food processor.

- Slowly add the light corn syrup. Strain the syrup through cheesecloth.

  (*Note:* It is easiest to place the syrup in the cheesecloth, bundle up the top, and, using a wringing motion, squeeze the syrup through the cloth. The result will be a bright green syrup with no bits of mint leaves.)

- Store in a squeeze bottle until service.

honey and orange blossom reduction sauce

6 ounces orange blossom honey
To taste orange blossom water

Note: The quantity of orange blossom water will vary according to its relative strength and the flavor of the specific honey used. Add enough flower water so that its presence is clearly felt through the flavors of the honey.

- Place the honey and orange blossom water in a saucepan over medium heat. Allow the mixture to simmer for approximately 5 minutes.

- Remove the honey from the heat. It will look a bit thin but will thicken as it cools.

crystallized rose petals

Rose petals 1–2 per dessert (1 rose should suffice)
4 ounces superfine granulated sugar

Note: If superfine granulated sugar is not available, simply use a spice grinder to pulverize granulated sugar.

1 tablespoon powdered egg whites

Note: Make sure to purchase rose petals that have been grown specifically for food industry use. These flowers are grown without the use of pesticides or other potentially dangerous chemicals that should not be ingested.

🌿 Pick the petals off the rose. Select petals that will not visually over-whelm the chocolate marquise.

🌿 Prepare the powdered egg whites per manufacture's specifications. 1 tbsp water to 1 tbsp meringue powder will be enough for a dozen or more rose petals.

🌿 Whisk together the dried egg whites and water.

Note: Working with dried meringue powder has two benefits:

1. It eliminates any danger of food-borne illness caused from eating raw egg products.

2. It allows for the lightest layer of liquid to coat the rose petals. In this recipe the egg whites act as a glue for the superfine granulated sugar. They aid in forming a thin, yet durable crust.

🌿 Dip each petal into the egg white mixture and then into the superfine granulated sugar.

🌿 Shake off any excess sugar and place each petal on a parchment paper-lined sheet pan.

🌿 Allow to dry at room temperature, preferably overnight.

🌿 Store in an airtight container until needed for service.

🌿 curry frozen yogurt

· ·

3 ounces granulated sugar
2 ounces honey
1½ tsp fresh lemon juice
1 vanilla bean
1 ounce pasteurized egg whites
⅔ ounce pasteurized egg yolks
2 cups plain yogurt
1½ tsp hot curry powder

🌿 The quantity of curry powder used will depend on its strength. Start with a bit less and adjust according to taste.

🌿 Place the curry powder in a dry pan and sauté until fragrant. Cool.

🌿 In a saucepan mix the honey, lemon juice, scraped vanilla bean, curry powder, and half of the sugar. Whisk the mixture together and bring to a boil.

- Reserve the vanilla pod for future use.
- Temper the hot mixture into the egg yolk and continue to mix until the mixture cools.
- Whip the white with the remaining half of the sugar until it reaches a stiff peak.
- Whisk yogurt until smooth and add in the sugar and yolk mixture.
- Fold in the egg white.
- Chill thoroughly.
- Churn in an ice cream machine.
- Cover and store in freezer.

pistachio brittle

4 ounces fondant
2 ounces glucose
2 ounces pistachios

- Place pistachios on a sheet pan and roast in a 350°F (175°C) oven until a light golden brown.
- Place fondant and glucose in a small sauté pan and set over medium-high heat. Stir occasionally and remove from heat once the mixture has become a light honey brown color.
- Pour the hot caramel onto a Silpat and let cool at room temperature.
- Once the caramel has hardened, break into shards and place in a food processor.
- Using short bursts, grind until a fine powder is formed.
- Sprinkle a thin layer of the powder on a Silpat and place in a 350°F (175°C) oven. Bake until the powder melts into a thin layer of caramel.
- Remove from oven and sprinkle roasted pistachios over the caramel. Pick up the caramel and twist into random shapes and spirals. Use caution as the caramel will be very hot.
- Store at room temperature until required for service.

PLATE ASSEMBLY

🌿 Place both the mint syrup and honey reduction sauces into squirt bottles. Use the sauces to form a border around the center of the plate.

🌿 Within this "frame" invert a coconut shell on the plate and top with the chocolate marquise. Place a rose petal on top of the marquise.

🌿 Add a quenelle of curry frozen yogurt to the left of the marquise and top with a shard of pistachio brittle.

🌿 Serve immediately.

 a taste of Asia

Entrée #1: mango and lemon grass consommé garnished with melon matchsticks

Entrée #2: steamed rice balls filled with adzuki red bean paste, roasted pineapple, and fresh lychee nuts, accompanied with three dipping sauces: tamarind, sweet soy, and wasabi

Entrée #3: fresh passion fruit sorbet served with coconut short dough chopsticks

This dessert is designed to mirror both the culinary cooking styles and flavors of Asia. The components of the plate are presented sequentially. Proper communication between the front and back of the house and, in turn, between the front of the house and the guest is vital for the true depth of this plate to be appreciated.

The dessert starts with a small portion of mango–lemon grass consommé. The consommé acts as an introduction to the rest of the plate. The soup is served at room temperature and has a wonderful clear, crisp essence to it. The mango and lemon grass washes over the palate accompanied by a few bites of fresh melon. The melon has been cut into matchsticks. The inclusion of fresh melon adds a burst of fresh fruit flavor, which harmonizes well with the flavors of the consommé.

The second component of the dessert is a trio of small steamed rice balls. The balls are made with traditional sticky sushi rice with a bit of honey. Each ball has a different filling inside: a traditional red adzuki bean paste, roasted pineapple, and fresh lychee nuts. The rice balls are served with a trio of dipping sauces, consisting of sweet soy, tamarind, and wasabi. The neutral flavors of the rice balls offer a great foil for the strong flavors of the dipping sauces.

The final course is a tangy, sour, palate-cleansing passion fruit sorbet served with chopsticks made of coconut short dough.

The flavors of this plate mirror those found in many Asian culinary and dessert entrées. As with many Asian plates, little or no fat is used. The overall flavors are clear and crisp, not muddied with the addition of oils, butter, or dairy. The plate starts with an introduction, a watercolor wash of flavors. The second course presents the guest with the strong flavors of the orient and, like many culinary plates, these strong flavors are accompanied with rice. The finale of the dessert cleanses the palate and leaves a lingering sweet taste on the palate with its coconut cookie chopsticks.

Asian plates often try to incorporate sweet, sour, bitter, and salt. This dessert incorporates those same flavors and by the time the guests are done with the sampler, they have experienced a full plate profile.

Plate Profiles

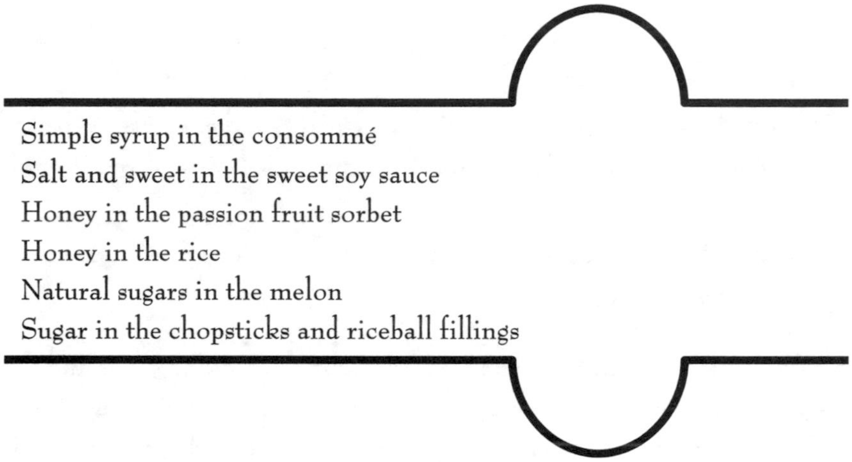

Simple syrup in the consommé
Salt and sweet in the sweet soy sauce
Honey in the passion fruit sorbet
Honey in the rice
Natural sugars in the melon
Sugar in the chopsticks and riceball fillings

FIGURE 11.5

Plate profile for a Taste of Asia: Top Notes.

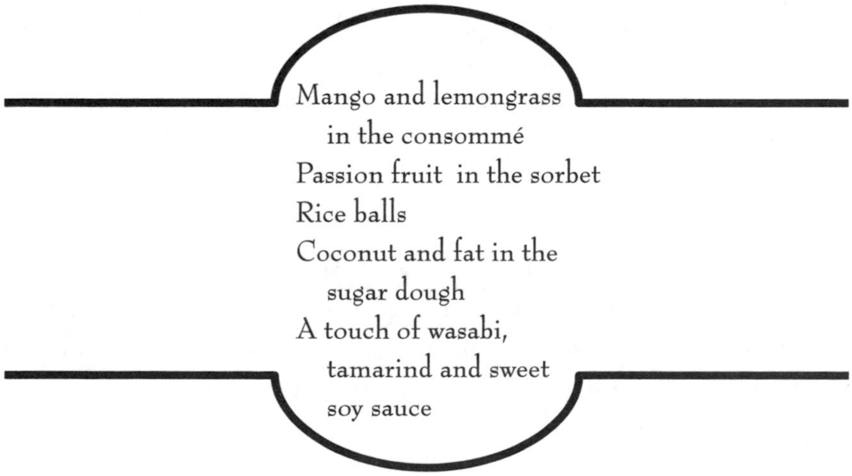

Mango and lemongrass
in the consommé
Passion fruit in the sorbet
Rice balls
Coconut and fat in the
sugar dough
A touch of wasabi,
tamarind and sweet
soy sauce

FIGURE 11.6

Plate profile for a Taste of Asia: Middle Notes.

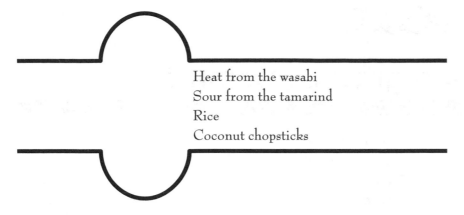

Heat from the wasabi
Sour from the tamarind
Rice
Coconut chopsticks

FIGURE 11.7

Plate profile for a Taste of Asia: Base Notes.

Flavor Profile

	SWEET/SOUR/ BITTER/SALT	AROMA	TRIGEMINAL RESPONSE
Entrée #1 Mango–lemongrass consommé	Sweet: consommé and fresh fruit Sour: consommé and fresh fruit	NA	NA
Entrée #2 Rice balls Adzuki Pineapple Lychee nut	Sweet: rice, bean paste, pineapple, and lychee nut Sour: pineapple	NA	NA
Dipping sauces: Wasabi Tamarind Sweet soy	Sweet: tamarind and sweet soy sauce Salt: sweet soy sauce Sour: tamarind	NA	NA Heat from wasabi
Coconut chopsticks	Sweet: sugar	NA	NA
Passion fruit sorbet	Sweet: honey Sour: passion fruit	NA	NA

FIGURE 11.8

Flavor profile for a Taste of Asia.

mango–lemon grass consommé

2 each ripe mangoes
2–3 stalks lemon grass
2 quarts water
5 ounces honey

- Cut the bottom off each stalk of lemon grass and remove the outer husks if they are tough and fibrous.
- Cut the bottom of each lemon grass stalk into coin-sized pieces and crush each piece with the side of a French knife.
- Place the lemon grass in a stockpot with the water and honey and bring to a simmer.
- Allow the mixture to steep until a strong lemon grass flavor is achieved.
- Purée the mango and add to the lemon grass base.
- Strain through cheesecloth.
- The resulting consommé should consist of flavors that move across the palate. The first impression should be of the lemon grass flavor, while the mango flavor follows closely behind. Overall, both flavors should not be overly sweet. The effect should be similar to a watercolor; simply a thin hint of the flavors is all that is needed.

coconut chopsticks

8 ounces pastry flour
2 ounces rice flour
4 ounces granulated sugar
8 ounces butter
3 ounces coconut, freshly grated
¼ tsp almond extract
½ tsp pure vanilla extract
2 ounces milk

- Mix the flours and the sugar together.
- Using a cutting or scissor-like motion with your fingers, rub the butter into the dry ingredients.

- Add the coconut, extracts, and milk to the dough and work the dough until it becomes smooth.

- Form the dough into a disk, wrap tightly with plastic, and refrigerate at least 30 minutes.

- Remove the dough from the refrigerator and roll out to a square that is approximately $1/3$ inch thick and at least 8 inches long.

- Using a French knife cut the dough into strips, forming chopsticks.

- Place carefully on a Silpat- or parchment paper-lined sheet pan and bake at 350°F (175°C) for 10–12 minutes or until golden brown.

- Once the chopsticks are cool, decorate with chocolate piping if desired.

sticky rice balls

. . . .

7 ounces sushi rice
12 ounces water
2 tbsp clover honey

- Place the rice in a chinoise mousseline and rinse until the water runs clear.

- Place rice and water in a sauce pan and allow to soak for 30 minutes.

- Bring the mixture to a boil, stir once, and cover with a lid and turn down the heat.

- Simmer for an additional 20 minutes.

- Take pan off the heat and let it stand for 10 more minutes, keeping the pan covered.

Fillings for Rice Balls

Red Adzuki Bean Paste

7 ounces dried adzuki beans
4 ounces granulated sugar
3 each star anise pods
2 each cardamom pods
pinch of salt

- Place the beans in a chinoise and rinse them with cold water.

- Put cleaned beans in a saucepan with 4 cups of water and the spices.

- Bring to a boil. Lower the heat and allow the beans to simmer until they are soft.
- Once the beans are soft enough to be easily mashed, add the sugar and continue to simmer for 20 minutes.
- Remove from heat and cool.
- Using a potato masher, smash the beans into a paste.
- Proceed with method of preparation for assembling rice balls.

Roasted Pineapple

½ fresh pineapple
1–2 tsp Chinese five spice powder
1 ounce brown sugar
1 ounce of sake

- Peel and core pineapple. Dice into small cubes (about ¼ inch) and place in hotel pan.
- Add Chinese five spice, brown sugar, and sake.
- Place in a 350°F (175°C) oven and roast, stirring occasionally, until pineapple begins to caramelize.
- Let mixture cool before filling rice balls.
- Proceed with method of preparation for assembling rice balls.

Lychee Nut Filling

12 fresh lychee nuts
2 ounces sake

- Clean lychee nuts.
- Marinate the lychee in some sake if desired.
- Proceed with method of preparation for assembling rice balls.

To assemble rice balls

- Use a sorbet scoop for easy portioning of the rice.
  - Place a portion of rice in the palm of your hand and add a tablespoon of desired filling. Carefully roll the rice over the filling to form a clean ball.
  - Dipping your hands often in cold water will make the rolling process much easier.
  - Store rice balls covered in the refrigerator until service.

tamarind sauce

4–8 ounces tamarind paste

Tamarind paste with seeds will yield the most flavorful results. Although there are many tamarind nectars and compounds available, many of them have a cooked flavor which tends to hide tamarind's wonderful sour notes.

Place the tamarind paste on the top of a double boiler. Stir occasionally as the paste is heating up.

Add simple syrup to taste.

Strain.

Store in the refrigerator until service.

wasabi sauce

2 ounces wasabi powder
1–2 ounces honey

There are many types of wasabi available. Try to get the best-quality powder possible, one with no fillers.

Add water to create a thick paste and let sit for 10 minutes to fully develop the flavor.

Add honey to taste.

Add additional water, if needed, until the desired consistency is achieved.

This is a potent sauce; only a little bit is needed on the plate.

sweet soy sauce

Sweet soy sauce is available in most Asian markets. It has the familiar salty notes of soy sauce, coupled with a rich sweetness. It has a thick, syrupy consistency. Nothing more is needed. It can be used, as is, directly from the bottle.

passion fruit sorbet

zest and juice of one lime
8 ounces passion fruit purée
6 ounces simple syrup

🌿 Whisk all ingredients together. Taste. The sorbet will be quite sour.

🌿 Add additional simple syrup if desired.

🌿 Pour into ice cream machine and churn.

Note: Best results are achieved if the sorbet can be placed in a hardening cabinet for from 10 to 15 minutes before being placed in the freezer.

PLATE ASSEMBLY

🌿 This plate is designed to offer the customer a sampling of Asian flavors. For this reason it is preferable to display each component individually rather than to group them together as a single dessert.

🌿 First, the consommé. This can be served in a small bowl. A half cup or so of the consommé is plenty. Use a bowl that allows the customer to see the beautiful melon matchsticks floating in the mango–lemon grass broth.

🌿 Second, the sticky rice balls. These are lined up along with their accompanying dipping sauces. The sauces are all pungent so not much is needed.

🌿 The third element is the sorbet.

🌿 This is placed separately from the rice balls, near the chopsticks, as if waiting to be picked up from the plate.

 # 21st century gingerbread

This dessert is based on my mother's gingerbread cake recipe. This dessert was a staple of many childhood autumn meals, served with applesauce and Chantilly cream. This modern version keeps many of the same elements but adds some unexpected flavors.

Entrée: gingerbread cake

Frozen: toasted cumin ice cream

Sauce: apple cider reduction with rye whisky

Garnish: woven apple blanket

Crunch: spicy molasses cookie

It is undeniable that gingerbread and apples go well together. This plate celebrates that relationship in many ways. The gingerbread, full of potent spices, takes center stage. The apple accompanies the cake in many guises. It is found in the reduction sauce as well as in the apple blanket. The various textures of the apple allow it to be experienced in the top, middle, and base notes of each bite.

The gingerbread is essentially a quick bread using the blending method. This version includes some grated fresh ginger, dry mustard powder, and a couple of twists of black pepper. These spices add some base notes to the dish. The ice cream is a variation of Chantilly cream. Like the Chantilly cream, the ice cream adds a rich, creamy texture to the dish. The cumin seeds are dry roasted until fragrant and then infused into the dairy–sugar mixture. They will be strained out of the mixture when the dairy is tempered into the yolks. The heavily savory toasted cumin flavor would probably not work as well if it were not part of a fatty and rich food product. Its presence in the French ice cream is ideal.

The apple cider reduction is apple cider reduced down until it is almost a syrup consistency. Using fresh apple cider, as opposed to apple juice, will add a full, round, tart flavor to the reduction. The rye whisky is added to the cider for its earthy slightly woody flavor and the alcohol base note it brings to the sauce.

The thin molasses cookie reflects some of the same spices found in the gingerbread cake while introducing a hint of crunchy molasses flavor. Its crisp texture ensures that the flavors will remain on the palate slightly longer than those of the cake. The cookie also provides a landing spot, a safe anchor for the scoop of ice cream that sits on top of it. The woven apple blanket consists of thin strips of candied apples. They have been "woven" together to form a blanket, which rests on top of the ice cream.

Visually the plate is designed so that the customer can experience the perfect bite in each forkful or spoonful. The stacking of the flavors also helps to create some visual impact.

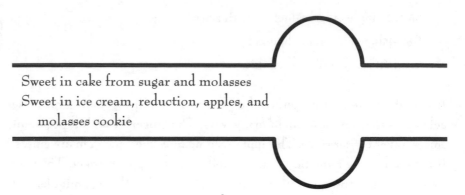

Sweet in cake from sugar and molasses
Sweet in ice cream, reduction, apples, and
   molasses cookie

FIGURE 11.9

Plate profile for 21st Century Gingerbread: Top Notes.

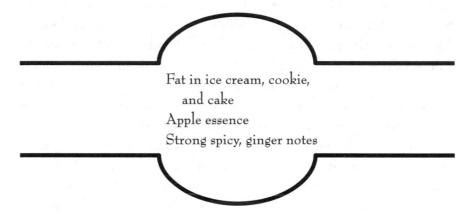

Fat in ice cream, cookie,
and cake
Apple essence
Strong spicy, ginger notes

FIGURE 11.10

Plate profile for 21st Century Gingerbread: Middle Notes.

Earthy heat from cumin, ginger,
   dried mustard, and black pepper
Sour note from apple reduction
Slight burn from rye whiskey

FIGURE 11.11

Plate profile for 21st Century Gingerbread: Base Notes.

Flavor Profile

	SWEET/SOUR/ BITTER/SALT	AROMA	TRIGEMINAL RESPONSE
Gingerbread cake	Sweet: molasses	NA	Heat from fresh ginger, black peppercorns, and dried mustard powder
Molasses cookie	Sweet: molasses and sugar	NA	Heat from fresh ginger
Cider reduction with rye whiskey	Sweet: natural sweetness of the apples Sour: also from the apples	NA	Slight burn from the rye whiskey
Toasted cumin French ice cream	Sweet: sugar	NA	A bit of earthy heat from the cumin
Woven apple blanket	Sweet: apples Sour: apples	NA	NA

FIGURE 11.12

Flavor profile for 21st Century Gingerbread.

RECIPES

 gingerbread cake

8 ounces all-purpose or pastry flour

$1\frac{1}{2}$ tsp baking soda

$\frac{1}{4}$ tsp salt

$\frac{1}{2}$ tsp cinnamon

$\frac{1}{2}$ tsp dried ginger

1 tsp fresh ginger, grated

2 twists black peppercorn

$\frac{1}{2}$ tsp dried mustard powder

$\frac{1}{4}$ tsp ground cloves

1 whole egg

12 ounces molasses

4 ounces melted butter

4 ounces hot water

🌿 Sift all dry ingredients.

🌿 Whisk together the egg and the molasses.

🌿 Add the melted butter to the wet ingredients and blend well.

🌿 Mix together the wet and dry ingredients.

🌿 When all of the ingredients are almost completely incorporated, add the hot water.

🌿 Place in a greased pan, or ungreased flexi pans in a 350°F (175°C) oven. Bake for 18–25 minutes or until the center of the cake bounces back when lightly pushed with your finger.

Note: Reduce baking time if the cakes are being made individually.

🌿 molasses cookie

• •

8 ounces softened butter
12 ounces sugar
1 whole egg
$2\frac{1}{4}$ ounces molasses
$\frac{1}{3}$ ounce ground ginger
$1\frac{1}{2}$ tbsp grated fresh ginger
$\frac{1}{3}$ ounces baking soda
$\frac{1}{4}$ tsp salt
12 ounces all purpose flour

🌿 Cream butter and sugar until lump free.

🌿 Add molasses, scraping the bottom and sides of the bowl.

🌿 When the sugars and butter are lump free slowly add eggs and ginger.

🌿 Sift together all dry ingredients.

🌿 Add dry ingredients to creamed ingredients and mix until just combined.

🌿 Shape dough into a disk, wrap, and chill for a few hours or overnight.

🌿 When the dough is chilled, roll out onto a lightly floured Silpat. The resulting dough should be not thicker than $\frac{1}{4}$ inch.

🌿 Bake at 350°F (175°C) for up to 10 minutes or until the dough is no longer shiny and feels slightly dry to the touch.

- Remove sheet pan from oven and, using pastry cutters, cut into desired shapes. Remove any scraps from the Silpat and set aside.

- Return the cookies to the oven.

- Bake an additional 5–9 minutes or until the cookies are completely set.

- Allow the cookies to cool before removing from the sheet pan.

Note: Do not throw away the scraps. They can be saved and used in a variety of ways: in place of cake crumbs, folded in a mousse, panna cotta, or ice cream, or sprinkled on the top of tuile or lace cookies before they are baked.

cider reduction with rye whisky

2 quarts fresh apple cider
4 ounces rye whiskey

- It is vital that this sauce begin with the highest quality apple cider you can find. Apple cider, as opposed to apple juice, is made from pressing juice out of fresh apples. Apple juice is often made from a concentrate or it begins with apple cider and then has additional water and sugar added to it. Pour the apple cider into a saucepan and place on medium heat. When the cider reaches a boil turn the heat down and keep it at a simmer. After the cider has reduced by half, add 4 ounces of rye whiskey to the saucepan. Continue to simmer the sauce until it starts to thicken.

- To test the consistency of a sauce, spoon a small amount onto a plate. This will cool the sauce quickly and give you an idea as to its consistency. If cooked for too long, reduction sauces have a tendency to become too syrupy. When they cool they then become almost candy-like. This can be avoided if the sauce is removed from the heat shortly before it reaches the desired consistency. Remember that the sauce will thicken as it cools.

- It will take awhile for the cider to reduce down to a syrup like consistency, but the resulting tangy, flavorful reduction is well worth the time invested.

toasted cumin french ice cream

8 ounces milk
8 ounces heavy cream
pinch of salt
4 ounces granulated sugar
4 ounces egg yolks
¾ tsp toasted cumin seeds, ground

- Place dairy, sugar, and toasted cumin in a saucepan and bring to a scald.

- Taste. If stronger flavor is desired, take the pan off the heat and cover with plastic wrap. Allow the mixture to steep at room temperature until the desired depth of flavor is obtained. Continue with method of preparation when flavor has reached the desired level.

- Temper hot dairy mixture into the egg yolks; use a thin wire whisk and try to incorporate as little foam as possible.

- Return to stove over medium high heat.

- Stir constantly with a heat resistant spatula until the mixture has reached nappe.

- Place in an ice bath.

- When base has cooled completely, churn in an ice cream machine.

- If possible, place in hardening cabinet for 10–15 minutes before storing in the freezer.

woven apple blanket

1 Granny Smith apple

- Slice a Granny Smith apple on a mandolin or a meat slicer. The resulting slices should be no thicker than ⅛ inch.

- Cut each apple slice into thin matchsticks.

- Weave the sticks into a lattice type of "blanket."

- Place the blanket on a Silpat-lined sheet pan.

- Bake at 250°F (120°C) for 25 minutes.

- Take the apples out of the oven and flip over.

🌿 Return the apples to the oven and continue to bake until the blankets are almost completely crisp. Remove from oven.

🌿 The apples will continue to dry and crisp as they cool.

PLATE ASSEMBLY

🌿 Using the back of a ladle spread a round of cider reduction in the middle of the plate. In the middle of the sauce, place the gingerbread cake. On top of the cake lay the molasses cookie, a scoop of toasted cumin ice cream, and the woven apple blanket.

Note: Prior to service scoop the ice cream on top of the cookies and place in hardening cabinet or freezer. This will insure that the ice cream will remain "glued" to the cookie in its journey from the kitchen to the guest.

 tomato trio

The following dessert explores the variety of tomato flavors. The plate profile of the tomato varies in each individual element of this dish. The idea is for the guest to start with a light wash of tomato flavor in the first element, move to a roasted tomato caramelized flavor in the second element, and finish off with a fresh tomato sorbet.

The tomato theme and flavor unites each of these individual elements as does the greater Italian context of the plate. In each component the tomato flavor is combined or contrasted with flavors from Italian cuisine. In the case of the tomato water the foam is made from corn. The roasted tomato is served on a polenta and olive oil cake with basil. And the sorbet sandwich is served between two Parmesan crisps accompanied by a balsamic reduction. There is no doubt that this type of dessert is not for everyone. For those with a sense of culinary adventure, the dessert allows the guest to experience the many and diverse flavors of tomato.

The plate is designed as a sampler starting with light flavors and moving to heavier. The light tomato flavors are presented in products that will dissipate quickly on the palate, while the heavier flavors are in products whose texture forces them to linger on the palate.

Entrée #1: Tomato water with corn foam

Entrée #2: olive oil polenta cake with jammy tomato marmalade and basil clear sauce

Entrée #3: tomato sorbet sandwiched between Parmesan tuile and served with a balsamic reduction

Plate Profiles

Sweet from corn foam, jammy marmalade,
sorbet, olive oil cake, and basil clear sauce
Salt in Parmesan cheese

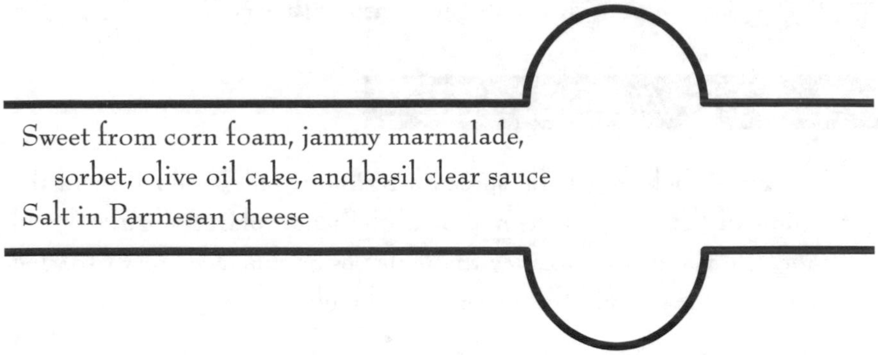

FIGURE 11.13

Plate profile of Tomato Trio: Top Notes.

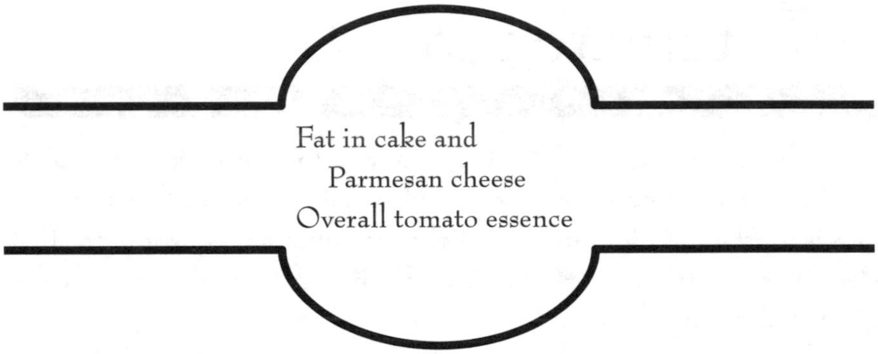

Fat in cake and
Parmesan cheese
Overall tomato essence

FIGURE 11.14

Plate profile of Tomato Trio: Middle Notes.

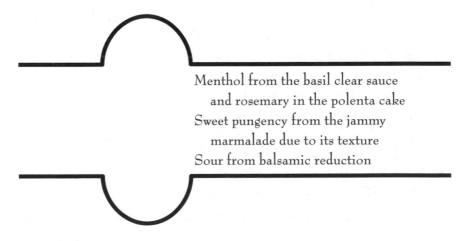

Menthol from the basil clear sauce
and rosemary in the polenta cake
Sweet pungency from the jammy
marmalade due to its texture
Sour from balsamic reduction

FIGURE 11.15

Plate profile of Tomato Trio: Base Notes.

Flavor Profile

	SWEET/SOUR/ BITTER/SALT	AROMA	TRIGEMINAL RESPONSE
Tomato water with corn foam	Sweet: natural sweetness from the tomato and corn Salt: just a touch in the water	A bit from the warm milk foam	NA
Olive oil polenta cake with jammy marmalade and basil clear sauce	Sweet: cake, marmalade, and clear sauce	NA	Menthol from basil clear sauce and rosemary in the polenta cake
Tomato sorbet sandwich with Parmesan tuile and balsamic reduction	Sweet: tomato sorbet Salt: Parmesan tuile Sour: balsamic reduction	NA	NA

FIGURE 11.16

Flavor profile for Tomato Trio.

RECIPES

tomato water shooter

1 lb vine-ripened plum tomatoes
pinch of sugar and/or salt, if needed

🌾 Blanch the tomatoes and remove their skins. Rough chop the tomatoes and place in cheesecloth. Tie the cheesecloth tightly, then tie it around the handle of a wooden spoon that is resting over the top of a large measuring cup or container. Place in a refrigerator and allow the tomato water to drip through the cheesecloth overnight.

🌾 The resulting water will be the base for the tomato water shooter.

🌾 Taste the water and add a small pinch of salt and/or sugar if desired.

roasted corn foam

1 ear fresh corn
16 ounces whole milk

- Husk and roast one ear of fresh corn
- When fragrant and slightly charred, remove from heat.
- Cut the kernels off the cob.
- Place cob and kernels in a saucepan with 2 cups of whole milk.
- Bring mixture to a boil
- Strain
- Return to stove and keep warm.
- Just before plating up, mix with an immersion blender.
- When needed for service pour the tomato water into a shot glass, filling the glass about 75% of the way. Spoon some foam on top of the water. The shot glass should now be about 90% full.

Note: The water should be served at room temperature.

olive oil polenta cake

6¾ ounces all purpose or pastry flour
4½ ounces cornmeal
1 tbsp rosemary
1 tbsp orange zest
1 tsp baking powder
¼ tsp salt
5 ounces mascarpone cheese
4 whole eggs
10 ounces granulated sugar
3 ounces olive oil

- Mix all dry ingredients together.
- Whisk mascarpone cheese until lump free. Add sugar and continue to whisk.

- Slowly add eggs to the cheese mixture.

- Fold together the dry and wet ingredients.

- Stir in olive oil.

- Place in flexi molds and bake at 350°F (175°C) until middle of cake bounces back when lightly pushed.

  Note: The bake time will vary according to the size of mold used. A 9-inch cake pan will take approximately 35–40 minutes to bake.

jammy tomato marmalade

1 lb roma, plum, or beefsteak tomatoes
2 ounces granulated sugar
pinch of sea salt
2 grinds of fresh black pepper

- Slice tomatoes in quarters and place in a hotel pan. Sprinkle the tomatoes with the salt, pepper, and granulated sugar.

- Roast tomatoes for approximately 25 minutes at 375°F (190°C).

- Remove tomatoes from hotel pan and place into a sauce pan. Scrape the hotel pan well, making sure to add all of the fond to the sauce pan

- Over low heat cook the tomatoes until they have completely broken down and reach a marmalade like consistency.

- Adjust seasonings if needed.

balsamic reduction

- Although referred to here as a reduction, a great aged balsamic can be used as is, straight from the bottle. An aged Aceto Balsamico will give the plate a depth of flavor not achieved with less expensive balsamic vinegars.

- A thinner balsamic vinegar can be used. Simply reduce it in a saucepan until it reaches the consistency of maple syrup. The addition of a small amount of granulated sugar will expedite the thickening process and round out the flavors of the vinegar.

tomato sorbet

Sour notes can be added in the form of lemon juice or balsamic vinegar. The result is extraordinary.

> 8 ounces roasted tomatoes (see jammy marmalade recipe)
> 3 ounces tomato paste
> 12 ounces water
> 6 ounces simple syrup
> pinch of sea salt

- Finely purée the roasted tomatoes.
- Whisk all ingredients together. Taste. Add a teaspoon of balsamic vinegar or fresh lemon juice if desired.
- Place in ice cream machine and churn.
- If possible, place sorbet in hardening cabinet for 10–15 minutes after churning. Store in freezer until needed for service.

parmesan tuile

Grate fresh Parmesan reggiano cheese. Spread the grated cheese into small circles on a Silpat. A thin layer of cheese works best. Bake in a 350°F (175°C) oven until lightly golden brown. The tuile cheese crackers will harden upon cooling.

basil clear sauce

> 4 ounces fresh basil leaves
> 2 ounces light corn syrup

- Blanch the basil leaves. Plunge them into boiling water and then place immediately into ice water. Remove the leaves from the ice water and pat them dry with paper towels.
- Place the leaves in a small robot coupe or food processor.
- Slowly add the light corn syrup. Strain the syrup through cheesecloth. (*Note:* It is easiest to place the syrup in the cheesecloth, bundle up the top and, using a wringing motion, squeeze the syrup through the cloth. The result will be a bright green syrup with no bits of basil leaves.)
- Store in a squeeze bottle until service.

PLATE ASSEMBLY

🌿 Fill a shot glass with a few ounces of the tomato water and top with a spoonful of corn foam.

🌿 To the side of the water shot, place the olive oil cake and cover with a generous spoonful of the jammy marmalade. Both the cake and the marmalade will taste best if served slightly warm. Place dots of the basil syrup around the cake.

🌿 Garnish a scoop of tomato sorbet with the Parmesan crisps and surround with a drizzle of balsamic reduction.

 # beet meets chocolate

The varied personality of the beet is showcased in this dessert. Beet's flavor changes according to the environment in which it is placed. When paired with chocolate, beets' muddy, earthy notes are evident. The result is a wonderfully rich, deep cake. In the orange panna cotta, the cleaner citrus notes of the beet are accentuated. The result is a refreshing complement to the chocolate plate.

The relationships of flavors in this plate are reminiscent of a repertory theatre group. No one flavor takes center stage. Each flavor supports the others. The diverse flavors of beet ties all of the components of the plate together. While the beet is an omnipresent background note, it does not overpower the other flavors on the plate. A guest looking for a chocolate "fix" will not be disappointed after having this dessert.

The colors of the plate are visually arresting, as are the contrasts of textures. The elements of the dessert are constructed so that the panna cotta and cake will be enjoyed in every bite.

The Guinness reduction with an orange "head" is a bit of visual whimsy. The reduction of Guinness maintains much of its original dark, rich chocolate brown color while the orange foam looks similar to the beer's thick foamy head. Water and orange juice form the base of the foam, which allows the sour tartness of the orange to shine through. The orange flavor picks up on the smooth orange notes experienced in the panna cotta. The sweet notes of the Guinness beer also echo the sweet chocolate notes of the cake and cookie.

Entrée: beet chocolate cake

Frozen: orange panna cotta with beet powder

Sauce: Guinness reduction with an orange head

Crunch: chocolate short dough cookie

Sweet from cake, beets, orange panna cotta,
Guinness reduction, and cookie

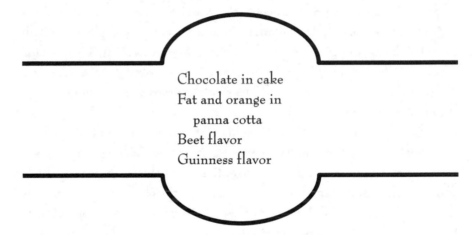

FIGURE 11.17

Plate profile for Beet Meets Chocolate: Top Notes.

Chocolate in cake
Fat and orange in
panna cotta
Beet flavor
Guinness flavor

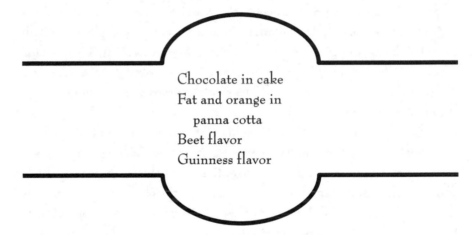

FIGURE 11.18

Plate profile for Beet Meets Chocolate: Middle Notes.

Bitter from chocolate cake and cookie
Alcohol burn from Guinness reduction
Slight sour from orange foam

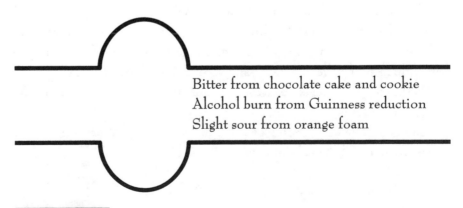

FIGURE 11.19

Plate profile for Beet Meets Chocolate: Base Notes.

Flavor Profile

	SWEET/SOUR/ BITTER/SALT	AROMA	TRIGEMINAL RESPONSE
Beet cake	Sweet: cake and beets	NA	NA
Orange panna cotta	Sweet: sugar Sour: orange, buttermilk	NA	NA
Guinness reduction with orange foam	Sweet: Guinness Sour: orange	NA	Slight alcohol burn from the Guinness
Chocolate cookie	Sweet: sugar Bitter: chocolate	NA	NA

FIGURE 11.20

Flavor profile for Beet Meets Chocolate.

RECIPES

beet chocolate cake

13 ounces pastry flour

1 lb 2 ounces granulated sugar

2 ounces cocoa powder

10 ounces water

$4\frac{1}{2}$ ounces vegetable oil

5 ounces butter, melted

4 ounces eggs

5 ounces buttermilk

$\frac{1}{2}$ ounce baking soda

$1\frac{1}{2}$ tsp vanilla extract

4 ounces roasted beet purée

Roasted Beets

Trim the tops and bottoms of three beets.

Rub each beet lightly with olive oil and wrap in aluminum foil.

- Place into a 350°F (175°C) oven for 50 to 70 minutes or until fork tender.

- Allow the beet to cool slightly and then peel.

- Purée in a robot coupe. The result will be slightly lumpy. Set aside.

- Sift together the dry ingredients except for the baking soda. Place in a mixer with a paddle on speed 1.

- Bring the vegetable oil, butter, and water to a boil and add to the dry ingredients. Continue to mix on speed 1.

- Once everything is fully incorporated, add the eggs slowly.

- Scrape down the sides and bottom of the bowl.

- In a small bowl, whisk together the buttermilk, the baking soda, and the vanilla extract.

- Add the liquid ingredients all at once to the batter in the mixing bowl. Continue to mix on speed 1 until well incorporated.

- Scrape the bottom and sides of the bowl.

- Spoon the batter into well-greased and/or parchment-lined molds. Fill each mold about 80%. On top of each cake spoon 1 tbsp of roasted beet purée. Using a bamboo skewer, a paring knife, or your finger gently swirl the beet purée throughout the batter.

- Bake at 350°F (175°C) until the center of the cake is firm. The baking time will depend on the size of your cake pan. Start checking individual cakes after 15–17 minutes.

- Let the cakes cool and then remove from mold.

orange panna cotta with a beet powder

¼ ounce powdered gelatin
10 ounces heavy cream
14 ounces buttermilk
½ vanilla bean
zest of ½ orange
3 ounces sugar

- Bloom the gelatin in ¼ cup of heavy cream.

- Bring the remaining cream, sugar, vanilla bean, and orange zest to a scald.

- Remove from heat and taste.

- Steep the mixture if required.

- Heat and dissolve the bloomed gelatin. This can be done on a double boiler or in a microwave.

- Add dissolved gelatin to the rest of the cream. Whisk in the buttermilk.

- Place mixture in an ice bath and continue to stir gently with a rubber spatula until the liquid just begins to thicken. It will have the consistency of yogurt.

- Pour into desired molds and chill for at least 3 hours.

- Remove panna cotta from molds and dust the top of each liberally with the beet powder just before service.

beet powder

1 raw beet, peeled

- Slice the beet on a mandolin and place the slices on a Silpat.

- Bake the beet slices in a 300°F (150°C) oven until dried.

- Allow beet chips to cool completely. They should be crisp enough to crumble easily in your hand.

- Grind beet chips in a spice grinder. Take the resulting powder and push it through a fine mesh sieve. Store in a tightly covered container at room temperature.

Guinness foam with an orange head

1 can of Guinness beer

- Pour all of the beer into a small saucepan.

- Reduce on medium heat until it reaches a syrupy consistency.

orange foam

2 cups orange juice
5 2-gram gelatin sheets

- Place 1½ cups of the orange juice in a 5-quart KitchenAid mixer bowl and place in the freezer.
- Bloom the gelatin sheets in cold water.
- Heat the remaining ½ cup orange juice and dissolve the bloomed gelatin in it. This can be done on a double boiler or in a microwave.
- Take the juice/mixing bowl out of the freezer and place in a 5-quart mixer with a whip attachment.
- On speed 1, slowly add the hot dissolved gelatin mixture to the cold mixture in the bowl. When all the gelatin has been added, turn the machine up to speed 3.
- Continue to whip until the entire bowl is full of orange foam. This will take from 5 to 7 minutes.
- The foam can remain out at room temperature until required for service.

chocolate short dough cookies

4 ounces granulated sugar
8 ounces unsalted butter, room temperature
1½ ounces whole eggs
6 ounces cake flour
6 ounces cocoa powder

- Sift together the cake flour and the cocoa powder.
- Place the sugar and butter together in a mixer with a paddle.
- Cream on speed 2 until the mixture is lump free. Scrape the bottom and sides of the bowl frequently.
- Slowly add eggs. Scrape bowl.
- Turn the machine to speed 1 and add the flour and cocoa powder all at once.
- Remove the dough from the machine as soon as the dry ingredients are completely incorporated.

- Place on a parchment-lined sheet pan and pat into a thin square. Wrap well and refrigerate for at least 1 hour before rolling out.

- Roll the dough to ¼-inch thickness and cut into desired shapes.

- Bake the cookies at 350°F (175°C).

   Hint: Because of the cookies' dark brown, almost black color it is often difficult to tell when they are done. The best way to check the cookies is to gently press their center. The cookies should feel dry to the touch.

PLATE ASSEMBLY

- Form a border around the outer rim of the plate with the Guinness reduction. Top with the orange foam.

- In the center of this "frame" place the chocolate beet cake. To the side of the cake place the chocolate short dough cookie and the panna cotta.

- Prior to service place the panna cotta onto the cookie and put in the freezer. This will insure that the panna cotta stays firmly in place when traveling from the kitchen to the guest.

 food of the gods

The history of chocolate is fascinating. Sweet chocolate, in a tablet or block form is a relatively new invention. Originally, chocolate was served as a drink, accompanied by ingredients indigenous to its environment. Products such as corn, chilli pepper, vanilla, and canela (Mexican) cinnamon were often added to the roasted ground cocoa nibs. It was then mixed with cold water and served as a beverage. A great delicacy, this chocolate drink was believed to give strength to its consumer. Montezuma was said to have drunk 50 cups of chocolate a day.

The various elements of this traditional drink are evident in this dessert. The canela cinnamon is added to the chocolate mousse. The mousse itself sits on top of a gelée of mango, lime, and ancho chilli pepper. The chilli theme is repeated in the jalapeños of the "salsa." The corn of the traditional drink is reflected in the corn meal tuile cookie. The cajeta sauce, made with a base of goat's milk, reflects not so much the history of chocolate as it does the Mayan environment from which it was born. Goat's milk is still used in contemporary Mexican cuisine. The salsa is an additional variation of Mexican cuisine—instead of tomatoes, strawberries, and instead of cilantro, fresh mint. The result is a slightly tangy, somewhat hot and altogether refreshing contrast to the richness of the mousse. The gelée's crisp sour flavors also contrast well with the mouth feel of the sabayon-based mousse.

Taken as a whole, the plate celebrates chocolate's history as well as the culinary environment of its birth.

Entrée: chocolate sabayon mousse with a mango–chilli gelée

Sauce: cajeta caramel sauce

Sauce: strawberry salsa

Sauce: mint syrup

Crunch/garnish: cornmeal tuile sun

Plate Profiles

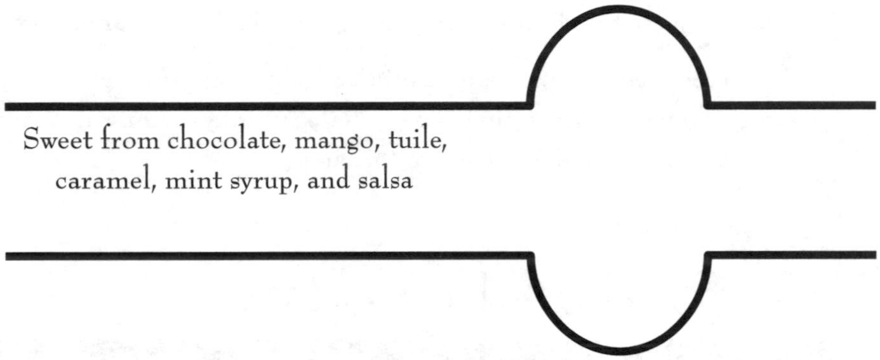

Sweet from chocolate, mango, tuile, caramel, mint syrup, and salsa

FIGURE 11.21

Plate profile for Food of the Gods: Top Notes.

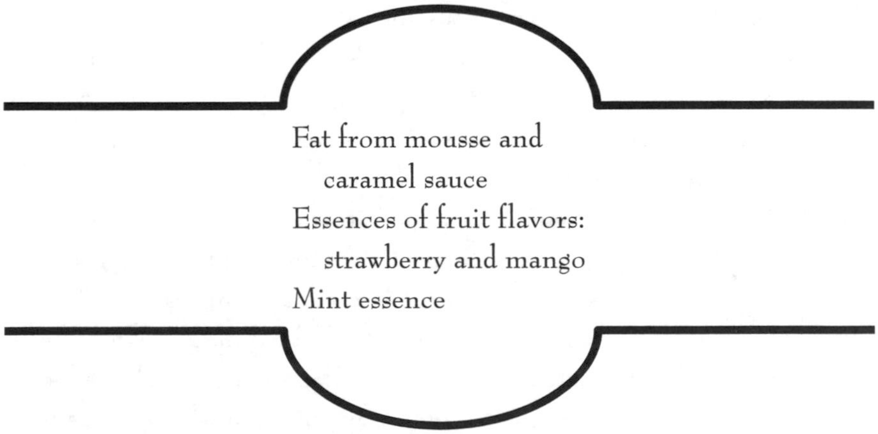

Fat from mousse and caramel sauce
Essences of fruit flavors: strawberry and mango
Mint essence

FIGURE 11.22

Plate profile for Food of the Gods: Middle Notes.

chapter 11   plated desserts

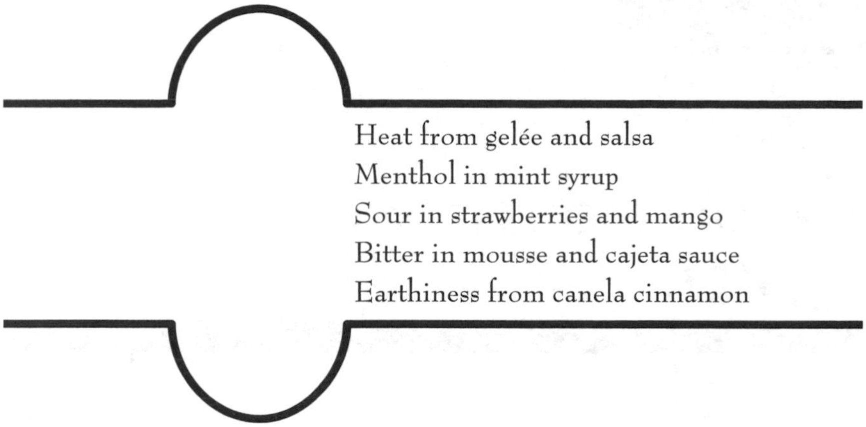

Heat from gelée and salsa
Menthol in mint syrup
Sour in strawberries and mango
Bitter in mousse and cajeta sauce
Earthiness from canela cinnamon

FIGURE 11.23

Plate profile for Food of the Gods: Base Notes.

Flavor Profile

	SWEET/SOUR/BITTER/SALT	AROMA	TRIGEMINAL RESPONSE
Chocolate sabayon mousse with mango/lime and chilli gelee	Sweet: chocolate and gelée Sour: lime in gelée Bitter: chocolate	NA	Ancho in gelée
Cajeta caramel sauce	Sweet: caramel and sweetened condensed goat's milk Bitter: caramel	NA	NA
Salsa	Sweet: strawberries, mango, and tequila	NA	Heat from jalapeño peppers Menthol from mint Burn from tequila
Mint syrup	Sweet: corn syrup	NA	Menthol from mint
Tuile sun	Sweet: sugar and corn meal	NA	Heat from ancho chilli

FIGURE 11.24

Flavor profile for Food of the Gods.

chocolate sabayon mousse with mango–chilli gelée

6 egg yolks
2 ounces granulated sugar
3 ounces tequila
6 ounces semisweet couveture chocolate
2 sheets gelatin
16 ounces heavy cream
1 tbsp ground canela cinnamon

Chop the chocolate and melt over a double boiler.

Whip the cream to soft peaks and place in the refrigerator.

Whip yolks and sugar on a double boiler until the mixture thickens and doubles in volume.

Slowly add the tequila to the yolk mixture while continuing to whisk.

Bloom gelatin in cold water.

Once the gelatin has bloomed, wring out the excess water and add the gelatin to the hot sabayon mixture.

Stir until the gelatin has completely dissolved.

Remove the sabayon mixture from the stove.

Whisk melted chocolate into the sabayon.

Fold in the whipped cream.

Place immediately in flexi molds. Leave room at top of each mold for the gelée.

Make sure that the bottom of each mold is completely flat. If necessary, tap the sheet pan against the worktable to remove any air pockets.

Freeze mousse while making the gelée.

mango–chilli gelée

8 ounces mango purée
½ lime zested
⅛ ounce (2½ grams) powdered gelatin
1 ounce lime juice
¼ tsp ancho chilli powder

- Bloom gelatin in lime juice.
- Add lime zest and chilli powder to the mango purée and whisk to combine.
- Heat lime juice/gelatin mixture to dissolve gelatin. This can be done on a double boiler or in a microwave oven.
- Add dissolved gelatin mixture to mango purée.
- Whisk to combine.
- Pour immediately on top of the frozen mousse.
- Tap the molds on the bench to remove any air bubbles.
- Return to the freezer until set.
- Remove mousse from molds and place on a parchment-lined sheet pan.
- Refrigerate mousse until required for service.

 # strawberry salsa

1 pint strawberries, cleaned
1 small bunch fresh mint
1 ounce tequila gold
½ fresh mango
⅓ fresh green jalapeño pepper

- Dice the strawberries and mango.
- Brunoise dice the jalapeño pepper.
- Chiffonade fresh mint.
- Add all ingredients together in a bowl and stir gently to mix.
- Allow salsa to sit for a few minutes for best flavor.

tuile sunburst

4 ounces melted butter
4 ounces sifted powdered sugar
4 ounces egg whites
2 ounces pastry flour
2 ounces yellow cornmeal

Whisk together butter and sugar until lump free.

Slowly add egg whites while continuing to whisk.

Add flour and cornmeal.

Note: See the Appendix for more information on tuile.

cajeta caramel sauce

12 ounces granulated sugar
7 ounces sweetened condensed goat's milk

Caramelize the sugar using the wet method.

Remove the sugar from the heat before the desired color is reached. Carryover heat will cook the sugar the rest of the way.

Once sugar is at the desired color, stir in the sweetened condensed goat's milk. Continue to stir until well incorporated.

Cool. Store in refrigerator.

mint clear sauce

4 ounces fresh mint leaves
2 ounces light corn syrup

Blanch the mint leaves. Plunge them into boiling water and then place immediately into ice water. Remove the leaves from the ice water and pat them dry with paper towels.

🌿 Place the leaves in a small robot coupe or food processor.

🌿 Slowly add the light corn syrup. Strain the syrup through cheesecloth. (*Note:* It is easiest to place the syrup in the cheesecloth, bundle up the top, and, using a wringing motion, squeeze the syrup through the cloth. The result will be a bright green syrup with no bits of mint leaves.)

🌿 Store in a squeeze bottle until service.

PLATE ASSEMBLY

🌿 Pipe chocolate lines on the left-hand portion of the plate. Randomly fill in the pattern with cajeta caramel sauce and mint syrup.

🌿 Place the chocolate mousse pyramid to the right of the sauce work and the salsa to the left.

🌿 Tuile sunburst will go on one side of the pyramid.

 # corny ice cream sandwich

This whimsical play on an ice cream sandwich is meant to be a pre-dessert. The portion is small, just a few bites. The dish is a combination of familiar and new elements. Most everyone has fond memories of childhood ice cream sandwiches. This sandwich is made of homemade ice cream and two shortbread cookies. The modern twist is introduced with the flavors of the dish.

The ice cream is made of a corn cream base, sweet, rich, and just a bit unexpected. The corn flavor is mirrored in the shortbread cookies, which are made with corn meal. The glazed berries offer contrasts in terms of color and texture. The slightly sour notes of the fresh fruit partner well with the rich ice cream. The basil syrup underscores a quiet Italian theme. Its crisp, grassy, menthol notes juxtapose well with the other flavors on the plate.

Entrée: corn ice cream sandwiched between two cornmeal shortbread cookies

Garnish: sugar-glazed fresh berries

Sauce: basil syrup

Plate Profiles

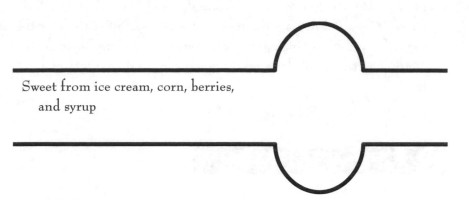

Sweet from ice cream, corn, berries,
and syrup

FIGURE 11.25

Plate profile for Corny Ice Cream Sandwich: Top Notes.

Fat in ice cream
Cornmeal in shortbread
Berry flavor
Basil flavor

FIGURE 11.26

Plate profile for Corny Ice Cream Sandwich: Middle Notes.

Sour from berries
Menthol from basil
Touch of corn from the shortbread

FIGURE 11.27

Plate profile for Corny Ice Cream Sandwich: Base Notes.

chapter 11   plated desserts

Flavor Profile

	SWEET/SOUR/ BITTER/SALT	AROMA	TRIGEMINAL RESPONSE
Ice cream sandwich	Sweet: ice cream and shortbread	NA	NA
Basil syrup	Sweet: syrup	NA	Menthol from basil
Glazed Berries	Sour: berries Sweet: sugar	NA	NA

FIGURE 11.28

Flavor profile for Corny Ice Cream Sandwich.

RECIPES

corn ice cream

1 ear of sweet corn
1 lb milk
1 lb heavy cream
pinch of salt
8 ounces granulated sugar
8 ounces egg yolks

- Shuck and roast one ear of fresh corn
- When fragrant and slightly charred, remove from heat.
- Cut the kernels off the cob and then place cob and kernels in a saucepan with the milk, cream, and sugar.
- Bring the mixture to a scald.
- Taste. If stronger flavor is desired, cover pan with plastic wrap and allow to steep off the heat. Once the corn flavor has deepened continue with method of preparation.
- Temper hot dairy mixture into the egg yolks.

Note: Strain the hot dairy–corn mixture through a chinoise mousseline while tempering. This will alleviate having to strain the corn cob and kernels later.

- Return to stove over medium high heat.

- Stir constantly until the mixture has reached nappe.

- Place in an ice bath.

- When base has cooled completely, churn in an ice cream machine.

- If possible, place in hardening cabinet for 10–15 minutes before storing in the freezer.

cornmeal shortbread cookies

5 ounces pastry flour
4 ounces yellow cornmeal
3 ounces granulated sugar
pinch of salt
4 ounces unsalted butter
2 each egg yolks
1 tbsp water
¾ tsp lemon zest

- Sift flour, yellow cornmeal, and salt together in a bowl. Dredge the zest in the dry ingredients.

- With a paddle on a 5-quart mixer, cream together the butter and granulated sugar.

- Continue to cream until lump free. Scrape the sides of the bowl frequently.

- Whisk together the water and the egg yolks.

- Add half of the liquid ingredients and continue to paddle. Scrape down the sides and the bottom of the bowl and add the remaining wet ingredients.

- Once the liquid ingredients are completely incorporated, add the dry ingredients.

- Form the dough into a disk shape and cover completely with plastic wrap.

- Place dough in the refrigerator. After 30 minutes the dough will be chilled enough to roll out.

- Roll out dough to approximately ¼-inch thickness.
- Cut dough into desired shapes and place on a parchment-lined sheet pan.
- Bake at 350°F (175°C) for about 8 minutes.

sugar-glazed fresh berries

· ·

½ pint each of strawberries and raspberries
1–2 ounces granulated sugar

- Clean and dry berries.
- Cut the strawberries into quarters, leave the remaining berries whole.
- Sauté the berries quickly over medium high heat.
- Once the berries are warm, sprinkle with a handful of granulated sugar and continue to sauté until a glaze is formed.
- Serve immediately.

basil syrup

· ·

4 ounces fresh basil leaves
2 ounces light corn syrup

- Blanch the basil leaves. Plunge them into boiling water and then place immediately into ice water. Remove the leaves from the ice water and pat them dry with paper towels.
- Place the leaves in a small robot coupe or food processor.
- Slowly add the light corn syrup. Strain the syrup through cheesecloth. (*Note:* It is easiest to place the syrup in the cheesecloth, bundle up the top, and, using a wringing motion, squeeze the syrup through the cloth. The result will be a bright green syrup with no bits of basil leaves.)
- Store in a squeeze bottle until service.

corny ice cream sandwich

PLATE ASSEMBLY

🌾 Place a small dot of basil syrup in the center of the plate. This will serve as the glue for the ice cream sandwich.

🌾 Lay one shortbread cookie on top of the basil syrup "glue."

🌾 Cover cookie with a scoop of corn ice cream.

🌾 Lay second cookie on top of the ice cream and press down lightly.

🌾 Using a spoon, drizzle a small amount of basil syrup to the right of the sandwich.

🌾 On the left side of the sandwich, sprinkle the freshly sautéed berries.

 # ode to provence

Herbes de Provence is a spice blend containing marjoram, rosemary, thyme, sage, savory, anise seed, and lavender. Once used solely in French classic cuisine, its full plate profile makes it the perfect accompaniment to plated desserts. The spice blend complements plates with light, clean flavors. The lavender in the mixture offers a light floral note, while the sage, rosemary, and anise seed all add a cooling base note.

This dessert uses the spice blend in a variety of ways. The panna cotta uses the entire blend while the other components utilize individual components of the spice mix. The fresh tarragon in the pound cake echoes both the flavor and cooling nature of the anise seed in the spice mix. The fresh thyme used to finish off the sautéed fruit is related to the blend's dried thyme.

The fleur de sel used around the rims of the lace cups pays homage to the cuisine of the Provence region.

Entrée: tarragon pound cake and fresh citrus sautéed with Muscat, accompanied with an herbes de Provence panna cotta

Sauce: lemon custard sauce

Crunch/garnish: fleur de sel lace cookies

Plate Profiles

• • • • • • • • • • • • • • • • • • •

Sweet from pound cake, panna cotta,
  Muscat glazed citrus, lace cookie,
  and thyme clear sauce
Salt from fleur de sel cookie

FIGURE 11.29

Plate profile for Ode to Provence: Top Notes.

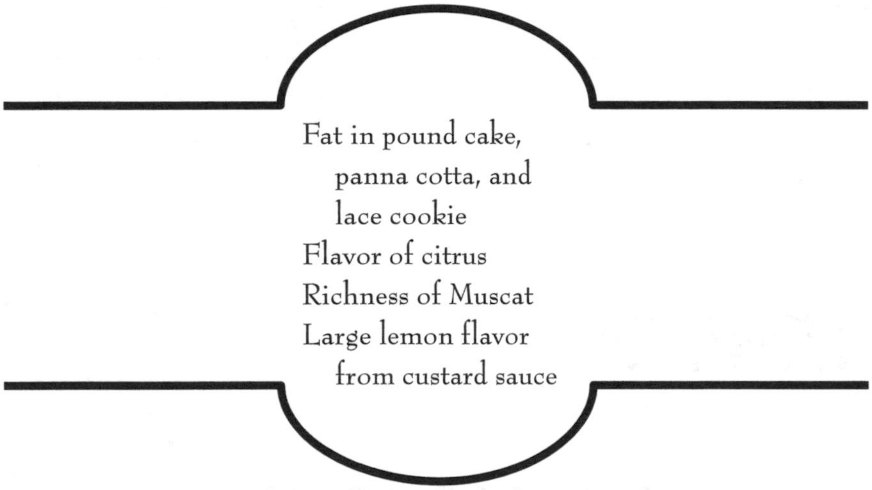

Fat in pound cake,
  panna cotta, and
  lace cookie
Flavor of citrus
Richness of Muscat
Large lemon flavor
  from custard sauce

FIGURE 11.30

Plate profile for Ode to Provence: Middle Notes.

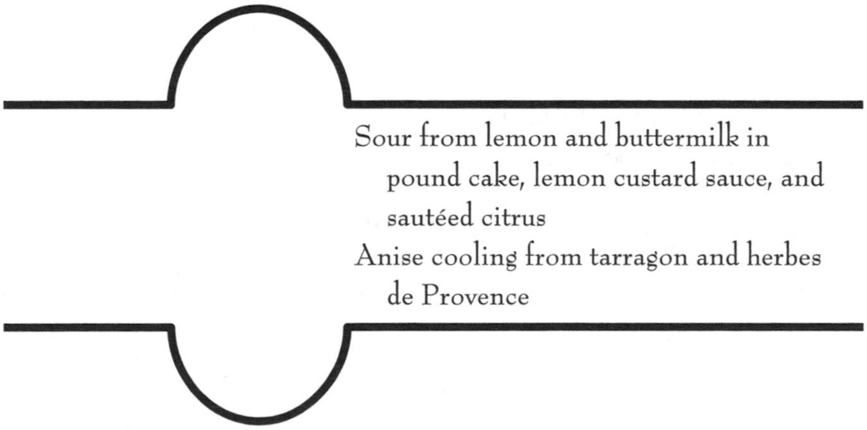

Sour from lemon and buttermilk in
  pound cake, lemon custard sauce, and
  sautéed citrus
Anise cooling from tarragon and herbes
  de Provence

FIGURE 11.31

Plate profile for Ode to Provence: Base Notes.

	SWEET/SOUR/ BITTER/SALT	AROMA	TRIGEMINAL RESPONSE
Lemon tarragon pound cake	Sweet: sugar Sour: lemon and buttermilk	NA	Anise cooling from tarragon
Lemon custard sauce	Sweet: sugar Sour: lemons	NA	NA
Citrus sautéed in Muscat	Sweet: Muscat Sour: oranges and grapefruit	Citrus fragrance	A bit of alcohol burn from the Muscat
Herbes de Provence Panna cotta	Sweet: sugar	NA	NA
Fleur de sel lace cookie	Sweet: cookie Salt: fleur de sel	NA	NA
Thyme clear sauce	Sweet: corn syrup	NA	NA

FIGURE 11.32

Flavor profile for Ode to Provence.

RECIPES

herbes de provence panna cotta

1 cup whole milk
¼ ounce gelatin
24 ounces heavy cream
3 ounces granulated sugar
1 tsp herbes de Provence

Bloom the gelatin with the whole milk.

Place the cream, sugar, and herbes de Provence in a sauce pan and bring to a scald.

Taste. Continue to steep off the heat if deeper flavor is desired.

- Stir the gelatin–milk mixture into the hot cream. Stir until the gelatin is completely dissolved. Return mixture to heat if needed.

- Place the mixture on an ice bath and stir gently until the mixture has just started to thicken. It will have the consistency of yogurt.

- Pour into the flexi molds and freeze until the panna cotta can be easily released from the forms.

- Pop the panna cotta out of the flexi molds and onto a paper-lined sheet pan.

- Place in refrigerator until service.

lemon–tarragon pound cake

$6\frac{3}{4}$ ounces pastry flour
1 tsp baking powder
$\frac{1}{2}$ tsp salt
4 ounces unsalted butter
$7\frac{1}{2}$ ounces sugar
2 whole eggs
$4\frac{1}{4}$ ounce buttermilk
zest of one lemon
1 tbsp fresh tarragon, chiffonade

- Sift the flour, baking powder, and salt together.

- Dredge the lemon zest in the dry ingredients.

- Cream together the butter and granulated sugar until lump free. Scrape the sides and bottom of the bowl often.

- Slowly add the eggs, scraping down the bowl between each addition.

- Alternately add the dry ingredients and the buttermilk.

- Place batter in flexi molds or bread pans and bake in a 325°F (160°C) oven.

- Baking time will vary according to the size of the pan used.

lemon custard sauce

· ·

3 ounces fresh lemon juice
zest of three lemons
1 whole egg
2 egg yolks
6 ounces granulated sugar
3 ounces unsalted butter

🌿 Heat the lemon juice together with the lemon zest and sugar in a sauce pan.

🌿 After the mixture comes to a scald temper it into the eggs.

🌿 Return the mixture to the stove and stir constantly until it reaches nappe.

🌿 Remove from heat and add butter.

🌿 Stir until the butter is melted.

🌿 Place sauce on an ice bath until completely chilled.

🌿 Pour into a sauce bottle and refrigerate until service.

sautéed citrus

· ·

3 grapefruit
3 oranges
4 ounces Muscat

🌿 Segment the grapefruit and oranges, being careful to reserve their juices.

🌿 Pour reserved citrus juices into a sauté pan and bring to a simmer.

🌿 Add the Muscat and continue to cook until the liquid becomes syrupy in consistency.

🌿 Add the segmented citrus fruit to the sauce and sauté just to warm the fruit. This should be done at service time.

Note: If the citrus fruit is cooked for too long it will break down and the visual impact of the whole segments will be lost in the final presentation.

fleur de sel lace cookies

4½ ounces unsalted butter
4½ ounces pastry flour
4½ ounces granulated sugar
7 ounces light corn syrup
1 ounce fleur de sel

- Place all ingredients, except the fleur de sel in a 5-quart mixing bowl.
- Cream with a paddle until fully incorporated.
- Place small marble-sized balls of the dough onto a parchment-lined sheet pan.
- The cookies will spread a great deal so make sure to leave enough room between cookies on the sheet pan.
- Bake in a 350°F (180°C) oven until golden brown, 12–15 minutes.
- Let cool for a minute or two and then form into abstract, free-form roses.
- Brush the outer rim of the rose with light corn syrup and sprinkle on fleur de sel.
- Store at room temperature until service.

 # thyme clear sauce

4 ounces fresh thyme leaves
2 ounces light corn syrup

- Blanch the thyme leaves. Plunge them into boiling water and then place immediately into ice water. Remove the leaves from the ice water and pat them dry with paper towels.
- Place the leaves in a small robot coupe or food processor.
- Slowly add the light corn syrup. Strain the syrup through cheesecloth.

  (*Note:* It is easiest to place the syrup in the cheesecloth, bundle up the top, and, using a wringing motion, squeeze the syrup through the cloth. The result will be a bright green syrup with no bits of thyme leaves.)

- Store in a squeeze bottle until service.

PLATE ASSEMBLY

- Using the back of a ladle spread a round of lemon custard sauce in the middle of the plate.

- Pipe a random design of thyme clear sauce on top of the lemon custard sauce.

- To the right of the sauce place the panna cotta.

- To the left of the panna cotta fan out slices of the pound cake and top with the sautéed citrus segments.

- Place fleur de sel lace cookie in between the panna cotta and the citrus segments.

appendix

🌿 1-2-3 or short dough

1 lb granulated sugar
2 lb butter, softened
3 lb pastry flour
3 each whole eggs

🌿 In a mixer with a paddle attachment, add softened butter (cut in chunks) and the granulated sugar.

🌿 Mix on medium speed until the mixture is soft and lump free.

🌿 Scrape the bottom and sides of the bowl often.

🌿 Slowly add eggs, one at a time. Make sure to scrape the bowl between each addition.

🌿 Turn off the machine and add the pastry flour all at once. Mix on speed 1 just until the flour is incorporated.

🌿 Once all of the flour is incorporated, turn off the machine.

VARIATIONS

Cocoa powder can be substituted for a portion of the flour. Do not add more than 8 ounces or the dough will be crumbly and unworkable.

🌿 Other flavor additions include: vanilla seeds, citrus zest, curry powder, star anise, or Chinese five spice.

231

- The key to wonderfully delicate short dough is in the mixing and handling.

- Make sure to mix only until the flour is incorporated.

- Work with the dough directly out of the refrigerator. Simply give the dough a few sharp whacks with a French rolling pin and it will quickly get to a workable consistency.

- Be careful not to dust the bench too liberally with bread flour, too much flour will toughen the dough. I like to use a combination of 50% bread flour and 50% granulated sugar. The sugar helps prevent the dough from sticking to the bench, adds a sweet crunch, and you don't have to worry about it toughening your end product.

- When storing the dough, place it out between two sheets of parchment paper. Storing it in a thin block makes it much easier to roll out.

 bavarian cream

5 sheets gelatin
1 lb milk
1 lb heavy cream
4 ounces granulated sugar
5 ounces egg yolks
infusion of choice

- Bloom gelatin sheets in cold water.

- Whip cream to soft peak and place in refrigerator.

- Make an anglaise with the remaining ingredients.

- Once the anglaise has reached nappe, quickly stir in the bloomed gelatin.

- Place mixture in an ice bath.

- Stir mixture to prevent the gelatin from setting. Be especially vigilant along the bottom and the sides of the bowl.

- Once the mixture has cooled and is just beginning to thicken, fold in the whipped cream.

- Pipe mix immediately into desired mold.

HINTS

☘ Remember that after gelatin has been bloomed and dissolved it is activated by cold temperatures. Therefore, pay close attention to the mixture once it is placed in the ice bath. You want the mixture to cool, to thicken slightly but not to become so thick that folding in the whipped cream becomes impossible.

☘ Remember that fat coats taste buds. Bavarian cream contains many fatty ingredients. The presence of heavy cream and egg yolks mean that your initial infusion must be strong. The flavor you taste in the anglaise will be diluted and/or dulled by the addition of the yolks and the whipped cream. To have a true flavor in the end product start with a strong infusion.

☘ Once the whipped cream has been folded into the anglaise base, pipe the mix immediately into desired mold (flexi molds work well) and then freeze. The frozen creams will be easy to pop out from the molds. Once they are released from the molds, place the Bavarian creams in the refrigerator on a parchment-lined sheet pan until service.

☘ caramel sauce

· ·

12 ounces granulated sugar
2 ounces butter
7 ounces heavy cream

☘ Caramelize sugar using either the wet or dry method.

☘ Just before sugar has reached the desired color, remove from the heat source.

☘ Quickly stir in the butter and cream.

☘ Continue to stir until the sauce is lump free.

VARIATIONS

For clear caramel sauces simply add water, juice, fruit purée, or liquor in place of the butter and heavy cream. For instance, in the above recipe, the 2 ounces of butter and the 7 ounces of heavy cream would be replaced with 9 ounces of raspberry purée when making a clear raspberry caramel sauce.

HINTS

🌿 Sugar holds a tremendous amount of carryover heat. For this reason it is important to remove the pan from the heat source before the caramel has reached the desired color. Be patient and allow the carry-over heat to cook the caramel the rest of the way. Once the desired color is reached, add the cream and butter.

🌿 Use caution when adding the cream and butter; the addition of these ingredients will produce a large cloud of steam. Make sure that you are not leaning over the pan when adding these items.

🌿 The sauce will need to be reheated once it has been refrigerated.

🌿 Caramelized sugar is one of the few products whose color is indicative of its flavor. The darker the caramel, the more bitter it will taste. For the most part, Americans are used to a rather anemic caramel, sugar cooked until it is a light honey color. Try taking the sugar a bit darker; it should be the color of a strong glass of iced tea (a good medium brown color). You may be surprised by the unexpected nutty/vanilla notes that emerge in the caramel's flavor.

🌿 chocolate sauce

4 ounces cocoa powder
8 ounces water
8 ounces granulated sugar
2 ounces semisweet couveture, chopped

🌿 Bring the sugar, water, and cocoa powder to a boil.

🌿 Whisk in the chopped chocolate.

🌿 Continue to whisk until the chocolate is melted.

🌿 Strain through a chinoise mousseline.

🌿 Chill in refrigerator.

🌿 Sauce will thicken as it cools and will need to be reheated to get it to a workable consistency for service.

Note: This is a wonderfully strong, bitter, slightly astringent sauce. It has a black color. Due to its almost completely lack of fat (except for the cocoa butter in the 2 ounces of couveture) it is a great accompaniment to main items that contain a lot of fat.

🌿 For added flavor, infusions can take place in step 1.

 fondant/glucose for sugar work

8 ounces fondant
4 ounces glucose

🌾 Place both sugars in a sauté pan or small saucepan. Cook over medium-high heat, stirring occasionally.

🌾 Once the sugar has reached the desired color, remove from heat and make desired garnishes.

VARIATIONS

❧ Substitute honey for the glucose. This will result in a much better-tasting garnish

❧ If desired, the sugar holds food coloring very well.

❧ Caramel powder:

    ❧ Once the fondant/honey mixture has reached a light caramel color pour onto a Silpat.

    ❧ Allow the sugar to cool at room temperature.

    ❧ Once the caramel is completely hard, break into small pieces and place in a food processor.

    ❧ In quick, short bursts pulse the caramel until it becomes a powder.

    ❧ The powder can be used as is to dust a plate or, alternatively, it can be sprinkled onto a Silpat and placed in a 350°F (175°C) oven.

    ❧ Bake the sugar until it is completely melted.

    ❧ Pull into desired free-form shapes.

HINTS

🌾 Success with sugar garnishes is often only a matter of correct temperature. If the sugar is too hot it will bead rather than form thin straight lines when dropped from a spoon or fork. If the sugar is too cold, it will be difficult to make delicate garnishes from it.

🌾 Be patient and with practice you will be able to tell quickly if the sugar needs to be heated up or cooled down.

🌾 No fancy equipment is needed for sugar work. A couple of metal forks, a dowel, and a ladle is all you need to spin sugar and form cork screws or cages.

french-style ice cream

1 pound milk
1 pound heavy cream
9 ounces granulated sugar
8 ounces egg yolks
desired infusion

- Place milk, heavy cream, sugar, and desired infusion into a saucepan and bring to a scald.

- Place egg yolk into a medium-sized bowl.

- Once the dairy mixture has reached a scald, taste. If the infusion is not strong enough, take the pot off the heat. Cover with plastic wrap and allow to steep until the flavor intensifies.

- Temper dairy mixture into the egg yolks. Use a piano wire whisk but stir gently so as not to create too much foam.

- Return pot to the stove and scrape constantly with a heat-resistant spatula. Pay special attention to the sides and corners of the pot.

- Once the mixture has reached a nappe consistency, remove from the heat and place immediately in an ice bath.

- When it is completely cooled, churn in the ice cream machine.

- Freeze until needed for service.

VARIATIONS

- Chocolate ice cream: add 5–6 ounces of cocoa liquor to the hot anglaise before the mixture is placed in an ice bath.

- Honey, brown sugar, molasses, or raw sugars can be substituted for the granulated sugar.

- Add-ins such as pieces of candies or roasted nuts should be added to the ice cream after it has been churned.

HINTS

- Be careful when tempering the eggs and the hot dairy mixture. Creating too much foam makes it difficult to see the dairy mixture once it is returned to the stove. This makes it easy to overcook the anglaise base.

✤ Remember that fat coats taste buds. When tasting the initial infusion bear in mind that additional fat is going to be added to the mixture in the form of egg yolks. Make sure that the diary/sugar/infusion blend is a strong one.

✤ lace dough

· ·

9 ounces pastry flour
9 ounces granulated sugar
9 ounces butter
9 ounces light corn syrup
nuts, seeds, grains as desired

✤ In a mixer with a paddle, cream together the flour, sugar, and butter.

✤ Add the corn syrup and any nuts, seeds, or grains you may desire.

✤ Roll into a log and store in refrigerator until ready to use.

VARIATIONS

❦ This dough works just as well plain as it does with the addition of nuts, seeds, or grains. When using nuts simply coarsely chop. Do not chop in a robot coupe or chop too finely or the end cookie will not have the desired spread. Fine nuts such as sliced, blanched almonds or pine nuts can be left whole as they will be slightly chopped by the paddle in the mixer.

❦ In addition to nuts, items such as quinoa, oatmeal, sesame seeds, or amaranth can be used. Cooked rice or cooked barley also make great additions to the batter.

HINTS

✤ These cookies spread a great deal in the oven. A marble-sized piece of dough will spread to a circle with a diameter of 2 inches. Take this spread into account when placing the dough on a Silpat or parchment paper.

✤ Let the cookie cool slightly before trying to mold it. Attempting to mold the cookie too early will result in it tearing.

✤ If a cookie with a sharp edge is desired, bake the cookies 80%. Remove from the oven and let cool slightly, cut to desired shape with a

French knife and then return the cookie to the oven to continue to bake.

🌿 Make sure to weigh out the corn syrup; it cannot be measured volumetrically. Line a bowl or measuring cup with plastic wrap, place on scale, and continue. When you are ready to add the corn syrup to the mixing bowl, simply gather the top of the wrap together forming a kind of sachet for the corn syrup. Place over the mixing bowl, pierce sachet with the tip of a knife and squeeze all of the corn syrup into the bowl.

🌿 soft gelée

9–12 grams of powdered gelatin/1 liter of liquid

🌿 Bloom gelatin in liquid and then heat until the gelatin is completely dissolved.

🌿 Pour into desired molds.

🌿 Refrigerate until set.

🌿 This is a fairly soft gelée. It will not hold a sharp form.

🌿 hard gelée

15–20 grams of powdered gelatin/1 liter of liquid

🌿 Bloom gelatin in liquid and then heat until the gelatin is completely dissolved.

🌿 Pour into desired molds.

🌿 Refrigerate until set.

🌿 This gelée will be firm enough to cut into a relatively small dice.

VARIATIONS

The type liquid used for these gelées is limited only by your imagination. Some suggestions:

❧ Infuse a lightly sweetened milk.

❧ Use the simple syrup left over from making fruit chips.

≈ Use poaching liquid.

≈ Use juices, liquors, coffees, chai mixes, teas.

≈ Use water "broths": water infused with vegetable skins and/or fresh herbs.

HINTS

✐ Experiment and adapt these recipes for the specific dessert you are making. You may find that you want a gelée that has more, or less, structure than the ratios given here.

✐ tuile paste

1 lb powdered sugar
1 lb egg whites
1 lb pastry flour
1 lb melted butter

✐ Melt butter.

✐ Sift powdered sugar directly into a large mixing bowl.

✐ Whisk together the sugar and the butter until the mixture is lump free.

✐ Slowly drizzle in the egg whites as you continue to whisk.

✐ Add the flour and whisk until there are no lumps.

✐ Store in refrigerator until ready to use.

VARIATIONS

≈ For chocolate tuile, substitute equal amounts of sifted cocoa powder for the flour (for example, take out approximately 8 ounces of flour and add 8 ounces of cocoa powder).

≈ This paste holds color very well; if desired, simply add a few drops of food coloring to the basic mixture.

≈ Fruit purée can also be added for both color and some added flavor; simply add the purée to taste.

≈ Tuile can be stenciled and then the coulis added directly on top of the cookie for an almost stained glass window effect.

≈ Sift cocoa powder over the tuile before baking for a marbleized look.

🌿 Tuile can be either stenciled or piped.

🌿 When stenciling tuile, place the Silpat directly on the work surface. This way you do not have to contend with the perpetually uneven sheet pan or the rims of the sheet pan.

🌿 When molding the tuile work quickly. It must be molded the second it comes out of the oven. Make sure that you have a landing spot cleaned off and any mold you may be using ready to go.

🌿 water-based foam

· ·

16 ounces of liquid
10 grams of sheet gelatin

🌿 Place 10 ounces of the liquid in the freezer.

🌿 Bloom the gelatin in the remaining 6 ounces of liquid.

🌿 Heat the gelatin/liquid mixture until the gelatin has dissolved.

🌿 Place the dissolved gelatin mixture in a 5-quart mixing bowl with a whip attachment.

🌿 Begin to mix on speed 1.

🌿 Slowly add the 10 ounces of cold liquid.

🌿 Once all of the liquid has been added, turn the speed up to 3.

🌿 Continue to whip for at least 5 minutes or until a firm foam appears on the surface.

🌿 The resulting foam can be used in a number of different ways:

• Spoon the foam off the top and use immediately. The result has a soft look to it and will last quite a while on the plate.

• Allow the foam to set in the bowl for a few minutes. The result can be scooped and/or quenelled and will stay quite firm.

• Scoop or quenelle the foam after it has set for a few minutes and freeze. The result is both lighter and a bit icier than a sorbet.

VARIATIONS

Any type of liquid can be used as the base for the foam.

HINTS

🖋 Be patient, depending on the type of liquid used the foam may take a while to stabilize.

🖋 If the foam becomes too firm, simply rewhip.

bibliography

ADRIA, FERRAN, JULI SOLER, and ALBERT ADRIA. *El Bulli 1998–2002*. Spain: El Bulli Books, 2002.

ALFORD, JEFFREY, and NAOMI DUGUID. *Hot Sour Salty Sweet*. New York: Artisan, 2000.

BAYLESS, RICK. *Mexico, One Plate at a Time*. New York: Scribner, 2000.

BRILLAT-SAVARIN, JEAN ANTHELME. *The Physiology of Taste*. New York: Knopf, 1949.

CORN, CHARLES, *The Scents of Eden: A History of the Spice Trade*. New York: Kadansho International, 1999.

DALEY, REGAN. *In the Sweet Kitchen: The Definitive Baker's Companion*. New York: Artisan, 2001.

DAVIDSON, ALAN. *The Oxford Companion to Food*. Oxford, UK: Oxford University Press, 1999.

DORNENBURG, ANDREW, and KAREN PAGE. *Culinary Artistry*. Hoboken, NJ: Wiley, 1996.

FIGONI, PAULA. *How Baking Works: Exploring the Fundamentals of Baking Science*. Hoboken, NJ: Wiley, 2004.

FLEMING, CLAUDIA. *The Last Course: The Desserts of Gramercy Tavern*. New York: Random House, 2001.

HILL, TONY. *The Contemporary Encyclopedia of Herbs and Spices*. Hoboken, NJ: Wiley, 2004.

MCGEE, HAROLD. *On Food and Cooking: The Science and Lore of the Kitchen*. New York: Scribner, 2004.

MILLER, MARK. *The Great Chile Book*. Berkeley, CA: Ten Speed, 1991.

MILLER, MARK, and MARK KIFFIN. *Coyote's Pantry*. Berkeley, CA: Ten Speed, 1993.

MILTON, JANE. *Mexican: Healthy Ways with a Favorite Cuisine*. London: Hermes House, 2002.

MORRIS, SALLIE, and DEH-TA HSIUNG. *The Practical Encyclopedia of Asian Cooking*. New York: Lorenz Books, 1999.

ORTIZ, ELISABETH LAMBERT. *The Encyclopedia of Herbs, Spices and Flavorings*. London: DK, 1992.

OSTMANN, BARBARA GIBBS, and JANE L. BAKER. *The Recipe Writer's Handbook*. Hoboken, NJ: Wiley, 2001.

RIELY, ELIZABETH. *The Chef's Companion: A Culinary Dictionary*. Hoboken, NJ: Wiley, 2003.

RIPERT, ERIC, and MICHAEL RUHLMAN. *A Return to Cooking*. New York: Artisan, 2002.

SONNENFELD, ALBERT, editor. *Food: A Culinary History from Antiquity to the Present*. New York: Columbia University Press, 1999.

TANNAHILL, REAY. *Food in History*. New York: Three Rivers, 1988.

YOCKELSON, LISA. *Baking by Flavor*. Hoboken, NJ: Wiley, 2002.

index

Bold faced numbers refer to recipes and/or method of preparation.